GLOBALIZATION AND THIRD WORLD WOMEN

Globalization and Third World Women
Exploitation, Coping and Resistance

Edited by
LIGAYA LINDIO-MCGOVERN

ISIDOR WALLIMANN

Syracuse University Press

First Paperback Edition 2012

12   13   14   15   16   17   6   5   4   3   2   1

∞The paper used in this publication meets the minimum requirements of the American National Standard for Information Sciences—Permanence of Paper for Printed Library Materials, ANSI Z39.48-1992.

For a listing of books published and distributed by Syracuse University Press, visit our website at SyracuseUniversityPress.syr.edu.

ISBN 978-0-8156-3305-1

British Library Cataloguing in Publication Data
Globalization and Third World women : exploitation, coping and resistance. — (Global connections)
1. Women—Developing countries—Social conditions. 2. Women—Developing countries—Economic conditions. 3. Women—Government policy—Developing countries. 4. Globalization—Social aspects—Developing countries. 5. Globalization—Economic aspects—Developing countries. 6. Globalization—Political aspects—Developing countries.
I. Series II. Lindio-McGovern, Ligaya. III. Wallimann, Isidor.
303.4'82'082-dc22

Library of Congress Cataloging-in-Publication Data
The Library of Congress has cataloged the hardcover edition as follows:
Globalization and third world women : exploitation, coping and resistance / [edited] by Ligaya Lindio-McGovern and Isidor Wallimann.
    p. cm. — (Global connections)
Includes index.
ISBN 978-0-7546-7463-4
1. Women—Developing countries—Social conditions. 2. Women—Developing countries—Economic conditions. 3. Globalization—Developing countries. I. Lindio-McGovern, Ligaya. II. Wallimann, Isidor, 1944-
HQ1870.9.G66 2009
305.409172'4—dc22

2009008824

Manufactured in the United States of America

Contents

List of Figure and Tables

Figure

Tables

Notes on Contributors

Shireen Ally is a Lecturer in the Department of Sociology, University of the Witwatersrand, Johannesburg. She received her PhD from the University of Wisconsin-Madison in 2006, having completed a dissertation on the politics of paid domestic work in contemporary South Africa. In 2008, she was seconded to the History Research Group at Wits University.

Christobel Asiedu is an Assistant Professor of Sociology at the Louisiana Tech University. She received her PhD in Sociology from the University of Illinois at Urbana-Champaign in May 2007. Her research interests include: Gender and technology, Gender and Development in Africa, and Gender and Globalization.

Leigh Brownhill is the author of *Land, Food, Freedom: Struggles for the Gendered Commons in Kenya, 1870-2007* (Trenton, New Jersey: Africa World Press, 2009). She is a co-founder of First Woman: The East and Southern African Women's Oral History and Indigenous Knowledge Network. First Woman has been recording the life stories of elderly Mau Mau women in Kenya since 1994. She has published widely on the subjects of gender and social movements in Africa.

Robert Dibie PhD, is Professor and Dean of the School of Public and Environmental Affairs (SPEA) at Indiana University Kokomo, USA. He is the external examiner of the Occupational, Environmental, Safety and Health (OESH) graduate program at the University of the West Indies, Mona Campus, Kingston, Jamaica. Professor Dibie is also the North American Editor of the *Journal of International Politics and Development* (JIPAD). He has published several books and more than eighty peer-reviewed journal articles in the area of environmental policy, civil society, public management, sustainable development, public policy, nongovernmental Organizations (NGOs), and ethics. Professor Dibie has presented research papers at over a hundred national and international conferences. He has also served as keynote speaker in many national and international forums, including the United States, Jamaica, South Africa, England, and Nigeria. Professor Dibie has also consulted for several universities and NGOs in the Caribbean Islands, United States, and Africa.

Ann Ferguson is a feminist philosopher who is an emeriti Professor of Women's Studies and Philosophy at the University of Massachusetts at Amherst. She has written two books and numerous articles in feminist theory, ethics and politics. The books are: *Blood at the Root: Motherhood, Sexuality and Male Dominance* (London: Pandora/Unwin Hyman, 1989) and *Sexual Democracy: Women,*

Oppression and Revolution (Boulder: Westview, 1991). She also co-edited a book in feminist ethics with Bat Ami Bar On, *Daring to be Good: Feminist Essays in Ethico-Politics* (Routledge, 1998).

Martha Gimenez is Professor Emeritus at the University of Colorado at Boulder. She has written and researched extensively on Marxist theory, as well as issues of gender, class and race. She is the co-editor of *Work Without Wages: Domestic Labor and Self-Employment Under Capitalism* (State University of New York Press, 1990), and has published articles in a large number of journals including *Ethnicities* and *Race, Gender and Class*.

Anne E. Lacsamana is an Assistant Professor in the Women's Studies Department at Hamilton College. Specializing in transnational feminist theory, Lacsamana's research focuses on U.S.-Philippine relations, with particular attention to the Philippine women's movement. She is the co-editor of *Women and Globalization* (Humanity Press, 2004) and has published articles and book reviews in journals such as *Nature, Society and Thought, Socialist Review, Critical Asian Studies*, and *Amerasia*. For the 2008-2009 year, Lacsamana was awarded an American Association of University Women (AAUW) Postdoctoral Research Fellowship to complete work on her manuscript *Revolutionizing Feminism: The Philippine Women's Movement in the Age of Terror.*

Shweta Majumdar is a PhD candidate in Sociology at the University of Connecticut. Shweta's research interest focuses on gender and human rights. She has published on Dalit organizing in the U.S. She recently won a Human Rights Institute grant to study widows in India.

Ligaya Lindio-McGovern, an Associate Professor of Sociology at Indiana University, USA, holds a PhD from Loyola University Chicago, USA. A former director of Women's Studies at Indiana University Kokomo, she is author of *Filipino Peasant Women: Exploitation and Resistance* published by University of Pennsylvania Press. She has also published several articles in various journals and edited books. She has conducted field research in various sites, such as British Columbia in Canada, Taiwan, Italy, Hong Kong, and the Philippines. She has been invited to speak in the U.S. and in other countries, like Switzerland, Canada, Netherlands, Spain on her research areas and special fields which focus on globalization and Third World women, Philippine labor export and international migration, women's movement, human rights and resistance, the globalization of reproductive labor and the health care labor market. She also held elected positions in professional organizations, such as the Society for the Study of Social Problems and the Midwest Sociological Society, USA (lmcgover@iuk.edu).

Bandana Purkayastha, an Associate Professor of Sociology and Asian Ameican studies, at the University of Connecticut, was educated in India (Presidency

College) and the U.S. She has published more than 25 peer reviewed articles and chapters which appeared in the United States, United Kingdom, Germany, and India which deal with issues of race, gender, class and human rights issues. Her recent books are *The Power of Women's Informal Networks: Lessons in Social Change in South Asia and West Africa* (co-edited with Mangala Subramaniam), a research monograph, *Negotiating Ethnicity: Second-Generation South Asian Americans Traverse a Transnational World*, along with two forthcoming books: *Living Our Religions: South Asian American Hindu and Muslim Women Narrate their Experiences* (with Anjana Narayan), and *Armed Forces and Conflict Resolution: Sociological Perspectives* (with Giuseppe Caforio and Gerhard Kuemmel). She is completing a book on Canadian Americans (with Susan Lucas), and one on human rights. She has served on a number of community organizations on issues of domestic violence, immigrant issues, and on the Academic Advisory Board of the Connecticut Health Disparities Project for the State of Connecticut. She won the State of Connecticut and AAUP citations for excellence in teaching, a UCONN Woman of Color award for excellence in achievement, leadership and service. She received citations of honor from the Governor and state legislature for the 2004 Connecticut Immigrants Day. She currently serves on the Executive Board of Research Committee-1 on armed forces and conflict resolution, as well as RC-32 on Women in Society of the International Sociological Association. She is the deputy editor of *Gender and Society*.

Robyn Rodriguez is Assistant Professor of Sociology at Rutgers University, New Jersey. Her research interests are in the areas of globalization, labor and trans/nationalisms. She is currently completing her book manuscript tentatively entitled, *Brokering Bodies: The Philippine State and the Globalization of Migrant Labor*. *Brokering Bodies* will be published by the University of Minnesota Press and is expected to be published in late 2009. Her scholarship has appeared in journals such as *Signs*, *Citizenship Studies* and the *Sociological Forum*. A long-time activist in the Filipino community organizing around labor, immigrant rights and women's issues, Rodriguez is currently active in building the National Alliance for Filipino Concerns (NAFCON), a national network of grassroots Filipino immigrant groups. Also, she has been recently elected to serve on the International Coordinating Body of the newly-formed International Migrants Alliance.

Terisa E. Turner is associate professor of Sociology and Anthropology at the University of Guelph in Ontario, Canada. She co-directs the International Oil Working Group, a NGO registered at the United Nations in New York. With the IOWG, she assisted in enforcing the United Nations oil embargo against apartheid in South Africa (1978-1990). Her books include *Arise Ye Mighty People! Gender, Class and Race in Popular Struggles* (1994) and *Oil and Class Struggle* (1980).

Professor Isidor Wallimann holds a PhD in Sociology from Syracuse University and an MA in economics and agriculture from Kansas State. He recently retired from his positions at the University of Applied Sciences Northwest Switzerland and from the University of Freiburg in Switzerland. He has published numerous books in English and German, such as *Estrangement: Marx's Conception of Human Nature and the Divison of Labor; Genocide and the Modern Age* (translated into Korean) and *On the Edge of Scarcity* (translated into German). As a visiting professor, he has been invited to universities in the United States, China, and Taiwan. He has lectured worldwide and served the Swiss National Science Foundation as an expert for social policy research programs. He is former Fellow of Indiana University Bloomington Institute of Advanced Study and a Visiting Professor of University North Texas, USA. (Isidor.Wallimann@tele2.ch)

Acknowledgements

This book is a response to the need to de-marginalize the experience of Third World women in the mainstream discourse on neoliberal globalization. We would like to express our sincere appreciation to those who helped in its completion:

To Indiana University Institute of Advanced Study (IAS), housed in Bloomington, under the able leadership of Professor John Bodnar and Ivona Hedin, for providing us a Visiting Fellowship grant that allowed Professor Isidor Wallimann, whose main residence is in Switzerland, to stay at Indiana University Kokomo for some weeks so we could collaborate in editing this book. It made our collaboration across continents much easier, and contributed to our meeting the publication deadline. The Institute's support affirmed the importance of this project and inspired us to reach the finish line.

To Dean Sue Sciame-Giesecke of the IU Kokomo School of Arts and Sciences who was very supportive during Professor Wallimann's fellowship with IAS and worked efficiently in providing him an office and internet access, along with the cooperation of Joyce Webb, Anna Aichele, Marsha White, and Carl Pennington.

To our colleagues and friends who wrote for us letters of support in our application for grants—William (Bill) Mello, Karl Besel, Matthew (Todd) Bradley, and Earl Wysong.

To the contributors of this volume who persisted with us in all the phases of the work.

To the anonymous reviewers who found this project important and shared valuable suggestions.

To Brittany Waite, SBSC student assistant, whose skillful and efficient clerical assistance was a tremendous help, especially in the second round of review.

To Neil Jordan, social science commissioning editor at Ashgate Publishing, for picking up this project after his predecessor left and for working with us to its completion.

Last, but not least, to our friends and families who gave us quiet inspiration and support.

In memory of
my loving mother, Monica Macasinag Lindio – 1914-2007
and dedicated father, Teofilo Lindio – 1912-1999
and to the First World mother, Margrit Wallimann, of Isidor

Chapter 1

Introduction

Neoliberal Globalization and Third World Women: Exploitation, Coping and Resistance

Ligaya Lindio-McGovern and Isidor Wallimann

Neoliberal globalization is not a neutral process, it is gendered, and has exacerbated domestic and global social inequalities.[1] Thus, a growing resistance against its destructive course and an active search for alternatives is in the making (Smith and Johnston 2002; Brecher, Castello, and Smith 2009; Naples and Desai 2002). Third World women who experience more adversely than First World men and women the negative impact of neoliberal globalization are actively taking part in this growing resistance. The dynamics of power in this dialectics of resistance and change offers insights to better understand neoliberal globalization, rethink the mainstream conceptualization about it, and how we can learn from each other on how to alter its course towards greater global social justice.

We disagree with some who argue that the use of the term "Third World" or "Third World women" is no longer applicable since globalization has increasingly integrated nations of the world. We disagree, first, because such argument tends to imply that neoliberal globalization is a neutral process. It fails to see the hegemonic power (mainly embodied in the G-7) that dominates the formulation of neoliberal policies that advance global capitalism or transnational capital which often, in its constant search for cheap labor and resources, violate the rights of working people and abuse the environment. Second, our use of the term "Third World women" recognizes the uneven impact of neoliberal globalization which has, in many instances, exacerbated gender, race/ethnicity and class inequalities. We use the term "Third World women" as a conceptual category for women marginalized and exploited in the process of neoliberal globalization anywhere, particularly in the non-industrialized world. Their resistance defies the hegemony that neoliberal policies fortify, although the struggle is often difficult and not without problems and risks, especially when the "neoliberal state" (Harvey 2007; Robinson 1996) responds with political and military repression. The concept "Third World women", therefore, appropriately recognizes the uneven impact of globalization

---

1 See for example, "Women and Globalization", special issue of *Journal of Developing Societies*, Volume 23, Issue 1-2, January-June 2007, Guest Editors: Ligaya Lindio-McGovern and Erica G. Polakoff.

on working people, depending on their and their nations' position and location in the global political economy. We find "Third World women" in poor and rich countries, in the North and South, in the core and periphery/semi-periphery as neo-liberal globalization continues to structure and re-structure class, race and gender inequalities. It is therefore important that the experience, voice, and politics of Third World women be de-marginalized and included in the mainstream analysis and knowledge construction about neoliberal globalization. This is the thrust of this volume.

We take this thrust, first, because, as David Harvey (2007, 3) argues, "neoliberalism has become hegemonic as a mode of discourse". Largely dominated by think-tanks and policy-makers in the North (Appadurai 2001), this hegemonic mode of discourse can be problematic as it creates a dominant ideational structure that can serve the very structures of power and ideologies that are to be challenged in the struggle for global social justice. Second, because learning from the experience of Third World women as they respond to the impact of neoliberal globalization can unearth knowledge from below rarely represented in policy-making and mainstream academic circles. This knowledge can be useful both for questioning neoliberal policies, policy transformation, and shaping strategies for change. At this juncture, it is important that we first define neoliberal globalization for clarification as the term globalization has been used and abused with different shades of meaning.

What is Neoliberal Globalization?

Neoliberal globalization designates the transformation of the global political economy based on neoliberalism as a "theory of political economic practices that human well-being can be best advanced" in economic arrangements that promote "private [ownership of the means of production], free markets, and free trade", whereby the "role of the state is to create and preserve institutional frameworks" and conditions that will facilitate such practices (Harvey 2007, 2). As an economic project, its basic doctrines of deregulation, privatization, economic liberalization, labor flexibilization and diminished state-supported social provisions (Harvey 2007, Lindio-McGovern 2007) are meant to create the appropriate conditions for the preservation and global expansion of capitalism that has maintained a wealthy transnational capitalist interests that in turn plays an active role in maintaining capitalist globalization (Sklair 2001). Deregulation reduces state regulation of the economy or restrictions on the mobility of capital and labor flexibilization to create an abundant supply of cheap, controllable and disposable labor force, and so create appropriate conditions that facilitate global capital expansion. Economic liberalization—that dismantles restrictions on the flow of goods, services, and foreign investment—promotes transnational capital expansion worldwide. Privatization—that puts public productive and service enterprises into the private sector, reducing state-subsidized social services and reducing public sector corporations—further opens up new spheres for transnational capital to control local economies especially of the Third World. The global power of transnational corporations thereby grows (Korten 2001; Lindio-McGovern 2007). The IMF (International Monetary Fund) and the World Bank that impose structural adjustment policies tied to development loans to the Third World and the WTO (World Trade Organization) that regulate trade have become supra-national structures of power that unfetter the reins of neoliberal globalization. They failed to improve the lives of the marginalized sectors of the global economy, and have even exacerbated their poverty and exploitation.

The major themes woven through the works of the contributors in this volume further illuminate an understanding of the gendered process of globalization and its contestations as they examine the experience of Third World women in both North and South, in Asia, Africa, Latin and Central America.

Globalization and Gendered Regional Inequalities

Most discussions on globalization and global inequality have centered on the global North and South disparity. Such discussions while important, blur the inequalities within regions that may also occur as neoliberalism intensifies gender, class and/or racial inequalities. While the uneven impact of neoliberal globalization has maintained a global core and periphery (North and South), it is also creating a regional core/periphery within the South. One conceptual site to examine the gendered nature of this regional inequality is the circulation of cheap and disposable waged reproductive labor necessary for the maintenance of productive labor, which under neoliberal rule, serves capitalism. Who supplies cheap reproductive labor and who is served? Within a region, an urban center develops where women from poorer countries of the region tend to concentrate to work as domestic workers in middle-class homes. Shireen Ally (Chapter 2 in this volume) calls attention to this phenomenon as she observes it in Southern Africa. Poor women seeking support for their families migrate from the poorer regions of Southern Africa—such as Zimbabwe, Basotho, Mozambique—to better-off South Africa providing the reproductive labor demands of mainly white, middle-class homes, concentrating in Johannesburg, South Africa's urban center. The presence of these women bifurcates the reproductive labor market and wage structure of reproductive labor where the migrant women are placed at the lower end. The post-apartheid South Africa's implementation of neoliberal policies (Ally in this volume; Benjamin 2007) has not benefitted women (and men) evenly within South Africa and within the region, perpetuating historically rooted raced and classed/ gendered structures. Ally's observation of regional inequality in Southern Africa corroborates with Lindio-McGovern's (2004) and Robyn Magalit Rodriguez's (Chapter 4 in this volume) views on Asia where the rise of the New Industrializing Countries (NICS) has sharpened and given a new face to its regional inequality. Taiwan's economy, for example, is partly being built on the back of Asian women from poorer countries in the region—such as the Philippines and Indonesia whose economies have been devastated by neoliberal policies—who provide cheap and disposable reproductive labor, alongside its imported low-waged contract male and female productive labor for companies. There are cases when the migrant women's reproductive labor is extended and blended with productive labor demands of Taiwanese petty capitalists, a way of making productive labor cheaper. Hong Kong—now under Special Administration of mainland China in the post-British colonial rule—has become an urban hub for Filipino and Indonesian reproductive workers pushed out by the economic pressures due to structural adjustment policies imposed on their home countries.

The regional inequality in the South exacerbated under neoliberal globalization is not entirely isolated or delinked from the social construction of inequalities within the richer capitalist countries that comprise the global North. Martha Gimenez's (Chapter 3 in this volume) notion of the "circulation of labor" as mirroring the intensified inequalities resulting from the "mobility of capital" under capitalist globalization provides an insight into how the presence of migrants from countries in the South partly makes possible the stratification of the labor market within a Northern country, exemplified for instance by the United States.

The mobility of capital under regimes of labor flexibilization has hurt both the working class in the North and South. The de-industrialization, for example, in the U.S. economy has resulted in greater unemployment for men, bringing more women to the workforce but mostly in the lower ranks of the occupational ladder. The expansion of the service sector under global capitalism along with the contraction of manufacturing jobs due to de-industrialization requires as well cheap labor, and women predominating in this sector provide both cheaper and more expendable labor. Migrant labor is used, legal and illegal, to further depress wages. But while the retrenched American workers may have some cushions—such as welfare or unemployment insurance—the men and women in poor countries in the South usually do not have such cushions, and their migration, then, is often part of a survival or coping strategy. Sometimes, their governments (as in the case of Philippines, Indonesia, Mexico) turn to labor export as a response to both unemployment and debt crisis resulting from the structural adjustment policies, thus facilitating their migration into an economic diaspora. With increasing feminization of international migration, this "circulation of capital" also increasingly gets gendered. Thus, as neoliberal policies of labor flexibilization, import liberalization, devaluation of local currency and cuts in state-subsidy in social services continue to destroy Third World economies resulting in increased unemployment and underemployment (Lindio-McGovern 2007), the preconditions for the "circulation of labor" is created in the South. And if we come to think that the neoliberal policies of the IMF, the WTO, and the "transnational practices" of transnational corporations (Sklair 2002) that propel neoliberal globalization are largely controlled by Northern powers, then we see where the neoliberal hegemony is centered. However, although centered in the North, this neoliberal hegemony has developed multiple centers of power, including the shaping of "neoliberal states" (Harvey 2007, Robinson 1996) in the South, creating semi-periphery hegemonies as well.

Another conceptual site to examine the gendered and classed nature of regional inequalities and in the North–South divide under globalization is the flow of sex trafficking in the sexual commodification of women. Bandana Purkayastha and Shweta Majumbar (Chapter 11 in this volume) argue that under globalization sex trafficking of women and girls has increased and Third World women's vulnerability to it also increased due to their intensified poverty resulting from structural adjustment policies. The flow of sex trafficking is generally from the global south to the industrialized global north, but regional patterns are also discernible as hegemonies there have a hand on its process and organization. Purkayastha's and Majumbar's investigation of sex trafficking in South Asia show that India, which is becoming an "economic powerhouse" in the region, has become a major destination of trafficked women and girls from the poorer countries, such as Pakistan, Bangladesh, and Nepal. Purkayatha's and Majumbar's observation parallels a pattern in the European region. Women from within Europe whose countries had been more negatively affected by neoliberal and structural adjustment policies resulting in massive job displacement for women—such as Russia and Ukraine (countries in transition from socialist to market economy)—have become vulnerable to sex trafficking to other destination countries within Europe, such as France, Germany, Switzerland, and the Netherlands (Farr 2005).

Neoliberalism in Women in Development Thought/Discourse

In his "Globalization and Development Studies", Philip McMichael (2005, 111) argues that globalization and development "are two sides of the same coin" and that, as "discursive concepts", they have an ideological component. Neoliberalism as an economic project—anchored on an ideological base that is essentially within the capitalist mode of thought—seems more attune to the women in development (WID) mainstream perspective. WID became a dominant thought in the early 1970s emanating from Esther Boserup's seminal work that located Third Women's socially disadvantaged position from their not being integrated into development (Lindio-McGovern 1997; Chow 2002). Largely rooted in the modernization perspective and from the Western liberal feminist perspective, WID advocated for the integration of Third World women into economic development through institutional reforms, education, technology and income-generating activities. Since WID did not basically question the nature of capitalist development into which women were to be integrated, nor the technocratic, top-down premises of the modernization perspective among the North or Western countries, the neoliberal ideology easily and subtly inserted itself into the women in development (WID) discourse and its practice. This subtle insertion makes it appear that WID is empowering Third World women, and therefore requires a careful analysis of development projects espoused by international development agencies that claim to empower women, while its embedded neoliberal ideology and practice may result in marginalizing many and even maintain or sharpen the class disparity among Third World women. Christobel Asiedu (Chapter 9 in this volume) provides a good example of a careful analysis of the how neoliberal system of thought embedded in a development program can result in an uneven impact of neoliberal globalization on women of different class status, while in subtle ways serve the expansion of transnational capital in the Third World, such as in Africa where she conducted her case study. Hence, just as neoliberal globalization interlocks into pre-existing structures of power and inequalities, it also interlocks itself into frames of thought that serve as basis for development policy and practice. But alternative perspectives or development frameworks emerge as well that may also have implications for change. So, in the latter part of the 1970s as a response to the limitations of WID, women and development perspective (WAD) called attention to how global capital accumulation exploited women even as they were integrated into it (Chow 2002). The emergence of WAD apparently coincided with the growth of export-processing zones that began to emerge in Third World countries where women predominated the labor-intensive transnational corporations' global assembly lines, such as garment and electronics (Caraway 2007). Integration of women into global capital accumulation did not liberate most Third World women, especially peasant and working class women, from exploitation and poverty after all. Change for liberation of working class women implies transforming capitalist relations of production. Then in the 1980s, the gender and development (GAD) perspective came to prominence, which recognized the presence of patriarchy within class and across class and the oppression of women in both the reproductive and productive spheres. Viewing development as a complex process shaped by political, economic and social forces, it advocated a holistic approach that included all aspects of women's lives for their empowerment (Chow 2002). It saw Third World women as agents of their own empowerment, not merely beneficiaries of development programs designed from above or by external agencies. DAWN (Development Alternatives with Women for a New Era) came about in 1984 as a response to the marginalization of Third World women's experience in women in development (WID) thought and practice (Sen and Grown 1987; Moghadan 2005). A Third World women's initiative, DAWN "affirmed that it is the experiences lived by poor women throughout the Third Word in their struggle to ensure the basic survival of their families and themselves that provide the clearest lens for an understanding of development processes" and advocated "alternative development processes that would give principal emphasis to the basic survival needs of the majority of the world's people" (Sen and Grown 1987, 10, 9). Asiedu's (Chapter 9 in this volume) proposal to empower women in sub-Sahara Africa—through the introduction of Information Communication Technologies (without viewing it as panacea) in ways that will be more responsive to the needs of the rural women most neglected in the development process—is a bottom-up approach, and within an integrated development model. It is aimed not only at economic empowerment but also at the social and political empowerment of African women—a development perspective that falls within the GAD and DAWN approaches. Robert Dibie's (Chapter 10 in this volume) comprehensive proposals for empowering women in Africa fall within the GAD perspective as well, as he pays attention to the African patriarchal culture and how it has shaped the economic, political and social development of Africa that has subordinated African women, and how that subordination is exacerbated under globalization. However, the general current state of women/gender and development discourse is faced with the challenge to evolve new critical analytical frameworks that can best capture the nuanced ways neoliberal ideology and practice re/configure into existing institutions and development programs of both governmental and non-governmental organizations in ways that may subtly preserve capital accumulation on a global scale rather than facilitate its radical transformation. Such a framework must critically question the argument that considers it a positive aspect of globalization when Third World women are turned into consumers of the products of multinational corporations, low-wage workers, or providers of cheap services, such as domestic work. Such critical frameworks are important as they may have implications for shaping resistance to neoliberalism through alternative development programs and policies that will truly empower Third World women. Such theoretical work would require more ethnographic studies and participation of Third World scholars who are often marginalized in mainstream academic discourses and theorizing about globalization.

Colonialism and Imperialism

Neoliberalism "has roots in the world-historical colonial project associated with the rise of capitalism" (McMicahel 2005, 111). Others argue from the Marxist perspective that globalization is simply a new form of imperialism (Sklair 2002), and would prefer to use the term imperialism than the term globalization because it sort of mystifies its imperial project. Mainstreaming Third World women's experiences in analysis and discussions of neoliberal globalization reduces colonialism and imperialism to seemingly neutral events and processes of globalization. Third World women whose nations had been colonial subjects embody in their experience of exploitation and oppression the gendered nature of the colonial project that was an instrument in the expansion of global capitalism. Anne Lacsamana, and Leigh Brownhill and Terisa E. Turner (Chapters 5 and 6 in this volume) bring back colonialism and imperialism into the discussion of and resistance to globalization. Lacsamana (Chapter 5) calls for a Filipina–American feminist thought and feminism that will address American imperialism that continue to affect the everyday lives of Filipinos both at home and abroad. A two-pronged feminist politics that links Filipina Americans to the anti-imperialist movement in the Philippines as they struggle to construct a non-subjugated identity in the U.S. are salient components of their agency. Such feminist politics must reclaim a historical consciousness that their national identity carries a continuing struggle of the Filipino people for liberation from the continuing clutches of American imperialism, transnational capital, and militarism in the Philippines. The Philippine women's movement itself had always articulated an oppositional stance and politics against imperialism and militarism towards national economic and political sovereignty as it traced its history of struggle from the anti-colonization revolutionary movement. Lacsamana calls attention to the intensification of human rights violations by the Philippine state in response to the growing organized resistance from various sectors of Philippine society to the neoliberal agenda that has increased rather than alleviated the economic pressures they have long suffered.

According to David Harvey (2005), imperialism operates on two logics or processes: "accumulation of capital" and "accumulation of power through dispossession". Accumulation of power through colonialism dispossessed the colonized of their land and control of their labor. Control of land (including its resources) and labor was necessary for the accumulation of capital, transforming pre-colonial communal lands, production and subsistence farming. Accumulation of power through colonialism, however, had to be maintained by force. The gendered process of these two logics can be gleaned from examining the experience of Third World women. In Leigh Brown and Terisa Turner (Chapter 6 in this volume) we see the gendering of these two logics of imperialism in the experience of Kenyan women. Their continuing struggle for land through creative, militant land occupations (which is central to their being able to feed their families) and control of labor (which they lost under British imperialist–capitalist rule) is an eloquent resistance to this imperial logic that is re-articulated in the neoliberal agenda. The Kenyan's women's experience and resistance is paralleled by Filipino peasant women and men whose resistance to their landlessness—which began in the colonization period and intensified under neoliberal globalization—includes land occupations, attempts at control of agricultural labor, and promotion of an ideology of "land belongs to those who till it" (Lindio-McGovern 1997). Elizabeth Eviota (1992) in her *The Political Economy of Gender: Women and the Sexual Division of Labor in the Philippines* and Lindio-McGovern (1997) in her *Filipino Peasant Women: Exploitation and Resistance* provide an analysis of how the imperial logic of accumulation of capital through accumulation of power through dispossession is gendered through the experience of Filipino women. Therefore tracing the historical roots of neoliberal globalization makes visible the common ground of Third Women's experience and the gendered, classed and raced nexus that links the Global North and the Global South.

Resisting Gendered, Classed and Raced Neoliberal Globalization

Transnational feminism that networks women across the world for global social justice can be a potent force for resistance and creating change to avert the destructive and dehumanizing nature of neoliberal globalization. The neoliberal project that further frees the reins of global capitalism and its impact on Third World women suggests the need to contextualize the politics of an activist transnational feminism that would be more responsive to the needs of working class women, both waged and unwaged, and poor women. Martha Gimenez (Chapter 3 in this volume) suggests forging a working class women's politics framed around and based on the location of working women in the relations of production and reproduction, as they are subject to the instability of the national and world economies. Brownhill and Turner (Chapter 6 in this volume) offer an analytical framework that expands the concept of "working class" to include the waged and unwaged since both are commoditized in the process of global capital expansion. Working class women's transnational feminism, especially among Third World women, can strengthen the global resistance to neoliberal globalization that reinforce inequalities between men and women and among women.

Third World women's transnational alliances, in some cases, go beyond the boundaries of class, however, as when they tackle environmental concerns (although environmental issues are not entirely devoid of class issues) or when they participate in the global resistance to imperial wars (Terisa Turner and Leigh Brownhill, Chapter 8 in this volume).

Third World neoliberal nation-states provide the micro-structures for the macro-structures of neoliberalism as embodied in the policies of WTO, IMF and the World Bank. Although it can be argued that the neoliberal state may be unstable and play contradictory roles (Havey 2007, Sassen 1998), the Third World nation state basically centralizes power in the implementation of the neoliberal agenda. Hence, Third World women's resistance in this volume implicates their nation-states. This is best illustrated in the politics of Filipina migrant workers organized under Migrante International that targets the Philippine state in their struggle for migrants' rights even though they are geographically outside of it since it is actively promoting labor export due to unemployment and debt crisis resulting from the implementation of structural adjustment and neoliberal development policies in the Philippines (Robyn Magalit Rodriquez, Chapter 4). The nation-state is still looked upon to guarantee migrants rights in their host societies. So do the migrant domestic workers in South Africa, from poorer neighboring states, who voiced their demands for protective legislations that would guarantee them equal labor rights as other workers in South Africa (Shireen Ally, Chapter 2).

As a target of resistance, the state must be transformed in order to accommodate women's demands. This is exemplified in the Kenyan women's collective efforts to work for constitutional reforms that would guarantee their demands for land and food security (Leigh Brown and Terisa Turner, Chapter 6), and in the Philippine women's movement in alliance with other groups to engage in the political campaign for the resignation of the incumbent president, Gloria Macapagal-Arroyo, on whose ruling political and military machinery is deemed accountable for the recent political killings of student, peasant, worker, clergy, media, women and youth activists (Anne Lacsamana, Chapter 5). The unseating of the incumbent president would be a way to move to a transition government that would pave the formation of a democratic coalition government that would end militarization and work for an alternative system of governance and development that will promote the economic and social upliftment of the majority of the Filipino people and a sovereign nation.

The core corporate state allied with transnational capital is implicated as well, as Third World women challenge corporate greed that ravages the earth's resources, creating an unsustainable future. This is demonstrated in the global action to keep oil on the ground, calling for a moratorium on oil drilling by Nigerian, Costa Rican, and Ecuadorian women, involving indigenous communities (Terisa Turner and Leigh Brownhill, Chapter 8). The women challenged core corporate states to play a more active role in assuming environmental responsibility and controlling the power of oil corporations, even as they try to undermine their corporate power through shut-downs, strikes and boycotts.

Taking the state as a target of resistance in their contentious politics for a more just and life-sustaining world, Third World women defy the neoliberal agenda of deregulation that increasingly deprives citizens of their right to a sovereign government that will serve their interest and needs, protect them from corporate abuse that commoditizes their labor, and corporate power that deprives them of equitable access to resources. Their state-oriented politics of resistance invites calling into question the argument that the state withers away in the process of neoliberal globalization. The state may play contradictory roles under pressures from competing interests, or play an instrumentalist role to transnational capital, or a protective, transformative role in response to militant, massive, intense pressure from civil society to create alternative social arrangements and institutional frameworks to neoliberal globalization. Some states indeed have assumed a transformative role to effect alternatives to neoliberalism, such as the case of Venezuelan government under the leadership of Hugo Chavez who have responded to the demands of the poor for control of resources (Terisa Turner and Leigh Brownhill, Chapter 8) and forming an alternative regionalism among states that want to take a different turn from the neoliberal path (Ann Ferguson, Chapter 7).

As neoliberal globalization impairs local Third World economies and human rights deteriorate as governments contain political activism, the promotion of inalienable economic and political rights becomes even more urgent. Economic rights—the right to have a decent employment free of exploitative and dehumanizing working conditions; the right to adequate access to basic resources of food, shelter, clean/potable water, and health care; the right to a sustainable environment; the right to land and other means necessary to sustain means of livelihood; the right to education—cannot be attained under the counter-insurgency of neoliberal regimes without protecting and promoting as well political rights—the right of people to organize collective action to bring about change, to engage in transformative action directed at the state, the right to a voice in policy making, the right to equal place in governance, the right to public assembly and the means to disseminate/access information to articulate their voice and stories. The social conditions Third World women face and the confrontation for change and resistance they are shaping bring to urgency to broaden our conceptualization of rights to see the importance of intertwining political and economic rights, both in the process of change and in the content of change. Both are to be struggled for.

Proactive resistance to neoliberal globalization requires alternative values, antithetical to the values espoused by neoliberalism, that can shape alternative social arrangements, such as alternative economies. Neoliberalism promotes and is nourished by the culture and spirit of individualism, which is incompatible with the pursuit of social justice that presupposes social solidarity and the willingness to embrace that which would promote the common good (Harvey 2005). Embedded in the politics of Third World women's resistance are alternative values that form the basis or foundation for the alternative institutional arrangements emanating from below. For instance, the "solidarity economy" that the Mexican women are shaping through the formation of a cooperative movement nurtures and articulates the values of community and collective sharing of resources, time, and labor while at the same time offers an alternative to corporate economy (Ann Ferguson, Chapter 7 in this volume). Their productive cooperatives create micro-structures of non-capitalist relations that serve as an alternative to petty capitalism that fertilizes the ground for global capital accumulation, and which at times may enrich petty capitalists through the cheap labor of poorer men and women and even children. Their trading cooperatives provide an alternative to the unequal free trade contained in NAFTA and other free trade regimes of globalization, such as the WTO (World Trade Organization), that extract resources from the Third World, taking away their sovereignty over their own resources. Solidarity economies from below need the support not only of non-governmental organizations, but also of the state if it wants to take a transformative role.

In his *The Great Turning: From Empire to Earth Community*, David C. Korten (2006) talks about the need for "birthing" an "Earth Community" that would be oppositional to the values of Empire. "Empire" pursues hierarchical relationships based on domination and control, concentrates resources and material wealth to the ruling elite, honors the destructive power of violence and war, values masculine dominance, suppresses power of the many below and their great human potential for mature self-determination, courage, fearlessness and hope that can mobilize them for change. "Earth Community" on the other hand values, promotes, and sustains relationships that are non-hierarchical, gender balanced, cooperative partnerships/human connectedness, is protective of the rights of all, promotes democratic decision-making based on mutual responsibility and accountability, re-distribute power and resources to empower the powerless and improve the lives of all, and actualize human potentials. The cultural project of "Earth Community" favors communal stewardship of resources for the benefit of future generations. Its economic project affirms the right of every person to a means of livelihood, local control, self-reliance, and fair trade and sharing. Its political project affirms people's right to participate in decision-making that affect their lives, promotes restorative justice that distributes power equitably for the benefit of the whole community. As Third World women form communities of struggle in their collective response to the impact of neoliberal globalization, they are in the process of shaping the "birthing" of "Earth Community" that will be responsive to their own needs, and particular historically–culturally–politically produced economic, social conditions.

What More Needs to be Done?

A lot more needs to be done. On the epistemological level, more ethnographic studies that unearth thick description of Third World women's resistance wherever they are needs to be done. In this process more exploration on how the principles of feminist research can be more explicitly utilized is called for.[2] This volume suggests there is value in examining neoliberal globalization from the experience of "Third World women" who bear more the brunt of its negative impact because of their position and their nations' position in the global political economy and gendered, raced, and classed systems it perpetuates. Cross-country studies inquiring areas not yet covered and other sectors of the economy need to be further investigated.

On the transformational activist level, certainly a lot more needs to be done. One area, as indicated in the transnational networks that the Third World women are already forging, is to explore the possibility of forming new regionalisms from below and inter-regional empowerment networks both from the grassroots level and the interstate level. This new regionalism and inter-regionalism will consist of alliances of organized groups of men and women who see the need to change the course of neoliberalism in their regions and organize dialogues to gather and analyse data of the experiences of grassroots men and women to identify commonalities and particularities of their experiences. Then raise these efforts on inter-regional level dialogues and networks to organize a global voice of resistance and alternatives to neoliberal globalization. The process and content of this new regionalism will be determined by the groups themselves. On the level of the states, government leaders who have some consciousness to avert the policies of neoliberal globalization can begin to form alliances that will strengthen their exchange of resources and alternative world views in forging alternative economies and trade relations. These initiatives that are already in limited ways incipient in Latin America can be strengthened and broadened to inter-regional alliances to include Asia, Africa, and the Middle-East.

What more needs to be done is daunting and certainly without difficulties and even risks. But the voices, experiences, and actions of Third World women documented and analyzed in this volume provide the insight and hope that change

---

2   For a detailed discussion of feminist research see Sharlene NagbyHesse-Biber and Patricia Lina Leavy, *Feminist Research Practice* (2007). London and New Delhi: Sage Publications.

is possible, and that a more just, more equitable, more sustainable world is achievable.

References

Appadurai, A. (ed.) (2001), *Globalization* (Durham and London: Duke University Press).

—— (2001), "Grassroots Globalization and the Research Imagination", in Appadurai, A. (ed.), *Globalization* (Durham and London: Duke University Press), 1-21.

Appelbaum, R. and Robinson, W. (2005), *Critical Globalization Studies* (New York: Routledge).

Brecher, J., Costello, T. and Smith, B (2009), "Globalization and Social Movements", in Eitzen, D.S. and Zinn, M.B (eds), *Globalization: The Transformation of the Social Worlds* (Belmont, California: Wadsworth Cengage Learning).

Caraway, T.L. (2007), *Assembling Women: The Feminization of Global Manufacturing* (Ithaca and London: Cornell University Press).

Chow, E. (2002), *Transforming Gender and Development in East Asia* (New York: Routledge).

Chow, E. and Lyter, D. (2002), "Studying Development with Gender Perspectives: From Mainstream Theories to Alternative Frameworks", in Chow, E. (ed.), *Transforming Gender and Development in East Asia* (New York and London: Routledge), 26-57.

Eviota, E. (1992), *The Political Economy of Gender: Women and the Sexual Division of Labor in the Philippines* (London and New Jersey: Zed Books).

Farr, K. (2005), *Sex Trafficking: The Global Market in Women and Children* (New York: Worth Publishers).

Harvey, D. (2007), *A Brief History of Neoliberalism* (New York: Oxford University Press).

—— (2005), "From Globalization to the New Imperialism", in Appelbaum, R. and Robinson, W. (eds), *Critical Globalization Studies* (New York: Routledge), 91-100.

Hesse-Biber, S.N. and Leavy, P.L. (2007), *Feminist Research Practice* (Thousand Oaks, London, New Delhi: Sage Publications)

Held, D., McGrew, A., Goldblatt, D. and Perraton, J. (eds) (1999), *Global Transformations: Politics, Economics and Culture* (Stanford, California: Stanford University Press).

Heyzer, N. (1986), *Working Women in South-East Asia: Development, Subordination and Emancipation* (Milton Keynes: Open University Press).

Korten, D.C. (2006), *The Great Turning: From Empire to Earth Community* (San Francisco and Bloomfield, Connecticut: Berrett-Koehler Publishers, Inc. and Kumarian Press).

—— (2001), *When Corporations Rule the World* (San Francisco and Bloomfield, Connecticut: Berrett-Koehler Publishers, Inc. and Kumarian Press).

Lindio-McGovern, L. (2007), "Neo-liberal Globalization in the Philippines: Its Impact on Filipino Women and Their Forms of Resistance", *Journal of Developing Societies* 23:1-2, 15-35.

—— (2005), "Alienation and Labor Export in the Context of Globalization: Filipino Migrant Domestic Workers in Taiwan and Hong Kong", *Critical Asian Studies* 36:2, 217-238.

—— (2003), "Labor Export in the Context of Globalization: The Experience of Filipino Domestic Workers in Rome", *International Sociology* 18:3, 513-34.

—— (1997), *Filipino Peasant Women: Exploitation and Resistance* (Philadelphia: University of Pennsylvania Press).

McMichael, P. (2005), "Globalization and Development Studies", in Richard Appelbaum and William Robinson (eds.), *Critical Globalization Studies* (New York: Routledge), 111-120,.

Moghadam, V. (2005), *Globalizing Women: Transnational Feminist Networks* (Baltimore, Maryland: The Johns Hopkins University Press).

Naples, N. and Manisha, D. (2002), *Women's Activism and Globalization: Linking Local Struggles and Transnational Politics* (New York: Routledge).

Polakoff, E. (2007), "Globalization and Child Labor: Review of the Issues", *Journal of Developing Societies* 23:1-2,259-83.

Sassen, S. (1998), *Globalization and Its Discontents* (New York: New York Press).

Sen, G. and Grown, C. (1987), *Development, Crises, and Alternative Visions: Third World Women's Perspectives* (New York: Monthly Review Press).

Sklair, L. (2002), *Globalization: Capitalism and Its Alternatives*, 3rd Edition. (New York: Oxford University Press).

Smith, J. and Johnston, H. (2002), *Globalization and Resistance: Transnational Dimensions of Social Movements* (New York, Oxford: Rowman & Littlefield Publishers, Inc.).

Chapter 2

Globalization and Regional Inequalities
Regional Divisions of Reproductive Labor: Southern African Migrant Domestic Workers in Johannesburg

Shireen Ally

Introduction

While mainstream studies of globalization have examined the global re-organization of production, they have not been as trained on its "intimate 'Other'," the global re-organization of *re*production (Truong 1996, 47). But, recent scholarship within feminist and migration studies has exposed the "female shadow of globalization" (Ally 2005), as transnational flows of productive capital are accompanied by transnational flows of migrant women who labor as domestic, reproductive workers. This has been theorized as resulting in an "international division of reproductive labor" (Parreñas 2000), as the work of caring for primarily white families in the North is performed mainly by women "of color" from the global South, for low wages and under poor working conditions.

But, globalization has not only exacerbated the North-South divide, but generated and compounded inequalities *within* the global South as well. Increasing transnational flows of migrant domestic workers along the South-South circuit are indicative and constitutive of globalization's exacerbation of *regional* inequalities. Some of the earliest work on the globalization of paid domestic work, indeed, examined it as a regional phenomenon. Nicole Constable (1997) explored the experiences of Filipina domestic workers in Hong Kong, while Christine Chin (1998) offered an excellent analysis of Filipina and Indonesian domestic workers in Malaysia.

But, despite this initial recognition of the regional labor diaspora produced by globalization, an entire literature followed by exploring transnational migrant domestic work as a phenomenon of North–South inequalities within globalization (see also Anderson 2000, Chang 2000). In the most recent book on transnational migrant domestic work, however, there has been a return to a focus on regional inequalities. By examining Indonesian and Filipina domestic workers in Taiwan, Lan (2006, 4) explores how "the destinations of migration are no longer exclusively toward core countries in the North," but how the "newly-rich countries in the

South" produce new relations and hierarchies of inequalities regionally, rather than North to South.

While critical, the literature exposing the transnational migrant flows of domestic workers within the global South has been limited almost exclusively to exploring regional inequalities within Asia. In part, this reflects the specific visibility and extent of regional inequalities within the Asian regional constellation of the South, compared to others. But, Southern Africa as a region has witnessed important politico-economic shifts in the past decade that has produced a similar constellation of regional inequality. Not surprisingly, as various countries in the Southern African region have experienced politico-economic restructuring attendant to globalization, there has been the intensification of transnational flows of migrant domestic labor. Francis Nyamnjoh's (2006) recent account of Zimbabwean "maids" in Botswana has been a pioneering attempt to begin an exploration of this trans-regional labor diaspora. Documenting the fact that in Gaborone (Botswana) alone, domestic workers come from Zimbabwe, Zambia, Malawi, Kenya, and Somalia, Nymanjoh begins to detail regional disparities within Southern Africa. He also suggests the ways in which an examination of the circulation of domestic workers between countries within the region maps relative regional inequalities.

But, to understand the ways in which regional inequalities are reflected in, and constituted by, migrant domestic labor across the Southern African region, the most instructive entry point is South Africa. South Africa's expanding economic and political influence within sub-Saharan Africa is undisputed. Following the end of apartheid, and South Africa's transition to democracy, its position as the most industrialized country in the region has been reinforced by various forms of economic liberalization attendant to globalization. Through negotiated free trade areas such as the Southern African Customs Union, and various multilateral agreements, including those of the WTO, South African capital mobility, investment, and trade across the region has intensified in the past decade (Miller 2005). Many analysts have declared the intentions and effects of such South African expansionism "sub-imperialist," as South African retailers and mining houses expand into the region in ways that marginalize local producers, extract resources, and repatriate profits without serious development investment (Bond 2004). "That the new and ever surging waves of migration [to South Africa] are linked to th[is] accelerated globalization of consumer capitalism is all too obvious," argues Francis Nyamnjoh (2006, 31).

As a result, nationals from almost every country on the continent can now be found in Johannesburg, the country's economic center. A growing literature explores the experiences of migration in Johannesburg for African migrants from every part of the continent (Morris and Bouillon 2001, Crush 2001, Crush and MacDonald 2001, Landau 2004). Much of this in-migration to Johannesburg is, however, specifically from the Southern African region (Crush and MacDonald 2001). While official Southern African Development Community (SADC) protocols are quite restrictive in terms of the free movement of peoples (Oucho and

Crush 2001), legal migration from Southern Africa to South Africa has reportedly grown almost tenfold since 1990 (Crush and MacDonald 2000). There are no reliable figures for illegal migration, but it is bound to be equally dramatic.

As the local media have been quick to point out, of the legal and illegal immigrants who have flooded into Johannesburg, many women are likely to be employed as domestic workers (*Mail and Guardian* September 2, 2004). This chapter explores these transnational flows of migrant domestic workers along the South–South circuit within Southern Africa, and suggests the implications of this transnational division of reproductive labor for understanding *regional* inequalities within globalization.

Migrancy and Paid Domestic Work in South Africa

Jacklyn Cock's pioneering and seminal study, *Maids and Madams* (1980), documented meticulously the terrible pay, oppressive working conditions, and dehumanizing sexism and racism endured by South African domestic workers under apartheid. Widely regarded as amongst the most marginalized and exploited women of the working class, South African domestic workers had labored under apartheid's peculiar regime of migrancy. As Mahmood Mamdani's *Citizen and Subject* (1996, 18-21) detailed, the forms of political governance that separated urban and rural contexts ensured a bifurcated South African state mobilizing citizenship as the basis for an urban regime of law and rights, in contrast to the rural regime of extra-economic coercion and a "tribalized native authority." For black domestic workers, this created a distinct relationship between citizenship rights and labor market positioning, which rendered them tenuous migrants, requiring "passes" in order to remain in the urban areas where they worked.

The transition to democracy beginning in the early 1990s restructured citizenship and South African domestic workers benefited from the extension of an impressive array of new legal technologies for their protection, including access to the same rights as all other workers, a national minimum wage, mandatory contracts of employment, and the extension of unemployment insurance. Research has shown that these forms of inclusion have not transformed the institution of paid domestic work in South Africa (Ally 2006, Fish 2006, see also King 2007). As importantly, paid domestic work for black South African women remains enduringly migrant, in an intranational and social, rather than transnational and political sense, as workers continue to straddle the divides between urban and rural contexts (Ally 2006).

But, while the majority of domestic workers in South Africa remain intranational migrants, the sector is also made up of transnational migrants, especially from the rest of Southern Africa. The history of immigrants in paid domestic work in South Africa is, however, not necessarily new.

Foreign White Women, to Local Black Men and Women, to...Foreign Black Women?

When, by the beginning of the nineteenth century, the expansion of white English colonial settlement (increased demand) combined with a limited supply of local labor, it gave impetus to a period in which white women immigrants were increasingly incorporated into the sector (Cock 1980). Large numbers of white European women, seeking a route of escape from the poor working conditions and limited occupational opportunities available to them in a highly class-stratified Britain, immigrated to colonial South Africa to work as domestics (Swaisland 1993).

Towards the 1880s, however, white immigrant women came to be an unreliable supply to meet the demand for domestic labor in the Cape (Swaisland 1993), initiating the demographic shift to predominantly black women in the Cape. On the Witwatersrand (Van Onselen 1982), the economic hinterland of the country, and in Natal, a coastal colonial outpost, white female domestics were replaced by initially, black men, and then later black women. While temporally and regionally discontinuous, by the 1930s the dominant demographic pattern of domestic service in South Africa as an occupation of black women, from within the borders of South Africa, had been established (Cock 1980, Boddington 1983, Gaitskell et al. 1984).

While this continues to remain the major demographic pattern of paid domestic work until today, women migrants from neighboring countries have, throughout the latter half of the twentieth century, also crossed the border to work as domestic workers in South Africa, most notably from Lesotho, but also from Zimbabwe, Mozambique, and Swaziland. The extent of these regional migrants' incorporation into paid domestic work in apartheid South Africa has not been fully documented. Instead, existing analyses of the history of paid domestic work in South Africa have focused almost exclusively on intranational migrants (Whisson and Weil 1971, Preston-Whyte 1976, Cock 1980, Gordon 1985, Gaitskell et al. 1984, Fish 2006, King 2007).

A very useful recent survey of domestic workers in Johannesburg, however, indicated that migrant domestic workers from the region do constitute a sector of the paid domestic work market (Peberdy and Dinat 2005). The survey found, interestingly, that all foreign domestic workers were from the Southern African region, almost 50 percent from Lesotho, almost a third from Zimbabwe, and the rest from Mozambique (6 percent), Botswana (4 percent), Swaziland (4 percent), Malawi (4 percent), and Zambia (2 percent).

While the extent of illegality makes it difficult to ascertain accurately the number of transnational migrant domestic workers in South Africa today, there is a pervasive feeling that the phenomenon has intensified in recent years. Francis Nyamnjoh's (2006) innovative exploration of regional migrant domestic work found that the vast majority of foreign domestic workers in Botswana (87.7 percent), especially Zimbabweans, came to Botswana between 2000 and 2003. To explore this in contemporary South Africa, I conducted an intensive qualitative study between

January and June 2007 to understand the contours of transnational migrant domestic work in Johannesburg, the country's largest and most populous city, and its implications for understanding regional divisions of reproductive labor within globalization.

Sampling transnational migrant domestic workers at churches, social gatherings, and residences in the inner city of Johannesburg, and the working-class neighborhoods surrounding it, in-depth interviews were conducted with 28 workers who felt comfortable enough to tell me their stories. They revealed not only their reasons for, and experiences of migration and paid domestic work, but the socio-political structuring of a supply of domestic labor from South Africa's poorer neighboring countries.

Transnational Migrants as Domestic Workers in Contemporary Johannesburg

'The Land of Milk and Honey'

One does not have to spend much time in the inner city neighborhoods of Johannesburg – Hillbrow, Yeoville, Braamfontein, and Berea – to find women (and men) who have left their homesteads in Lesotho, Zimbabwe, Mozambique, Botswana, Zambia, Malawi, Swaziland, and Namibia, and who currently work as domestic workers in the affluent suburbs of Johannesburg, and even its working-class ones.

Some have been in South Africa as migrant domestics for more than twenty years. The Malawian and Zambian men in the sample had arrived in South Africa in the 1980s, and one even in 1976, to work for families more comfortable with "houseboys." Women from Lesotho, Zimbabwe, Botswana, and Swaziland had also been working as domestics in Johannesburg for at least 15 years. But, a fair proportion (36 percent) of the migrant domestics in the sample arrived in South Africa after the transition to democracy in 1994, and constitute a new segment of transnational migrant domestic workers.[1]

These include Zimbabwean, Basotho, and (to a much lesser extent) Mozambican women[2] who have fled stagnating and deteriorating economic conditions and

---

1   While 36 percent of the migrant domestics were recent immigrants, it is still unclear what proportion of domestic workers in South Africa are foreign migrants. Peberdy and Dinat's (2005) survey found that approximately 6 percent of domestic workers in Johannesburg were from countries other than South Africa, but many labor experts suggest that with the extent of illegal immigration, the figure is likely to be much higher.

2   Two of the women in this sample were Zimbabwean and Mozambican respectively, but did not work for South Africans as domestics, but rather for their countrymen and women.

uncertain political futures in their home countries, many illegally, to find better prospects in what some called 'the land of milk and honey.'"[3]

Women, especially from Zimbabwe and Lesotho, with limited education and few work-related skills faced shrinking economies in their home countries. In Zimbabwe, an economic implosion saw the unemployment rate rise to 80 percent in 2005 (*Business Report*, February 19, 2007) and annual inflation to over one million percent by May 2008,[4] with major shortages of basic commodities, including bread, milk, and petrol. In Lesotho, village economies dependent on the remittances of male migrant miners in South Africa faced serious disruption when South African gold mining operations dramatically shrunk in the 1990s. While sub-contracted multinational textile firms created low-wage jobs for many young women, some sought alternative sources of employment. Many of the new migrant domestics in Johannesburg are therefore Zimbabwean and Basotho women fleeing deteriorating economic conditions and lack of jobs in their home countries.

But, just as importantly, many of the recent migrants have equally come to Johannesburg pulled by the lure of an expanding and urbane city life, pregnant with exciting opportunities. Anna Mukwedeya,[5] a 28-year-old Zimbabwean woman from a shanty town bordering Harare, for instance, explained that she came to Johannesburg because many of her cousins had been to the city, and had returned with stories of a pulsing urban energy on the streets of Johannesburg, an exciting social life, and the many opportunities for testing one's hand at a variety of entrepreneurial ventures. Anna, having always dreamed of owning her own hair salon, and seeing the possibility of the realization of that dream become more distant every day in Zimbabwe, decided to leave Harare temporarily in order to "find a way" in Johannesburg.

Mmantho Moshesh, a 25-year-old woman from a rural village in the highlands of Lesotho, was similarly drawn to Johannesburg's prospects. With drought having made the prospects of survival through subsistence agriculture in Lesotho unlikely, she had tried to find work in Maseru, Lesotho's capital city. But, not having finished high school, she struggled, and imagined a bigger, better life for herself than the confines of Lesotho seemed to provide. When she learned through a friend that a surreptitious plan was afoot to abduct her for marriage, she resolved to leave what she imagined as a parochial life in Lesotho to explore the "big city" of Johannesburg, with its "big buildings, and many, many people, and lots and lots of opportunities."

Whether pushed by the lack of opportunities in their home countries, or pulled by what seemed the abundance of opportunities in "the land of milk and honey,"

---

3   Many workers in the sample referred to South Africa in this way, but for a few, they did so sarcastically.

4   Reported by Tendai Biti, Platform for Public Deliberation, Thursday May 22 2008, Wits University Great Hall.

5   The names of all workers are pseudonyms, to protect guarantees of anonymity.

when they finally made their way to Johannesburg, many of these women found themselves encountering a situation very different than they had imagined.

Being *"Makwerekwere"*

Far from "the land of milk and honey," most of the women who made their way to Johannesburg found themselves immediately confronted by a hostile state, a hostile local population, and a hostile economic environment. Having to negotiate with the South African government's Department of Home Affairs, responsible for issuing temporary visas and work-seeking permits, became a horrifying experience for more than a few women. Threatened with deportation, border officials and those staffing the main Home Affairs offices within the city elicited sexual favors and money in exchange for papers.

Sylvia Mapondo, a 20-year-old Zimbabwean woman, left her son behind in the care of her mother in Bulawayo, and paid a border runner who escorted her and six others on a three-day journey across the crocodile-infested Limpopo river into South Africa. Staying at a dilapidated house in Musina, inside South Africa, they were raided by the police, who wanted sexual services in return for not sending her back home. "If I didn't do it, they were going to send me back, and then I would have to do that whole thing all over again," explained Sylvia with tears in her eyes.

Similarly, the hostile and violent reception of some of the women by the South African state was matched by the reception they received from ordinary South Africans. "They call you 'makwerekwere' and tell you to go back to Zim where you come from," related Elizabeth Tshifadzwa. A derogatory and insulting term for a foreigner, "makwerekwere" is used in South Africa to dehumanize black African migrants (Nyamnjoh 2006), delegitimate their presence, and mark them out for xenophobic attitudes, and sometimes, attacks.

Mahmoud Issa, a Malawian who had worked for the same family for fifteen years in Crosby, a township in the west of the city, was assaulted one evening while walking to catch a taxi to Yeoville, where he socialized with friends. The young thugs who dragged him along the road, beat him up, and left him wounded on the street, repeatedly called him "makwerekwere" and claimed the punishment was for "stealing our jobs and stealing our women." Mahmoud, painfully recalling the incident to my research assistant, explained mournfully, "I am a Muslim, and I have my wife here, so I don't mess around with South African women, but still they called me a 'makwerekwere' and said I was stealing their women."

The extent of xenophobia amongst South Africans towards, especially, foreign black Africans, has been well analyzed (Sichone 2001). A coercive economy of unemployment in South Africa, between 36 percent and 41 percent, creates intense competition for jobs. While coming to Johannesburg in the hope of better prospects at the heart of the continent's most vibrant economy, migrants found themselves instead in a very tight labor market and a hostile economic environment, in which transportation, accommodation, and food are expensive, and where competition for the available jobs very intense.

For women with limited education and experience, the low-skill, low-wage construction and security sector jobs available to their male counterparts were not as easily available to them. Seasonal agricultural work, which some of their friends and family had taken up, did not appeal to some of the women who wished to remain in the city. In this context, many of the women migrants, from Zimbabwe and Lesotho especially, found one form of work in Johannesburg that was readily available – domestic work.

"The Job is Tough, but it is Building my Future"

With nearly a million South African women employed in domestic work, it is the largest single sector of women's employment in the country (Ally 2004). With such demand, the migrant women who eventually found themselves in paid domestic work did so relatively easily. Some had tried their hand at entrepreneurial activities, but found it difficult to sustain without access to credit, or found themselves crowded out by the ever-expanding informal sector activity on the streets of the degenerating inner city. Some had secured other forms of employment, usually working for other migrants, sometimes on the streets. Many realized within a few weeks of being in the city that the demand from urban households for reliable cleaning and child care services made for a viable form of employment. As one worker, Sarah Ndungu explained:

> In Harare, you can do domestic work, but it does not pay very much and you can get treated very badly, because you work many, many hours. So, in Jo'burg, I first did not want to do this kind of work. But, my neighbor in my flat she had a job [as a domestic worker]. When she wanted to go back to Zim, she told her madam I could work for her. That's how I got this job.

Workers reported that employers were more keen on hiring Zimbabwean domestics rather than local South Africans because, as workers paraphrased their employers' attitudes, "we [Zimbabweans] are more educated," "more loyal, trustworthy," "more clean," "speak better English," and "are cheaper." Basotho workers suggested similar employer stereotypes in preference for Basotho, compared to South African, workers: "Basotho are more clean," "more respectable and quiet," "don't demand as much," "work for less money," and "are more full of respect."

This construction of ethnic-national stereotypes to hierarchically order the domestic labor market has been documented in other instances as well (Pratt 1997). Here, the specific construction of national differences by employers was also reproduced by South African domestic workers themselves as they disparaged foreign women for allegedly taking their jobs and working for much less. An official of the national union,[6] in fact, reproduced employers' logic claiming that "these Zimbabwean and Mozambican workers come here and they work for peanuts, and they are making it very difficult for us [South African domestic workers] to get the minimum wage."

While some migrant domestics, especially Basotho, were earning relatively good wages,[7] there were a large proportion (54 percent) of workers, mainly Zimbabwean, Basotho and Mozambican, in this study who earned less than R400 [USD 57][8] per month. Similarly, while several experienced generally good working conditions, with reasonable hours, and access to leave, many worked under quite abusive conditions.

Sylvia Mapondo, working for an employer in the dilapidated suburb of Troyeville, was forced to scrub the toilet using a toothbrush, and sleep underneath the kitchen sink on an old and bug-infested mattress. Sylvia struggled to find affordable accommodation in the city after she and her Congolese boyfriend at the time were evicted from the rundown inner city apartment where they stayed, and for a while lived in a one-bedroom apartment with her boyfriend and eight of his family, until the relationship ended, and she was stranded in the city without an income or place to stay.

The employer she eventually came to work for in Troyeville, offered her a "rent-free" spot beneath the sink, and "free" food, as well as R250 [USD 29] a month, in exchange for her full-time services as a maid, cook, and stand-by shopkeeper in the little café he ran out the back room of the decaying house. For giving out the wrong change to a customer one day, she was locked in a room for two days with only water and a half a loaf of stale bread. While Sylvia's was the worst case of abuse encountered in this study, most workers faced some or other form of abuse. Many, especially Zimbabwean workers, worked long hours, for poor pay, and many subject to sexual abuse. While many complained, they also repeatedly emphasized that the work they did was crucial for their current and future livelihoods.

Sarah Ndungu was typical in this, as the relatively good wages she earned of R1600 [USD 228] per month allowed her to rent a small apartment in Berea, a high-density low-income residential area of the inner city, feed and clothe her one infant son, and the 18-year-old sister from Zimbabwe who lived with them to take care of the little boy during the working day, as well as send crucial remittances back home, which when converted to Zimbabwean dollars, represented a small fortune. Sarah explained:

---

6   SADSAWU (South African Domestic Service and Allied Workers Union).

7   One worker earned R2500.00 [USD 357] per month, and four earned approximately R1500.00 [USD 214] per month.

8   These conversions are based on the exchange rate at the time of writing, of seven South African Rands (R) to one U.S. Dollar (USD).

> With the sometimes R200 [USD 29] I can send back every month, I have now over four years, built a house on the homestead of my parents, and I have bought chickens and paid for new fencing for the coup, plus they have grown a big vegetable garden with the money, and even sell some of the cabbage at the market on Saturday. People, when they come from the other areas they are very jealous that we have so much and have built such a prosperous life. This job is tough, but it is building my future.

Most workers explained the crucial function of their remittances – which when converted into Maloti, Pula, or Zimbabwean dollars – made them relatively prosperous in their home countries, and allowed for the guarantee of a better future when they returned home. Mmantho Moshesh, a young Basotho woman, having scorned the provincialism of Lesotho, working live-in for employers who have never allowed her more than one week's worth of leave per year, is also building something to return to:

> I have been sending some of my money home every month for my family so they can eat. They would not survive without it, and they are sending my one niece to school with it. But, I am also keeping a little bit, because these few rands here, it is worth a lot in Lesotho, and I want to have my own tavern when I go back. I have already a lot put away for this, and I know I will have a bright future back home for the work I am doing here right now [translated from Sesotho]

Despite the optimism of many workers, of surviving difficult working conditions now, for the security of a better future later, for the workers in this study who had been working as migrant domestics for more than fifteen years, the prosperous future was always deferred, and they endured instead difficult working conditions with little protection in the "new" South Africa.

"They Need your Labor, but they Don't Want You"

South Africa's immigration policies are notoriously restrictive, and its implementation sometimes brutalizing. With a strong aversion to receiving unskilled and semi-skilled immigrants, the South African state has made deportation, or detention at its repatriation center, Lindela, a common experience for many undocumented migrant domestics. Judith Atanasio, a Mozambican domestic worker in Melrose, one of Johannesburg's most affluent suburbs, was arrested in Rosebank one evening for being in the country illegally, and sent to the Lindela repatriation center. While meant to be temporary, Judith was kept at Lindela under difficult conditions for three weeks, experiencing alleged brutality at the hands of Lindela staff regularly during that time. A week after being deported she found her way back in to the country, and reported her employer's reaction on her return:

She shouted at me first. She said where was I for a month? She had some big party. She needed me. Then, she found another maid for that time. But, she said to me I must be lucky because that girl stole some earrings, and I came to the door just before she could get someone else. Think about it. She did not want to know where I was for a month. She was just happy I was there that morning because she had another party and needed my labor. The whole of South Africa – they need your labor, but they don't want you [translated from Portuguese].

Workers in this study repeatedly emphasized the intense depersonalization that issued from employers' interest in their labor, but complete disinterest in them as persons. One worker put it succinctly: "They don't care if you get deported, or what you went through to get *Egoli* [to Johannesburg]. They just care that the clothes are washed and ironed, the house is clean, and the food is cooked."

Of course, two employers of long-time migrant domestics had facilitated permanent residence status for their workers, and the workers spoke affectionately of their employers, while at the same time remaining quite critical of their employers' efforts. Martha Moseneke, a domestic worker for more than 12 years from Botswana, whose employers assisted her in getting permanent residency for herself and her son expressed a more complicated understanding of her employers' benevolence:

They have been very good to me and my child. But, I was with them for 10 years, and raised their daughter as if she was my own. When they had a second child, they knew they needed me. I was already explaining to them how I will have to go home for my son and because I don't have proper papers any more. It's like that, you see. They needed me.

But, many migrant domestic workers were treated as disposable by their employers. Only 45 percent of the domestic workers in this sample who had arrived in South Africa after 1994 stayed in any job for longer than a year. Many cited deportation as a major reason for the break in employment. Others referenced employers' sense of the disposability of foreign domestic workers as cheap labor. Elizabeth Tshifadzwa energetically mocked an employer, mimicking the South African accent and the employers' mannerisms as she dramatized for me and my research assistant the perceived attitude of South African employers: "I like Mugabe. He sends me a new maid every month, every time half the price of the one before." Elizabeth was joking, but in some ways not. Many workers like Judith explained how, after being deported, or going home for a visit and re-entering the country illegally, they returned to their employment only to find their employer having hired another desperate migrant domestic worker, sometimes at lower wages.

Restrictive immigration policies, therefore, combined with strong employer demand for domestic workers and the desperation of women who face unemployment and poverty in their home countries, produces a potent cocktail. Migrant women from neighboring countries bear much of the risk and cost

– financial, psychological, and physical – of maintaining a supply of cheap domestic labor to South African households. Furthermore, with no legal recourse or protection available to them as workers in South Africa, they experience a precarious political status that creates a dual labor regime based on citizenship status.

Labor Rights and Wrongs

In a striking irony, South African domestic workers are beneficiaries of one of the most extensive and impressive efforts anywhere in the world to formally regulate paid domestic work, but the vast majority of foreign domestic workers remain excluded from labor rights for the sector because they are mainly illegal immigrants.[9] South African domestic workers are entitled to the same rights as all other workers, plus a national minimum wage, mandatory contracts of employment (with strict prescriptions for minimally acceptable working conditions), and even social security benefits (unemployment insurance and a pension fund), but most foreign domestic workers who are in the country illegally and/or do not have work permits are not covered by these protections.

Union officials identified this as a source of the inefficacy of the legislation to protect South African domestics. "If the employer wants to avoid paying the minimum wage, or UIF [unemployment insurance], they hire a Zimbabwean," said an office-bearer of the national union. While this may not necessarily be the case, the political exclusion of most foreign migrant domestic workers from the legislative protections for the sector due to the problems of illegality certainly creates a dual labor regime, in which South Africans with citizenship are entitled to different conditions of work than most migrant domestics are likely to receive. Many South African domestic workers do not necessarily benefit from the legislative protections (Ally 2006, Fish 2006, Grossman 2004), but employers of undocumented migrants enjoy state-mandated impunity in settling on unregulated wages and working conditions with their domestic workers.

Foreign domestic workers found this dual labor regime unacceptable, and emotively called for their inclusion within these legislative protections. "We are being so much exploited by South African madams. South African domestic workers they are having these laws to protect them and minimum wages. We Zimbabweans we are being so exploited without these laws," one worker told my research assistant. But, in the same breath, many workers questioned the ability of labor rights to challenge their exploitation. Elizabeth Tshifadzwa, a recent arrival in Johannesburg, summarized some workers' thoughts with a hint of humor:

---

9   75 percent of the workers in this study were in the country illegally, and a further 15 percent had papers to be in the country, but did not have work permits, and were therefore not covered by the legislation.

Yes, we should be covered by the legislation just like South African domestic workers. We are working just like they are. But, they are, some of them, also getting exploited, but they are afraid to take their employer to the court to get proper money, so it makes you wonder, what will it help if we get these laws to protect us Zimbabweans also. Worse!....At least the employers can't deport South Africans for taking them to court. If we start asking for minimum wages, can you imagine? There will be a train running to Lindela every day packed with all of us who work in the houses! [Laughs] Better we just keep our head down and keep working....one day, I will be home and rich with these lemon's [nickname for her employers] money.

This failure of workplace protection, together with a very punitive immigration regime, primes most migrant domestic workers for an unstable and uncertain life, always between exploitation and deportation, poverty and the promise of prosperity, work and family, and home and away.

Legacies of Regional Inequality, Reinscribed

For some of the women in this study, especially Basotho and to some extent Zimbabwean, life as a migrant domestic worker in South Africa began as far back as the late 1970s. They had worked as domestic workers in South Africa from the 1960s, when the apartheid economy was booming. This was not unusual. For much of South Africa's modern history, a regional labor diaspora has reflected and constituted regional hierarchies. During apartheid, labor flows within the region were strictly disciplined, channeled largely to service the interests of South Africa's racial capitalism. Surrounding countries such as Lesotho, Swaziland, Botswana, and Mozambique effectively functioned as 'labor reserves' for South African mining operations during this period (see Maloka 2004). But, while it was mainly men who migrated to work on South Africa's mineral mines to build its eventual wealth and prosperity, women also migrated to work in centers of the economy like Johannesburg. Their work as beer-brewers and sex workers has been documented (Bonner 1990), but their labor as domestic workers has not been fully studied or recognized.

For the migrant women in this study who first came to Johannesburg under apartheid in the 1970s and the 1980s, and found work as domestics, paid domestic work did not allow them to live the dreams of a better future they too had imagined. For Sophie Mokoto, a 52-year-old mother of three, the devastating effects on Lesotho's economy of the combined effects of globalization and the slowdown in South Africa's mining operations, had created a precarious situation for her two youngest children, both still in school. She continues to invest in extended family to ensure a homestead to return to in Lesotho, but needs to keep working in Johannesburg to sustain an income for getting her two children through school. She does not imagine a future in Lesotho for either of them, and wants to remain working in Johannesburg just long enough to see them "find their way" in South Africa.

Inasmuch as the regional inequality between South Africa and its neighbors, produced by the racially exploitative apartheid system, structured Sophie Mokoto's entry into paid domestic work in Johannesburg in the 1970s, these regional inequalities have been reinscribed in the contemporary period. The disruptive effects of macro-economic shifts toward export-oriented development and liberalization now structures the entry into paid domestic work of many of Sophie's country-women, and the intensification of migration from countries like Zimbabwe and Mozambique.

While Cherryl Walker described many of apartheid South Africa's politically independent neighbors as "labor-exporting states of the subcontinent" (Walker 1990, 168), this role and function has been reproduced in the post-apartheid period of globalization. The net exit of capital from South Africa to the region as part of South Africa's neo-liberal economic restructuring has been explored (Miller 2005). But, there is an equal net entry of labor to South Africa from the region, and the implications of that labor mobility for understanding regional inequalities has not yet been fully examined. Furthermore, these processes are intensely gendered. Recent studies indicate that female migrants to South Africa are now beginning to outnumber male migrants (Dodson 2001, Mate 2005), and this study shows that many of these female migrants find themselves constituted as a domestic work force.

When labor migrancy is in service of the basic reproductive functions of cooking, cleaning, and child-care in the intimate spaces of family life, on the one hand, and is so intensely gendered, on the other, as in paid domestic work, the regional labor diaspora in South Africa is part of the constitution of regional hierarchies beginning from the private sphere. Paid domestic work remains one of the most important areas opened up by feminist inquiry not necessarily because of the characteristic low wages, poor working conditions, and general marginalization of the sector, but in its implications for understanding the gendered divisions of reproductive (cleaning and caring) labor in the home, and its intersections with the politics of race and class (Rollins 1985, Glenn 1988).

As Angela Davis (1981), amongst others, argued, the paid domestic work of African-American women in white American homes represented the resolution of the gendered division of reproductive labor between men and women through the creation of a new division of reproductive labor – between middle-class white women employers and their working-class black domestic workers – a reconstituted form of unequal power on the basis of race, and with it, class. Migrant women from the Southern African region are increasingly being utilized as a paid domestic labor force in South Africa, suggesting a reconstituted form of unequal power, this time between nations. In South Africa, the apartheid-era racial division of reproductive labor between affluent white women and their poorer black domestic workers is being reproduced as a regional division of reproductive labor – between a relatively prosperous South Africa, and its poorer black neighbors.

But, while national states – sending and receiving – have been implicated in actively structuring the supply of south-east Asian women domestics to Europe (Anderson 2000), the United States (Chang 2000), Canada (Bakan and Stasiulis 1995) and the rest of Asia (Chin 1998), in Southern Africa, the reproductive labor supply is structured and sustained by historical and continuing regional inequalities. The regional labor flows within the Americas (of Caribbean, Central and South American migrant women's servicing of the reproductive labor needs of the U.S.), for instance, is structured by the legacy of historic inequalities from the colonial era, exacerbated and reinforced under globalization. Through this socio-economic rather than direct political structuring, African-American women were replaced by mainly immigrant women of color from poorer nations within the region, and the intra-national raced and classed division of reproductive labor became an inter-national one within the region. Southern Africa has witnessed a similar restructuring of the division of reproductive labor, but rather than a new phenomenon, it represents an intensification of existing patterns in ways that suggest the exacerbation of regional inequalities within globalization, rather than simply those of the North–South divide.

Conclusion

In 2003, Pei-Chia Lan presciently documented the "maid trade in the global south," (171) through an examination of transnational migrant domestic work within Asia. Despite other studies that explored a similar *regional* restructuring of reproductive labor within globalization (Constable 1997, Chin 1998), the "maid trade" is today mainly discussed as an effect of globalization between North and South. In Southern Africa, however, historical patterns of migrancy have confronted new forms of inequality within globalization, intensifying circuits of transnational migrant domestic work within the region.

The laboring bodies of Zimbabwean, Basotho, and Mozambican women increasingly service the reproductive labor needs of mainly white, middle-class households in more prosperous South Africa. While black South African women continue to work as domestic workers in a raced and classed intra-national division of reproductive labor, migrant domestics from within the region desperate for survival, or keen on exploring their prospects in "the land of milk and honey," exist at the other end of a dual domestic labor regime in the country. With demand constructed by employer stereotypes that cast Zimbabweans or Basotho women as more amenable to domestic work, and supply ensured by worsening economic conditions in their home countries, they enter paid domestic work at differential wage rates compared to South African domestic workers, and under a different political regime.

In a curious irony, while the South African state is lauded for its effort to construct one of the most impressive efforts anywhere in the world to protect South African domestic workers, its political hostility towards unskilled and semi-skilled immigrants from the region conditions some of the exploitation and abuse faced by migrant domestics, as they struggle to gain legal status in the country and therefore are not protected. Nonetheless, as a result of the tenacity and persistence of these women, as they endure hazardous journeys and difficult work, Southern Africa is being refashioned by migrant women domestic workers.

Southern Africa's cities are being remade by the women who leave their home countries to work in more prosperous countries within the region. In doing so, they are not just restructuring regional divisions of labor, but reconstituting African urban modernity. As Mbembe and Nuttall (2004:364) importantly recognize in their analysis of this urban modernity,

> Johannesburg...with its own syntax, its arteries, its depth, its darkness, and the crucial figure of the migrant worker...the migrant worker...is the paradoxical cultural figure of African modernity.

As migrant women labor in service of the regional inequalities within Southern Africa, they become vital in constructing the globalized modernity of cities like Johannesburg. Not simply victims that are pushed and pulled by the ebbs and flows of globalization, forced across borders, into abusive relations, and exploitative work, they are actively re-shaping the region – from the urban spaces of its cities to the intimate spaces of its homes. Their lives make legible the reinscription of regional inequalities under apartheid in the contemporary era of capital and labor mobility, and in doing so, they reshape the future of South Africa's public and private landscapes.

References

Abu-Habib, L. (1998), "The Use and Abuse of Female Domestic Workers from Sri Lanka in Lebanon," *Gender and Development* 6:1, 52-56.

Ally, S. (2004), "Domestic Labor Pains," *South African Labor Bulletin* 28:5, 50-51.

—— (2005), "Caring about Care Workers: Organizing in the Female Shadow of Globalization," *Labor, Capital, and Society* 38:1-2, 185-207.

—— (2006), *'Maid' with Rights: The Contradictory Citizenship of Domestic Workers in Post-Apartheid South Africa* (Unpublished PhD Dissertation. University of Wisconsin-Madison).

Anderson, B. (2000), *Doing the Dirty Work? The Global Politics of Domestic Labor* (London: Zed).

Bakan, A.B. and Stasiulus, D. (1997), *Not One of the Family: Foreign Domestic Workers in Canada* (Toronto: University of Toronto Press).

Boddington, E. (1983), *Domestic Service: Changing Relations of Class Domination, 1841-1948: A Focus on Cape Town* (Unpublished Masters thesis, University of Cape Town).

Bond, P. (2004), "The ANC's 'Left Turn' and South African Sub-Imperialism," *Review of African Political Economy* 31:102, 599-616.

Bonner, P.L. (1990), "'Desirable or Undesirable Basotho Women?' Liquor, Prostitution and the Migration of Basotho Women to the Rand, 1920-1945," in Walker (ed.).

Chang, G. (2000), *Disposable Domestics: Immigrant Women Workers in the Global Economy* (Cambridge: South End Press).

Chin, C.B. (1998), *In Service and Servitude: Foreign Female Domestic Workers and the Malaysian 'Modernity Project'* (New York: Columbia University Press).

Cock, J. (1980), *Maids and Madams: A Study in the Politics of Exploitation* (Johannesburg: Ravan Press).

Constable, N. (1997), *Maid to Order in Hong Kong: Stories of Filipina Domestic Workers* (Ithaca: Cornell University Press).

Crush, J. (ed.) (2001), *Immigration, Xenophobia, and Human Rights in South Africa*. SAMP Migration Policy Series No 22 (Cape Town: Idasa).

Crush, J. and McDonald, D. (eds) (2001), "Special Issue: Evaluating South African Immigration Policy after Apartheid," *Africa Today* 48:3, 1-13.

Davis, A. (1981), *Women, Race and Class* (New York: Random House).

Dodson, B. (2001), "Discrimination by Default? Gender Concerns in South African Migration Policy," *Africa Today* 48:3, 73-89.

Fish, J.N. (2006), *Domestic Democracy: At Home in South Africa* (New York and London: Routledge).

Gaitskell, D., Kimble, J., Maconachie, M., and Unterhalter, E. (1984), "Class, Race, and Gender: Domestic Workers in South Africa," *Review of African Political Economy* 27-28, 86-108.

Gamburd, M. (2000), *The Kitchen Spoon's Handle: Transnationalism and Sri Lanka's Migrant Housemaids* (Ithaca: Cornell University Press).

Glenn, E.N. (1986), *Issei, Nisei, War Bride: Three Generations of Japanese American Women in Domestic Service* (Philadelphia: Temple University Press).

Gordon, S. (1985), *Talent for Tomorrow: Life Stories of South African Servants* (Johannesburg: Ravan Press).

Grossman, J. (2004), *The Denigrated Compassion and Vision of the Backyard: South Africa's Domestic Workers in the New Global Village* (Unpublished paper).

Hondagneu-Sotelo, P. (2001), *Doméstica: Immigrant Workers Cleaning and Caring in the Shadows of Affluence* (Berkeley: University of California Press).

King, A.J. (2007), *Domestic Service in Post-Apartheid South Africa: Deference and Disdain* (Aldershot: Ashgate).

Lan, Pei-Chia (2006), *Global Cinderellas: Migrant Domestics and Newly Rich Employers in Taiwan* (Durham: Duke University Press).

Landau, L. (ed.) (2004), *Forced Migrants in the New Johannesburg: Towards a Local Government Response* (Johannesburg: University of the Witwatersrand).

Maloka, E.T. (2004), *Basotho and the Mines: A Social History of Labor Migrancy in Lesotho and South Africa, c. 1890-1940* (Dakar: Codesria).

Mamdani, M. (1996), *Citizen and Subject: Contemporary Africa and the Legacy of Late Colonialism* (Princeton: Princeton University Press).

Mate, R. (2005), *Making Ends Meet at the Margins? Grappling with Identity, Poverty, Marginality and Economic Crisis in Beitbridge Town* (Dakar: Codesria).

Mbembe, A. and Nuttall, S. (2004), "Writing the World from an African Metropolis," *Public Culture* 16:3, 347-372.

Miller, D. (2005), "New Regional Imaginaries in Post-Apartheid Southern Africa – Retail Workers at a Shopping Mall in Zambia," *Journal of Southern African Studies* 31:1, 117-145.

Morris, A. and Bouillon, A. (eds) (2001), *African Immigration to South Africa: Francophone Migration of the 1990s* (Pretoria: Protea and IFAS).

Nyamnjoh, F.B. (2006), *Insiders and Outsiders: Citizenship and Xenophobia in Contemporary Southern Africa* (London: Zed Books).

Oucho, J.O. and Crush, J. (2001), "Contra Free Movement: South Africa and the SADC Migration Protocols," *Africa Today* 48:3, 139-158.

Parreñas, R.S. (2000), "Migrant Filipina Domestic Workers and the International Division of Reproductive Labor," *Gender and Society* 14:4, 560-580.

_____ (2001), *Servants of Globalization: Women, Migration, and Domestic Work* (Stanford: Stanford University Press).

Peberdy, S. and Dinat, N. (2005), *Migration and Domestic Workers: Worlds of Work, Health, and Mobility in Johannesburg*, Migration Policy Series No. 40 (Cape Town: Southern African Migration Project).

Pratt, G. (1997), "Stereotypes and Ambivalence: the construction of domestic workers in Vancouver, British Columbia," *Gender, Place, and Culture: A Journal of Feminist Geography* 4:2, 159-178.

Preston-Whyte, E. (1976), "Race Attitudes and Behaviour: The Case of Domestic Employment in White South African Homes," *African Studies* 35, 71-89.

Rollins, J. (1985), *Between Women: Domestics and Their Employers* (Philadelphia: Temple University Press).

Sichone, O. (2001), "The Making of Makwerekwere; East Africans in Cape Town," paper for the workshop, "Interrogating the new Political Culture in Southern Africa; Ideas and Institutions," Harare, 13-15 June.

Silvey, R. (2004), "Transnational Domestication: Indonesian Domestic Workers in Saudi Arabia," *Political Geography* 23, 245-264.

Swaisland, C. (1993), *Servants and Gentlewomen to the Golden Land: The Emigration of Single Women from Britain to Southern Africa, 1820-1939* (Providence and Oxford: Berg).

Truong, T.D. (1996), "Gender, International Migration, and Social Reproduction: Implications for Theory, Policy, and Research, and Networking," *Asian and Pacific Migration Theory* 5:1, 27-52.

Van Onselen, C. (1982), "The Witches of Suburbia: Domestic Service on the Witwatersrand, 1890-1914," in Van Onselen, C. (ed.) (1982), *Studies in the Social and Economic History of the Witwatersrand 1886-1914, Volume 2: New Ninevah* (Johannesburg: Ravan).

Walker, C. (1990), "Gender and the Development of the Migrant Labor System, c. 1850-1930," in Walker, C. (ed.), *Women and Gender in Southern Africa to 1945* (Claremont: David Philip).

Whisson, M.G. and Weil, W. (1971), *Domestic Servants: A Microcosm of 'the Race Problem'* (Johannesburg: South African Institute of Race Relations).

Chapter 3

Global Capitalism and Women

From Feminist Politics to Working Class Women's Politics[1]

Martha Gimenez

Introduction

As capitalism changes the economic, social and political terrain in which the world's working populations struggle to survive, it is more important than ever to examine how these processes are changing women's lives and women's politics. Those processes cannot be properly understood if one takes, as a point of departure, the ideological way in which they have been politically constructed. I have replaced the widely used but misleading term, "globalization," with global capitalism to stress the need to understand theoretically and politically the nature of the current processes of change that have united the world under the rule of unfettered capitalism. The world is not undergoing today a benign process of unification under the auspices of anonymous market and social forces. The fall of the Iron Curtain and the Berlin Wall meant the end of political barriers to the emergence, in actuality, of the capitalist world market which Marx and Engels had foreseen in the Manifesto (McCarney, 1991: 30). It is in the context of these processes of accelerated economic and cultural transformation, that changes in the conditions facing working women must be examined. Marxist feminist theory can contribute by illuminating the capitalist processes altering the lives of all women, particularly working women today.

There is an abundant literature about how global capitalism victimizes most working women while creating, at the same time, conditions favorable for the rise of women's resistance. All over the world there are numerous instances of women's grassroots efforts to struggle around a variety of issues such as education, reproductive rights, health care, and economic survival (see, for example, Rowbotham and Linkogle, 2001 and Naples and Desai, 2002). Global capitalism, however, has other contradictory and important effects upon women which need to be theorized to inform future research into the possibilities and limits for the

---

1 I have discussed some of these ideas in Martha E. Gimenez, "Marx and Feminism in the Era of Globalization," in *Socialism and Democracy*, Vol. 18, No. 1, January-June 2004.

political mobilization and organization of women in the U.S. This is why, in this chapter, I focus neither on women's victimization nor women's agency, but on the structural and ideological consequences of global capitalism upon working women. More specifically I focus on the effects of changes in the social relations in the context of which social classes and strata within classes are reproduced. These changes, I will argue, deepen the class divisions among women and are likely to have profound and contradictory effects on women's experiences, consciousness, and the future viability of feminism as a political ideology capable of energizing and mobilizing women in the United States.[2]

Inequality, Reproduction, and Women's Opportunities Under Global Capitalism

One of the most salient and well known effects of global capitalism is the increase in economic and political inequality within and between nation states. The uncontrolled circulation of capital, legitimated by neoliberal ideologies that celebrate the intrinsic goodness of free markets and deny the necessity of state intervention to ameliorate the negative consequences of economic change have intensified class differences and increased the power and wealth of the capitalist classes. In the poorer countries, the dominant political classes' uncritically accepted the neoliberal economic gospel; they implemented structural adjustment policies imposed by the World Bank and the IMF; they privatized national industries, natural resources, utilities and social services, imposing the so-called "flexibilization" of labor contracts, a measure that put an end to working class gains in job stability and pay. Unavoidably, such policies intensified income and wealth inequalities.

The wealthier capitalist countries are not exempt from this process of concentration of wealth and income in the hands of the very few: in the United States, for example, in 2001, 33.4 percent of all privately-held wealth was in the hands of the top 1 percent of households, while 51 percent was in the hands of managers, professionals and small businesses altogether comprising 19 percent

---

2   My analysis rests upon the Marxist notion of class, understood as a relationship between capitalists and workers, mediated by their relationship to the means of production. At the level of analysis of the mode of production, there are two main classes: owners of the means of production and non-owners, the vast majority of the people who must sell their labor to survive. At the level of social formations (e.g., regions, nation states), each class is stratified according to the social and technical division of labor and divided in terms of socioeconomic statuses (SES) based on income, occupation and educational differences. Most of the discussion in this chapter proceeds at the level of social formations, where working women are divided by class (e.g., capitalist women working in business or bureaucracies do not share the same interest as women who are factory or office workers), and by socioeconomic status (i.e., differences in education, income and occupation which produce antagonisms among women who, in terms of their relationship to the means of production, share the same class position).

of households. This means that 20 percent of households owned 84 percent of the wealth, leaving 16 percent for the bottom 80 percent of households.[3]

The circulation or mobility of capital, which deepens inequality everywhere, is mirrored by the circulation of labor. Migration is not a new economic survival strategy, but the intensification in the circulation of capital and the economic upheavals it produces have, at the same time, increased intra-national and inter-national migration flows. Migrants traveling back and forth between their place of work and country of origin, add to the increasing numbers of people circulating around the globe for personal and political reasons.

It is individuals from the top (e.g., CEOs, top executives, professionals, etc.) and the bottom (e.g., low skill, manual workers) layers of the social classes that circulate the most. The most negatively affected are the working classes, especially working women and their families. We must keep in mind that the well-being of most women is tied to the economic fate of the men of their class. As male wages decline, as male unemployment grows and profit seeking employers replace male with female labor, women's responsibility for the economic survival of their families expands. In poor countries, women's economic strategies include now, more than ever, migration within and across national borders, for globalization has resulted in the immiseration of working class women (Aguilar, 2004: 406) and the feminization of the proletariat. The "feminization of migration" hints at the enormity of the changes in family organization and women's roles and expectations taking place today both in wealthy and poor countries because "in both developing and developed regions, the stable, organized, and mostly male labor force has become increasingly "flexible" and "feminized." Keeping the cost of labor low has encouraged the growth of demand for female labor, while declining household budgets have led to an increase in the supply of job-seeking women" (Moghadam, 1999: 369).

Overall, in the 1990s, 50 percent of the world's migrants, about 60 million, are believed to be women; over half of all Filipino immigrants to all countries were women; women comprise about half of all migrants leaving Mexico, India, Korea, Malaysia and African countries, and over half of the migrants arriving to the United States, Canada, Sweden, the United Kingdom and Israel throughout the 1990s (Ehrenreich and Hochschild, 2003: 5-6). Western and Asian wealthy countries are the chosen destination of millions of women who are unable to find employment in their countries of origin. This unprecedented mobilization of women across vast distances and national borders reflects the deteriorating conditions facing most male workers in their countries of origin. The switch to export led economic development in the developing countries, together with the effects of structural adjustments imposed by the IMF and the World Bank undermined the power of organized, mainly male labor and resulted in a more flexible, feminized labor force, together with growth in the informal sector, temporary employment

---

3   G. William Domhoff, "Wealth, Income and Power," in *Who Rules America?* http://sociology.ucsc.edu/whorulesamerica/power/wealth.html.

and self-employment (Moghadam, 1999: 369). Undoubtedly, population growth must be viewed as a contributing factor to poverty and migration but demographic factors must be considered with caution. Contrary to the neo-Malthusian belief that poverty would decrease and wages would rise if the working class were to control its natural increase, it must be kept in mind that "the demand for labor is not identical with increase of capital"... and "the supply of labor is, to a certain extent, independent of the supply of laborers" (Marx, [1867] 1967: 640). Capital accumulation, which rests upon unceasing changes in the forces of production, as it absorbs come kinds of labor declare others obsolete thus unceasingly producing and reproducing a reserve army of labor or surplus population, some of whose members might choose migration as a survival strategy. This analysis presupposes Marx's distinction between "labor power" (the capacity to work) and the owners of labor power, the workers themselves; the demand for labor and the level of wages are not determined by the size of the workforce (except under exceptional conditions and temporary conditions) but by economic and political criteria (Gimenez, 1979: 22). At any given time, therefore, growth of the surplus population tends to outpace economic growth and increases in the demand for labor, a phenomena usually ideologically understood in purely demographic, Malthusian terms, a perspective that naturalizes the historical effects of the laws of capital accumulation (Marx, [1867]: 612-712; Gimenez, 1998: 461-465).

The relative decline in economic opportunities for male workers is not exclusive to the poorer countries. In the United States, for example, declining male earnings, downsizing, de-industrialization, outsourcing, growth in temporary and contingent work, etc., have pushed countless working women to the labor force. In the U.S. today, the proportion of married couples, with or without children, where men are the sole breadwinners has declined steadily for the last 65 years. In 1940, men were the sole breadwinner in 94 percent of married couples with children under 17. In 2000, men are the sole breadwinner in only 29 percent of these families. Two-paycheck and two-career families are now the norm and women's earnings are keeping millions of families above the poverty level.

This does not mean, however, that there have been no improvements in the status of women in the United States. In the 1960s, civil rights, antiwar and other social movements, including the women's liberation movement changed the political landscape and opened real opportunities for women and racial/ethnic minorities. These processes of change, however, have had contradictory results; they contributed to the liberation and emancipatory objectives of the more privileged women, while strengthening the oppression of working class women. Today, there are more businesses owned by women, and the proportion of women in executive, managerial and professional occupations has grown since the 1970s. However, despite considerable advances in women's education, employment and income, most women work still in sex-segregated occupations and can be found in the lower levels in the occupational hierarchies. Working women are still more likely to be nurses, dieticians, elementary school teachers and low level white collar workers. Just as the opportunities and quality of life of college educated and relatively privileged working women improve, they have worsened for the vast majority who remains trapped in low paying, sex-segregated jobs: "the majority of women are still working class, languishing in low-wage, insecure jobs, with little prestige and stability and no benefits" (Luce and Brenner, 2007: 122). There is no better indicator of the deepening class and socioeconomic status differences among women than the growth in the number of corporations like Merry Maids, which provide domestic servants for upper and upper-middle class women and their families.

It is here that we find the confluence between two apparently independent processes of global capitalism:

1. Processes that generate male and female unemployment and poverty in poor countries, pushing millions of working women to migrate and seek employment in the United States and other wealthy countries.
2. Changes in the U.S. economy that eliminated millions of well paid, blue collar male jobs and pushed millions of women into the labor force, thus substantially increasing the demand for service workers willing to do the domestic work that middle class working women cannot do and more privileged women will not do.

The combined effects of stagnating male wages, increase in women's employment and increase in the number of immigrant women willing to do service work, regardless of their skills and education, is altering the organization of domestic labor or, from the standpoint of Marxist feminist theory, the domestic social relations of reproduction. In the long run, this reorganization is likely to have contradictory ideological effects. Among the more privileged, upper strata of working women, it has the potential to undermine their support for feminism and feminist politics. Among middle and working class women, there is the possibility of greater openness to women's politics. Last, but not least, among the domestic workers themselves, immigrant and native, white and non-white, it creates the conditions potentially favorable for political mobilization and unionization.

I define the domestic relations of reproduction as the relations between the agents of reproduction (e.g., the relations between married or cohabiting men and women and their children; the relations between couples and their paid domestic workers, etc.) mediated by their relationship to the conditions of reproduction (e.g., the house, its contents and grounds; the money and other resources necessary to provide for household needs; household tools, implements, appliances, etc.). The degree of women's economic dependence on their husbands' or partners' income; the extent of their own economic resources and contributions to the household; the use of domestic workers and the quantity and quality of domestic labor they can purchase affect their relative power, and the quality of the domestic relations of reproduction. This terminology might appear cumbersome; wouldn't it be easier to refer to the effects of the increased availability and affordability of domestic workers as changes in the domestic division of labor within the family? Family, however, is an ideologically loaded concept that obscures the nature of the social processes that go on within it. Ideologies about romance, motherhood, gender, family roles, social norms and expectations about husbands and wives, parents and children shape the common sense understanding of family and family life. These ideologies surrounding the family exclude from consideration what the domestic social relations of reproduction actually accomplish. Whatever the family structure, size, sexual preferences of the adult members, class location, and location in the racial and ethnic structures may be, the social relations of reproduction reproduce social classes and strata within classes. Instead of asking whether or not working women, native born or immigrants, are appropriately fulfilling their gender and care taking roles, it is important to ask, how are social classes reproduced? How are the physical and psychological energies of workers of all kinds, and managers, and capitalists and small business owners, etc., replenished every day? How are the new generations of members of these classes reproduced so that when they grow old and die there are others who will take their place? In what context are gender, racial and ethnic identities formed? Asking such questions leads us to focus on the social relations within which classes and strata within classes are reproduced and to wonder about the ideological impact, on the present and future generations, of changes in the social relations of reproduction.

A focus on families and family roles leads social scientists to view the results of transnational migration as the creation of "care deficits." A "care deficit" is created in the wealthy countries, as more women seek and find full time employment and cannot care for their homes and families. Simultaneously, a "care deficit" is created in the poor countries, because women who migrate leave uncared for children and elderly parents at home in order to give strangers' children and homes, thousands of miles away, the love and care they should have been bestowing upon their own families. In an important and informative article, for example, Professor Salazar-Parreñas (2003) writes that there is a care crisis in the Philippines, where the children of migrant women experience a variety of problems. The women themselves are vilified by the media and the government for not fulfilling their nurturant role, though between 43 and 54 percent of the Filipino population is supported by migrant women's monthly remittances to their families. This article is important because it highlights the contradiction between the new experiences that global capitalism is imposing upon migrant women, and the persistence of traditional expectations about women's family roles. This situation is likely to remain unchanged, in the Philippines and other countries which are also source of large outflows of migrant women, because the efficacy, strength or persistence of traditional values or ideologies depends on whether or not people continue to live according to those values.

In poor countries, neoliberal economic policies have succeeded in excluding the majority of the population from benefitting from economic growth. Most people continue to struggle for a living under conditions that remain relatively unchanged, in which the traditional ideologies continue to make sense. At the same time, as national job markets shrink, overseas opportunities open for employment in service jobs traditionally reserved for women. Working class women are forced to transcend the limitations of gender ideologies and family expectations in order to find employment wherever it may be available. The contradictory effects of global capitalism both sustain the strength of traditional ideologies among those left behind, while at the same time undermining them, by forcing masses of people, mostly women, to violate their injunctions in order to support their families.

This analysis of care deficits in the family, heightened demand for domestic workers and service workers in wealthy countries, and government insensibility to the conflicting demands that tear migrant women's lives apart is important but insufficient to understand the implications of current processes of change. It describes the visible effects of underlying changes in the capitalist organization of social reproduction.

The Gendered Social Reproduction of Class and Potentials for Struggle and Resistance

Under capitalism, the process of working class reproduction in all its aspects is left mainly to the ingenuity of the workers themselves; it is private and the extent to which the state takes some responsibility depends on the outcome of class struggles and political compromises. Employed wage and salary workers are able to create relatively stable living conditions for themselves and their children, the future members of their class. Those who cannot find work or find work at poverty or near poverty wages, reproduce the future members of the poverty population which in the U.S., in 2006, numbered 36.5 million, including 12.8 million children under age 18.[4]

The conflict between domestic and paid labor demands place most working people, particularly working women, in a very difficult position. Global capitalism intensifies this conflict by creating the conditions that push an ever increasing proportion of women to the labor force, whether in their own countries or elsewhere. By 2004, 59.2 percent of American women were in the labor force (a light decline from 60 percent in 1999); 71 percent of mothers with children under 18 are in the labor force and 35 percent of working wives contribute 35 percent of the family income.[5] At the same time, global capitalism provides also a solution, through the growth in the numbers of legal and undocumented immigrant women, open to exploitation in low paid service occupations in the public sector and low paid domestic work such as, for example, nannies, maids, baby sitters, cooks, etc.

In the Philippines, Mexico and the many other countries which have become exporters of female labor, underlying the "care deficit" is a crisis in the

---

4   U.S. Bureau of the Census, Poverty: 2006 Highlights. http://www.census.gov/hhes/www/poverty/poverty06/pov06hi.html.

5   Women in the Labor Force: A Databook [Highlights]. *U.S. Department of Labor - Bureau of Labor Statistics.* http://www.bls.gov/cps/wlf-databook2005.html.

reproduction of the working classes. While their social reproduction was never secure, migration, especially the migration of women, forces the relatives left behind to care for children and the elderly, developing survival strategies that could potentially result in collective solutions at the grass roots level. This situation calls for state intervention through welfare policies providing support to unemployed or underemployed fathers left in charge of their children and/or to the relatives or elderly parents who step in to care for children whose mothers work abroad.

State priorities in poor countries, however, are biased against the interests of those too poor and too powerless to challenge, politically, the status quo. It is left to the ingenuity of the people left in care of their children and the elderly to devise strategies for care and survival, strategies which have the potential to create community based or collective solutions. Fundamental to activate this potential would be a change in the way the situation is framed in public discourse. A discourse that frames the issue as one of "care deficit" reproduces the traditional nurturant female role and does not transcend the privatized nature of social reproduction under capitalism. An alternative discourse could highlight the importance of household or domestic labor as the labor that reproduces the working classes; instead of criticizing migrant women, it would explore possible alternative social relations of reproduction designed to ensure the health and education of future generations of workers. Such a discourse could, hypothetically, lead to a different and positive appreciation of the sacrifices migrant women make and could contribute to the reorganization of the relations of reproduction in ways that could trigger processes of grassroots organization and self-reliance.

If the tasks required for reproducing the present and future generations of workers are ideologically delinked from gender expectations and, instead, are understood as forms of socially necessary labor of crucial importance for the well being of the working classes and the nation as a whole, this change in articulating their significance could help alleviate ideological and social pressures on migrant women, thus opening the way for the exploration of community or collective solutions. Changes in dominant ideologies or discourses are not easy and cannot be achieved overnight – but women's organizations in the U.S. and in the countries that export female labor, like the Philippines, could begin the hard work of degendering the social relations of reproduction, and legitimating collective forms of social reproduction in which men and women, kin and non-kin members of the community would be engaged.

In wealthy countries, like the U.S., that people resolve the conflict between family and work by substituting their own labor with the labor of others, or by lowering household cleanliness standards and eating out is not a new phenomenon. What is new is the growth in the supply of household workers who sell their labor either on an individual basis or through corporations such as the Merry Maids. Global capitalism is democratizing the use of domestic servants in the U.S. (Ehrenreich, 2002: 85-103). Formerly a privilege of the wealthy, who have always had an array of household workers (butlers, housekeepers, governesses, nannies, maids, cooks, gardeners and chauffeurs), the use of domestic workers is spreading from the wealthy and the upper middle classes to the rest of the population, especially in the main urban centers where immigrants tend to flock. The spread of the use of domestic workers is altering, in the context of middle class households, the nature of domestic relations of reproduction between men and women. The issue of domestic labor and the conflict between men and women, parents and children, about who does what, when, and where; and the conflict between paid work and domestic work were a cornerstone of feminist theorizing in the late 1970s and 1980s and continue to be one of the contributing determinants of gender inequality. I will not claim that, by shifting most of these tasks to the labor of paid workers, those conflicts are fully resolved. All that the use of domestic workers accomplishes is to minimize marital or partner conflict while maintaining the privatized nature of social reproduction under capitalism unchanged. My concern is different and has to do with the ideological and reproductive effects of this massive reorganization of the mode of reproduction upon the women who hire domestic workers, upon their children, especially the daughters, and upon the women, mostly immigrant, who work as domestic workers.

Social Reproduction and Feminist Ideology and Policies

What is the potential ideological effect, upon women who hire domestic workers, of the experience of doing away, to a large extent, with all or most of the demands of household work? This experience has the potential to change women's self-understanding, identity, awareness of possibilities, and relative openness to feminist politics. My hypothesis is that women who, as children, grew up in a household where domestic labor was done by paid workers, while their mothers were full-time workers focused mainly on the social aspects of reproduction (e.g., child socialization, play, education, etc.) are likely to find it difficult to empathize with or understand fully the inequalities that continue to shape most women's lives. Combining family and work responsibilities is likely to seem easy to young women raised in such a home environment, where having domestic workers is a taken-for-granted aspect of everyday life. The argument I want to make, therefore, is that global capitalism has the potential to undermine – among a substantial proportion of U.S. working women – the ability to mobilize politically as women, by undermining the experiential grounds for their receptivity to feminist ideology and politics, especially those forms of feminism that stress not just women's inequality in the world of work, but women's inequality and oppression in their own homes.

Feminist ideology in the United States reflected special historical conditions which made it unavoidable for women to select gender as their primary identity rather than class, work, race, ethnicity, nationality or other potential identities. The very success of the American economy in providing paid employment for working class women, reduced the supply and increased the cost of household help, especially the live-in kind. After the Second World War, the employment of domestic workers ceased to be the badge of middle class status but remained, primarily, the customary privilege of the capitalist and the upper-middle classes. Middle class, educated American women thus experienced the kind of domestic oppression that their counterparts in poor countries seldom knew, for in poor countries there is an oversupply of poor girls and young women for whom domestic service is the first step out of the farm or out of poverty and into the world of work. This experience of domestic oppression was one of the forces that fueled the late 1960s women's movement and the development of socialist and Marxist feminist theories (Gimenez, 1990: 25-45). As global capitalism increases the supply of domestic workers, thus lowering their cost, the use of domestic workers for childcare, cooking, housecleaning, elder care and so forth, is likely to increase. This practice, it can be plausibly argued, is likely to weaken and perhaps eliminate, particularly among women who hire full-time domestic workers, the experiences of domestic inequality and oppression necessary for women's self-perception in terms of their gender, and for their support for feminist ideologies and politics.

Full-time work is also likely to have important ideological effects. Women's employment, which has increased to the point that almost 60 percent of women are in the labor force by changing women's experiences and self-understanding, has the potential to open up the possibility that women may begin to see themselves primarily as working women, whose issues have to do not only, or necessarily, with their gender but with their location in the occupational and class structures as female workers. This could be considered a welcome potential change, conducive to the emergence of a working women's feminism.

So far, this discussion has been centered around the middle and upper-middle strata. However, most women workers are part of working class, dual pay check, not dual career families and the main reason why they work is likely to be economic necessity. These households are not likely to use domestic servants like the more affluent dual career or single earner households. Their way of coping with the conflicting demands of household work and waged work is likely to be declining health (because of the consumption of fast foods) and quality of life. Working class women's employment and income increase their power in the home but do not undermine the economic importance of marriage or a stable partnership. And how about the potential ideological effects, among immigrant women, of doing domestic work or low paid service work in a place so distant from their homes, culturally so different? All immigrant women, whether students or workers, are caught between competing loyalties: to their homeland and families, on the one hand, and to themselves, for their decision to immigrate is also a decision to change and develop in ways unforeseen in their childhood. What can feminism offer to them?

Feminist ideologies, whether liberal, radical, or socialist, rest upon the conceptual foundation of a transnational, abstract notion of woman. This standpoint is captured in the slogan "women's rights are human rights," put forth in the 1995 Beijing declaration.[6] The inclusion of women and girls within the scope of international human rights documents and agreements is an important step in feminist struggles. This commitment to human rights for women as human beings – including the right to

---

6 *Fourth World Conference on Women Beijing Declaration.* http://www.un.org/womenwatch/daw/beijing/platform/declar.htm.

work, own property, get credit, education, and job training; to political participation, to freedom of thought and religion, to health, sexual expression and reproductive self-determination – fosters awareness of the magnitude of the problems facing women today, and about the barriers to improving women's lives.

Postmodern feminists and non-western feminists are critical of universalistic notions of women's rights because 1) they rest on an essentialist understanding of women and their needs; 2) they express the views of privileged western women and 3) they ignore the substantive differences of class, race, ethnicity, culture, national origin, etc. among women. From the standpoint of postmodern and many non-western feminists, then, the western feminist agenda centered on individual rights is unworkable and unacceptable.

In the U.S. today, immigrant women workers and students face two main feminist alternatives: 1) universalistic feminist goals expressed in documents produced by the United Nations and innumerable NGOs all over the world and 2) the postmodern and non-western feminist critique of those goals, which give priority to cultural, religious, and national differences and identities. This polarization of views reflects, at the level of ideology, the uneven material development of global capitalism and the enormous gap between the material conditions that shape the experiences and political consciousness of relatively privileged western and western educated women, on the one hand, and the vast majority of the globe's female population, on the other. Western feminists can stress the importance of individual rights and individual self-determination because they do not live within tightly knit communities and extended kinship networks in which kin ties are also economic ties. And postmodern western feminists celebrate the fluidity of identities and the primacy of culture, race and ethnicity over class, because they do not experience the constraints many cultures impose upon women, and because their secure economic positions renders class theoretically invisible.

Neither ideological path offers a politically acceptable alternative to immigrant women workers and students. To self-identify as women, in pursuit of equal economic, political and civil rights is important individually, but insufficient to attain collective improvements in their location, as a group, in the economic and racial/ethnic stratification of this country. To self-identify in terms of racial, ethnic or cultural identities can be both empowering and, at the same time, self-defeating. Why? Because acceptance of the racial/ethnic minority label means that their work related grievances can be heard only if framed in the context of civil rights violations, not in the context of violations of their rights as working women. Self-identification as women leads to the same paradoxical situation: woman and/or minority woman are identities acceptable within the dominant political discourse; working class and working class women do not fit, particularly if women do not have a union to back their claims.

Marxist–feminist theory offers an alternative perspective that both preserves and transcends this polarity, an alternative based on the universality rooted in the material conditions that shape the lives of most women in the planet: their location in the organizations of production and reproduction. The vast majority of the world's women work for their economic subsistence and the economic survival of their families. Their work reproduces the world's working classes. Most women, regardless of differences associated with culture, religion, nationality, race, etc., are working women who are subject to the ups and downs of the capitalist national and world economies. Their common location in the relations of production and reproduction is a universal, yet historical, material base, for their potential mobilization and political organization not as women and not as workers, but as working women.

Conclusion

As global capitalism alters the employment opportunities of the world working classes, it simultaneously changes the organization of social reproduction; i.e., the network of social relations within which present and future members of different social classes are physically and socially reproduced, daily and generationally. In poor countries, the effects of these processes fall most heavily upon the rural and urban working populations. The relative decline in employment opportunities for working class men has led to the "feminization" of international migration and the rise of a "care deficit," which leaves the care of children and the elderly in the hands of fathers and relatives. Working class relations of reproduction are thus changed in ways that could potentially increase state involvement and awareness of the need to assume responsibility for the future generations of workers. However, given the capitalist trend to substitute living labor with dead labor objectified in machinery and technology, it is unlikely that states, usually eager to foster investments, will respond in ways favorable to the reproduction of a healthy, educated and skilled working class. It is up to women's organizations to challenge the gendered ideological understanding of the effects of female migration, and to posit instead, the valorization of reproductive labor, delinked from gender expectations and politically constructed as a valuable socially necessary labor which should be a social, rather than private responsibility.

In wealthy countries, the increased availability and use of domestic workers by a broad strata of the working population is likely to lessen present and future generations of relatively privileged working women's receptivity to feminist politics beyond claims for individual rights that transcend class divisions such as, for example, reproductive rights and equal employment and educational opportunities. Global capitalism, then, deepens class, socioeconomic and racial/ ethnic inequality among women but, as it increases women's employment, it also opens the possibility for the emergence of a different form of women's political consciousness which, at this time, I call "working women's feminism." Capitalism, I argue, has the potential of producing contradictory ideological effects, dividing women's interests, undermining feminist concerns with women's oppression "as women" while opening, at the same time, the possibility for the emergence of a new feminism, one that acknowledges and seeks to transcend the real antagonisms among working women, whether native born or immigrant.

As the paid labor of household workers changes the domestic division of labor and the constraints more privileged working women face in their daily lives, their work and home experiences change qualitatively, thus modifying their self-perception as well as their children's views about gender roles. As women's experience of oppression moves from the home to the workplace, there is the potential for the rise of a new feminism which, like the old, will continue to be predicated upon the contradictions inherent in capitalist societies, now intensified by the effects of global capitalism. However, this might be an excessively optimistic scenario; as more American women live lives relatively unconstrained by household responsibilities, this might altogether undermine their openness to feminist ideologies and politics, except those which are unlikely to challenge their class and job privileges.

I have identified the changing contexts where women work and live and have presented some considerations about the potential effects of these changes upon women's consciousness. But structural changes do not generate ideologies automatically; it is important that women concerned with the need for a new women's movement may start dialogues between working women, immigrants and native born, white and non-white. These dialogues should challenge the dominant cultural and political discourses because they endorse identity politics, delegitimating class as a key dimension of everyone's life, and do not acknowledge the individual and social significance of work, including the socially necessary private and social reproduction work done by tens of thousands of workers, mostly immigrant women of color, engaged in cleaning and service work. Such dialogues should make visible working women's class location, identifying shared interests as workers while acknowledging also, in a straightforward manner, the class interests that divide them. Working class feminism may seem utopian today. But identity politics have structural limits that need to be acknowledged. Legislation against gender, racial, and immigrant discrimination and in support of equal opportunity does not change the material realities of job scarcity, working class exploitation, and racial/ethnic oppression. Capital's mobility and capacity to close plants, downsize and outsource with impunity has undermined the class power of working men and women. But working women employed in service occupations, for example, both in domestic and public settings, are engaged in socially necessary labor, a labor that cannot be outsourced or downsized without dire social consequences. Objectively, this gives them some leverage but objective conditions are not sufficient; social movements spring to life as society changes and alters the outlook of many people at the same time. In the meantime, what women activists can do is to raise consciousness about the social significance of the work women do and about the importance of keeping in mind that gender and racial/ethnic identities are, within the context of American politics, the ideological ways in which consciousness of exploitation and oppression start. Consciousness-raising may seem old fashioned today but society has changed in ways that perhaps make it imperative to start all over again, this time with a broader comprehension of the macro level, global processes that affect working women's lives.

References

Collins, J. and Gimenez, M. (eds) (1990), *Work Without Wages: Domestic Labor and Household Survival in the United States* (New York: SUNY Press).

Ehrenreich, B. and Hochschild, R. (eds) (2002), *Global Woman: Nannies, Maids and Sex Workers in the New Economy* (New York: Henry Holt and Company).

Ehrenreich, B.E. (2002), "Maid to Order," in *Global Woman*, 85-103.

Gimenez, M. (1990). "The Dialectics of Waged and Unwaged Work: Domestic Labor and Household Survival in the United States," in Collins (ed.)

McCarney, J. (1991), "The True Realm of Freedom: Marxist Philosophy after Communism," *New Left Review*, 19-38.

Naples, N. and Manisha, D. (2002), *Women's Activism and Globalization: Linking Local Struggles and Transnational Politics* (New York: Routledge).

Parreñas, R. (2002), "The Care Crisis in the Philippines: Children and Transnational Families in the New Global Economy," in *Global Woman*, 39-54.

Rowbotham, S. and Linkogle, S. (2001), *Women Resist Globalization: Mobilizing for Livelihood and Rights* (London: Zed Books).

Chapter 4

Migration, Transnational Politics, and the State
Challenging the Limits of the Law: Filipina Migrant Workers' Transnational Struggles in the World for Protection and Social Justice

Robyn Magalit Rodriguez

Extra-legal struggle is how change happens. Without organizing and doing rallies and campaigns, the government would not do anything! Getting legal representation requires that you get a lawyer which is very difficult. Extra-legal action is necessary both abroad and in the Philippines. Majority of Filipinos are dependent on migrants so that means that the struggle we [as OFWs] go through abroad, affects [our families] here too.

(Ceny, domestic worker in Hong Kong and MI International activist)

Introduction

This chapter's title draws inspiration from Ceny, a domestic worker employed in Hong Kong and an active member of a Migrante-International (MI) member organization. MI is a transnational alliance of grassroots Philippine migrant workers' organizations that is the focus of this chapter. I met Ceny in the Philippines while she was in between contracts. After visiting family members, Ceny spent the rest of her time at MI's headquarters in Quezon City helping coordinate mass mobilizations around different campaigns including one demanding that the Philippine government intervene in the release of a Filipina, previously employed as a domestic worker, who was jailed in Saudi Arabia.

Mary Jane Ramos was imprisoned after killing her employer. After suffering a series of rapes over the course of three-days by her employer, Ramos killed him in self-defense. Though the Saudi Arabian government cleared Ramos of any malicious wrongdoing, it refused to release her from jail. She would not be allowed to return to the Philippines until she paid $40,000 in so-called "blood money" to her former employer's family. In Saudi Arabia, it is customary for the perpetrator of a crime to monetarily pay their victim's family even when a court clears them of criminal intent. Ramos and her family did not have enough money to pay off her "blood" debt. She was therefore left to languish in jail in Saudi Arabia. The Philippine government, meanwhile, did nothing to facilitate her release.

Ceny's statement is a poignant one, especially in light of the kinds of struggles, like that of Mary Jane Ramos, that Filipina migrants face around the world. Many migrant activists describe themselves as "modern day slaves." Filipina migrant workers are subject to highly exploitative working and abusive living conditions. Additionally, given migrant women's tenuous legal status as either legal or undocumented foreign workers, they are left vulnerable under the laws of their host countries. The uneven application of international human rights norms in different national contexts, furthermore, limits Filipinas' legal protections. Hence, as Ceny suggests, "extra-legal" action is necessary. For her, the law is limited in its ability to protect migrants' rights.

Given the limits of the law in Filipina migrants' countries of employment, how are they able to secure better working and living conditions, if at all? Moreover, how do Filipinas struggle to survive beyond everyday, individualized acts of agency? In other words, in what ways do Filipinas collectively mobilize to fight for their rights and welfare?

In this chapter, I examine the transnational organizing of Filipina migrants through the global alliance of grass-roots Philippine migrant groups, MI, as a means of answering these questions. MI offers an important case-study of the novel ways Filipina migrants can successfully organize and mobilize across national borders to assert their rights and to fight for their improved welfare.

The data I present in this chapter is based on my participant-observation of MI's headquarters in Manila, Philippines for three months in 1997 and an additional seven months in 2001. During that time, I observed and participated in a range of MI's campaign and research work. For instance, I observed as MI campaigned on behalf of Mary Jane Ramos (the campaign Ceny was part of). Additionally, I observed MI International's mobilization of return migrants and their family members to vote for progressive political candidates representing the Bayan Muna Party in the 2001 national elections. I also assisted MI in its research work and its other day-to-day tasks. This work allowed me access to their materials (including for instance, press statements, newsletters, brochures, and other organizational documents) which in turn allowed me to better understand organizational processes.

Additionally, I draw from observations conducted during a regional meeting of MI's affiliated groups in the Asia-Pacific region organized in December 2006 that was held in Cebu (Philippines) as well as observations of an international meeting convened by MI in Hong Kong in June 2008.

Before I discuss Filipina migrants' activism in MI, I will briefly discuss the context for the globalization of women workers from the Philippines.

The Globalization of Filipinas

Global Restructuring and Neoliberalism

Processes of globalization and alongside it, the dominance of neoliberal orthodoxy, have given rise to new forms of racialized and gendered labor demand around the world. Deindustrialization in advanced, "core" economies like the United States, and other Western nations, has meant the global restructuring of key industries which have off-shored manufacturing to peripheral, Third World sites where capital takes advantage of cheaper labor. In the U.S., we need look no further than the clothes on our backs for evidence of this process of global restructuring. Though garments manufacturing supplied many jobs to women in the United States for many decades, many have been closed and relocated to the global South. While U.S. consumers pay one price for an item of clothing, workers in the Third World are paid only a small fraction of the cost of that same item. Manufacturers and retailers, meanwhile, enjoy huge profits.

If deindustrialization is resulting in the contraction of some industries, it is also resulting in the expansion of others in the "core," including the service industry. From business services (cleaning companies) to personal services (which includes domestic workers), major firms as well as ordinary people, are requiring particular forms of service labor. This labor, however, is often defined in different national contexts amongst the "core" of the world system as being performable only by gendered foreign migrants. At the same time, neoliberalism and the state's scaling back of public services globally is producing its own sets of gendered and racialized labor demand including demands for care workers (nannies), who are often required to perform domestic service.

Deindustrialization in the core has produced a relative economic boon to some erstwhile peripheral economies who are now graduating to the status of "Newly Industrialized Country" or NIC. NICs in particular, have thrived as they have played host to erstwhile "core" factories. Significantly, these factories' hiring practices are often informed by the same kinds of gendered logics that shaped hiring when the factories were in the "core." To continue with the example of the garments industry, if women were hired to make clothing in the U.S., they are hired to make clothing in countries throughout NICs of Asia. As more and more women in the NICs are entering the labor force and as families enjoy higher incomes, citizens in the NICs have come to require personal services like caregivers and domestic workers. The workers sought to perform these jobs are increasingly secured from poorer neighboring countries.

The Role of the Philippine State

For states like the Philippines, globalization and neoliberalism and the new labor demands it requires, have become both an economic and political opportunity. Perennially crisis-ridden, the Philippines has emerged as what I call in my work, a labor brokerage state, that profits economically from the export of its citizens who regularly remit their earnings back home and that benefits politically by offering employment, albeit overseas, to its people.

Indeed, over the last decade, Filipina women have outpaced Filipino men as a percentage of the yearly total population of out-migrants from the Philippines. Filipinas find themselves working in gender-typed and gender-segregated occupations, generally as domestic workers, care givers and entertainers, but also as nurses, service workers, clerical workers, and factory workers. They are deployed to over 100 countries around the world ranging from the traditional immigrant-receiving countries like the United States, Canada, the United Kingdom and Australia, as well as NICs like Hong Kong, Taiwan, Singapore and South Korea, wealthy oil-producing countries like Saudi Arabia and the United Arab Emirates and even other developing countries like the island nation of Palau.

Living and Working Conditions

Parrenas illustrates how the Rome and U.S.-based migrants she interviewed experience "contradictory class mobility." That is, they are unable to find work in the Philippines despite their professional training and are better able to secure employment abroad. However, employment abroad often comes at the cost of having to accept lower-status work as domestics.

Not only do these women experience contradictory class mobility, they also contend with insufficient regulation at their sites of employment. Since they often work and live within the confines of their employer's private homes and are employed on an informal basis, the boundaries between work and leisure are frequently violated. Parrenas points out: "Live-in domestic workers, for example, often complain about the absence of set parameters between their work and rest hours." (Parrenas 2001) Indeed, if migrant women are undocumented, they are even more vulnerable to exploitation as they may be threatened with deportation by their employers if they protest their working conditions.

Even in the case when domestic workers are documented and their employment is ostensibly regulated through employment contracts that define set wages and working hours, Constable finds in her study of Filipinas in Hong Kong that they ultimately have little recourse to legal protections. Migrants' employment contracts are supposed to regulate their work and rest hours as well as define the wages the earn, however when migrants attempt to raise concerns about contractual violations to the Hong Kong government, "the onus of proof is on the worker," (Constable 1997) and the proof becomes difficult for domestic workers to muster.

Canada's Live-In Care Program (LCP) would seem on its surface to offer a better resolution to Filipinas' dilemma as either unregulated and undocumented workers or regulated workers with limited rights as temporary residents. Through the LCP the Canadian government imports foreign care-givers, 82 percent of whom are from the Philippines (PWC, March 5, 2002). Given entry on a temporary basis, the LCP requires that women live-in with a family for 24 months. During those 24 months of employment, caregivers are prohibited from applying for other kinds of work. After completing the 24 months of employment, caregivers are then eligible to apply for permanent immigrant status and ultimately citizenship. Then they are able to petition their family members to join them in Canada. Unlike the temporary contractual employment that women perform in places like Italy or Hong Kong, the LCP does offer women with the possibility of residency and ultimately a pathway to citizenship.

During their required 24 months of employment, however, caregivers are expected to perform duties for their employers at any hour of the day, 24 hours a day, 7 days a week. Caregivers are effectively held captive by their employers for two years, earning in some cases as little as $2.00 an hour (FNSG 2005). One Canadian legal scholar argues that the LCP program, and the restrictions it places on migrant women, is inherently abusive and that there are few legal avenues for women to contest their working and living conditions. She concludes that the LCP program is a reminder, "that although the law may be a powerful tool to effect significant changes, it is often not enough" (Santos 2002). In other words, though immigration law in Canada ostensibly offers women a pathway to citizenship and would seem more liberal as compared with the restrictive immigration laws of other countries, Santos argues that these laws are fundamentally flawed because they fail to protect migrants from abuse and exploitation while they complete the terms of the law's employment stipulations.

The circumstances Filipina contractual migrant workers face in other countries of the world are even more difficult because the states where they are employed mete out severe punishments for contractual violations. A 2005 news report describes how three hundred overseas Filipinos, women and men, are suffering in deportation cells in Saudi Arabia. It is illegal for migrants to break their employment contracts there, yet, when migrants find themselves working and living under abusive conditions, their only recourse is to leave their jobs. Escaping intolerable working conditions renders Filipinos "illegal" and therefore eligible for incarceration and deportation. Once in jail, they have no options for legal action, and must simply languish there indefinitely until they are sent back to the Philippines (People's Journal, August 20, 2005). Even in the case of professional workers, like nurses, Ball finds that Filipinas are on the bottom rungs of a racialized work hierarchy whereby "[t]he conditions of employment and the extent of personal freedom vary by nationality, and by the relative wealth of sending nations" (Ball 2004).

What these various studies of Filpina migrants illustrates is that as "foreigners," trapped in gender-typed jobs that are highly exploitative, Filipinas face a general condition of legal insecurity as employment and legal status are so tightly bound. To be employed in many cases, is to have legal status; to leave employment is to be rendered illegal and therefore to be stripped of what are already very limited legal protections. To be undocumented is to be rendered even more vulnerable as neither national laws nor international rights regimes can ensure one's welfare.

Even in the cases when women have legal status, the national laws in their countries of employment as well as everyday social practices on the part of employers and other host people renders them marginalized both legally, as I suggest above, and socially. Migrants' social marginalization can ultimately prevent them from being able to seek advocates from amongst host people including legal representation if there are in fact legal avenues for them to seek redress for exploitation. Additionally, migrants often actually live with their employers (as in the case of domestic workers or caregivers) or under the watchful eyes of the employers on residential compounds. This is often the case for Filipinas who are housed in communal housing arranged by their employers, for instance. Filipina migrants therefore lack meaningful interaction with host people, including potential advocates. Indeed, language and other cultural barriers might also prevent linkages with those who would be allies.

The Limits of the Law

The increasing significance of temporary, foreign labor to various countries around the world raises critical questions about the nature of rights for migrant workers. As rights continue to be moored to formal membership or citizenship in a nation-state, migrants face the problem of being legally marginalized in their countries of employment because they are non-citizens. Even as some host states may extend rights to migrants, they are often only partial. Moreover, those rights are contingent on migrants' legal status. Undocumented migrants' abilities to make claims on a host state are severely limited.

Meanwhile, international human rights regimes do not appear to offer an alternative regulatory framework from which migrants can frame their rights claims. Rochelle Ball and Nicola Piper point out, "The view of a global spread of conventions surrounding human rights, which leads to the claim that the advances of values attached to human rights would render the concept of citizenship almost irrelevant, seems to be rooted in European philosophy and regional systems such as the European Union (and EU citizens only), but cannot necessarily be extended to other regions, such as Asia, or to all types of migrants" (Ball and Piper 2002). Without reifying the notion that "human rights" is a modern, Western concept recognized and practiced solely by nation-states in the West, and thereby implicitly rendering non-Western nation-states as backward places where people do not enjoy rights, the point to be underscored is that rights, whether they are nation-based or rooted in international human rights conventions, cannot be enjoyed by migrants in many places around the world.

For Ball and Piper, given the limits of citizenship rights within host countries and international human rights regimes, that is, given the "limits of the law," new sorts of struggles become important. They suggest, "[t]here is evidence of increasingly transnational networking between migrant worker NGOs in both sending and receiving countries. These steps towards forging of service and advocacy alliances have great potential in making the needs and rights of globalised workers more broadly recognized and ultimately attended to" (Ball and Piper 2002). MI is a good-case study of the sort of "transnational networking…in both sending and receiving countries" that Ball and Piper describe.

MI makes the Philippine state its primary target for demands-making. Significantly, amongst MI's members are groups organized by migrants' children and family members. MI coordinates the mass mobilizations of Philippine migrants as well as their family members left behind against the Philippine government in the homeland as well as consular and embassy offices around the world. From MI's perspective, if the trouble is that Filipina migrants lack rights in their host countries or have little chance at asserting international rights regimes, they do retain membership, and therefore "rights" as citizens of the Philippines. As Philippine citizens, they have a better sense of the Philippines' political terrain and an understanding of the state's pressure points both in the Philippines and outside in the form of Philippine embassies and consular offices. They use their understanding of Philippine politics to compel the Philippine state to either reform migration policies or to even intervene extraterritorially on migrants' behalf.

In the section that follows, I offer first a sketch of how MI is organized, then I will examine specific campaigns it has organized around.

MI International

Background

Headquartered in the Philippines, MI has ninety affiliated organizations from almost every major region of the world. Though MI is not comprised exclusively of migrant women but they have been in key leadership positions. Through their engagement in the MI network, Filipina migrants bring domestic work (and other home-based care-related work) into the public sphere. They thereby denaturalize domestic work as an extension of women's innate other-orientation which foreign employers use to exploit and abuse them. MI insists domestic work is a legitimate form of employment which ought to be subject to state regulation rather than an intimate space to be protected from external intervention. Moreover, in contrast to nationalist, paternalistic and maternalistic middle-class and church-based activists who campaign for employment bans on domestic work or entertainment because it is "shameful" employment or because they believe women who choose to work in these jobs exercise poor judgment, MI activists struggle to maintain women's dignity.

Though MI does call for an end of the state's active promotion of labor migration, it is a call for the end of structural inequalities within and between states that effectively force people migrate. As Maher suggests, "women in sending countries need the material conditions to facilitate their full citizenship, including access to education, capital, and social services. They need legal institutions that value them and function to protect their rights, such that migration as a means of escape is no longer necessary," (Maher 2004). Indeed, it is full citizenship that MI women (and men) activists fight for.

MI creates and sustains its global network of affiliates by being flexible about the sorts of groups it seeks to both incorporate and create. On one hand, MI attempts to bring pre-existing organizations into its fold. MI activists will approach so-called "traditional organizations" that is, linguistic or home town associations (a typical organizational form amongst Philippine migrant workers) to participate in MI as a member. MI members are expected to share a commitment to collectively identified campaigns that are local to migrants' countries of employment (i.e. demands for minimum wages, struggles for human rights) or that involve fights for migration and other related reforms in the homeland. In South Korea, for instance, KASAMMAKO, a MI member alliance, is comprised of groups including the Capampangan Brotherhood Association (whose members hail from the Pampanga province in the Philippines) and the Bicol Association (also a regionally-based group).

On the other hand, MI launches new organizing efforts in different countries by adopting any of a number of organizational forms. Though migrants' political engagements are often limited by their host countries, migrants have creatively evaded their host states in order to build MI. MI activists' organizing efforts have been malleable, negotiating with the legal restrictions host states place on migrants' ability to form communities. For example, in many countries the only legal (or at least tolerated) form of social organization allowed are those associated with churches. Hence, MI activists have worked closely with progressive clergy to form prospective MI organizations. It is not surprising then that UNIFIL, an alliance of migrant groups in HK that is a member of MI, has long been headquartered in the Anglican St. John's Cathedral.

MI does not limit its organizing to the labor diaspora. In a speech at a summit for migrants' children, a young MI activist noted that, "It's important for children of migrants...to articulate their issues for their rights and welfare." The issue of family separation as a consequence of migration is a point of mobilization for MI in the Philippines which organizes the relatives of migrants and migrants' children into their own groups like the Kilusan ng MI ng Pamilya sa Pilipinas (Movement of Migrant Families in the Philippines, or KMPP) and Migrante-International Youth.

What links these seemingly disparate organizations across the globe is their shared analysis of both the causes and consequences of Philippine migration, namely, that the Philippine state has promoted the export of labor over other kinds of developmental initiative and has therefore cause the separation of Filipino migrants from their families. As written in an MI brochure, "We dream of a society that will never be torn apart just for the need to survive." Hence, amongst the objectives MI identifies for itself is the following: "Oppose the export of labor as a development paradigm. Build self reliant economic development to generate jobs internally, and promote social equity and justice." The lived experience of separation fuels migrants' and their family members' involvement in MI to struggle for the reunification of their families and ultimately to fight for redistributive social change in the Philippines that would give them the opportunity to enjoy dignified and sustainable livelihoods in the homeland.

Significantly, MI affiliated organizations are comprised of self-organized, grassroots migrant groups rather than the NGOs Ball and Piper discuss in their work. MI activists are in fact quite wary of what they call "NGOism" and its potentially depoliticizing effects. While there are NGOs that support MI's work, they cannot become MI member organizations. Their exclusion from MI membership is meant to ensure that migrants themselves are taking leadership in articulating their own needs and leading their own campaigns. Hence, when Ceny describes MI's work as being "extra-legal" she also means that MI is engaged in forms of political mobilization beyond the typical forms engaged in by NGOs involved in migrants' issues.

For instance, MI engages the Philippine state not by making formal petitions to government officials, but by rallying in front of Philippine embassies and consular offices in their countries of employment and demanding that the state advocate on their behalf on terms defined by migrants themselves. Indeed, migrants dealing any number of issues in one country can rely on MI's affiliated organizations based in the Philippines and around the world to hold solidarity actions in front of Philippine government offices to press the state to address their issues.

There is a plethora of NGOs outside of MI's ambit oriented toward providing direct service to migrant workers or advocating on migrant workers' behalf in the Philippines and throughout the world. These NGOs, however, are generally reluctant to take the kinds of direct action including protests, rallies and other kinds of public mobilizations against the Philippine government that MI member organizations do.

Though MI's approach to organizing and collective mobilization might be considered unconventional from the perspective of NGOs, MI has been successful in winning important gains for Filipina workers. Indeed, not only has MI been able to force the Philippine government to respond favorably to its demands, it has also been able to win important concessions from their host governments. The organizational capacity that migrant activists develop through their work in MI provides them with the skills and know-how to engage directly with their host governments. In the next section, I will examine key sets of campaigns around economic and human rights that it has engaged in to illustrate how it mobilizes around migrants' rights

Campaigns

Economic rights, it would seem, are rights migrants would struggle over in the host countries since it is in host countries where migrants' employers are located and it is host countries' employment and labor laws that govern migrants' wages and work conditions. MI, however, not only mobilizes migrants in struggles in their host countries, but indeed, it targets Philippine state representatives to pressure host governments to protect migrants' rights.

In the case of Filipina caregivers in Taiwan, for instance, an MI affiliated organization called for the dismissal of Philippine state representatives who failed to intervene on migrants' behalf in a wage dispute:

> We therefore call for the dismissal of Mrs. Lydia Espinosa and Paul from MECO (Manila Economic Cooperation Office)[1] for selling out Jovita and Marilyn. They acted as representatives of the employer, broker and even the Hsinchu [Taiwanese] Labor Bureau (MI Sectoral Party-Taiwan Chapter).

In addition to launching a campaign for these officials' dismissal, MI activists also launched a campaign demanding a standard employment contract for all migrants working in Taiwain as illustrated in the following quote:

> The tasks presented to the organization for the next two years include campaigning for a standard employment contract for all foreign workers. This is to ensure that all side agreements imposed in the Philippines and/or Taiwan should be made void or non-binding (MI, Taiwan).

The "side agreements" MI-Taiwan alludes to include bilateral agreements between the Philippine and Taiwanese governments on minimum wages for Filipino migrants.

To contest these kinds of "side agreements," migrants have struggled against Philippine migration officials in the Philippines to ensure that they earn fair wages while they are overseas. For instance, MI launched a campaign in the Philippines against the Department of Labor and Employment calling for its head to step down. According to MI,

> With the Philippine's own Labor Chief agreeing to slash wages of Filipino migrant workers, it's not surprising if other foreign employers and governments take her cue. In effect, this government sends the message that Filipino workers are negotiable for lower wages (MI International 2002).

In a similar campaign, MI raised a public outcry against the Philippines' main migration bureau, the Philippines Overseas Employment Administration (POEA) when it announced that the Japanese government had agreed to open up two hundred positions for nurse and caregiver "trainees." MI was outraged by this and issued the following statement:

---

1   Given the Philippines' one-China policy, rather than having a formal embassy in Taiwan, it has MECO which essentially carries out diplomatic functions.

If the Arroyo administration pushes through with this plan, it means that Filipino nurses and caregivers sent to Japan will receive lower wages than their Japanese counterparts. After their three year 'training' stint, it's likely that many will simply be deported out of Japan given the extremely difficult Japanese language test the nurses and caregivers must take before 'qualifying' to work as regular nurses and caregivers (International 2005).

What this statement suggests is that MI recognizes that migrants' wage rates are not merely dependent on the minimum wage rates set by foreign government or wages offered by employers, but that the Philippine state is accountable in ensuring that migrants get fair wages. The Philippine state must be accountable to migrants whether it means intervening in sites of employment on their behalf or through Philippine migration officials' commitment to only deploy migrants to those countries where migrants will be guaranteed decent wages.

In 2007, Filipino nurses sat in a New York State courtroom, indicted on criminal charges for patient endangerment because they had walked off their jobs. They left their place of employment to protest low wages and bad working conditions. According to James Millena, a nurse-turned-doctor. "We were brought to the staff house where we stayed for two months for free and saved money we needed when we move to an apartment...I shared the room with other Filipino nurses. We took turns sleeping on the bed and on the floor. It wasn't comfortable, but I didn't complain." He also revealed that he was assigned to handle 100 patients by himself throughout his shift (National Alliance for Filipino Concerns 2007). The nurses however were being countersued by the facility where they worked after the nurses themselves filed suit against the labor recruitment agency that had facilitated their migration to and employment in the U.S.

After their legal strategy stalled, the nurses decided to take the issue nationally through NAFCON (which has links to MI)—to "avoid corrupt politics" and to:

> help [the nurses] meet their basic demands- including dropping of all criminal and civil charges against them in the State of New York, seeking compensation for all backwages including unpaid overtime wages, re-suspension of the Sentosa recruitment license by the POEA, and investigation by the State of New York on Sentosa Care LLC operations against existing anti-human trafficking law and the thirteenth amendment outlawing slavery (NAFCON, May 2007).

Mobilizing both in the Philippines and the United States, MI affiliated organizations demanded that the Philippine government intervene on their behalf.

MI's protest activities in the U.S. included major press campaigns, public forums, an on-line petition generating nearly three thousand signatures (many of whom claimed to be nurses) and even participation in the Philippine Independence Day Parade in New York City. Indeed, MI efforts appear to have been instrumental in getting the nurses' issue addressed by the New York Times. In the Philippines, MI along with the Alliance of Health Workers, BAYAN Philippines, and the Health

Alliance for Democracy participated in protest actions that targeted the Phililppine based-offices labor recruitment agencies (National Alliance for Filipino Concerns 2007). The protests led to the government's blacklisting of the recruitment agency to stop its future deployments of workers. When the Philippine government rescinded the blacklist order, which the MI activists attribute to political pressure from U.S. lawmakers (with whom the recruitment agency putatively had links), MI refused to let up on their campaign and it is on-going.

MI organizations' transnational response to the Sentosa nurses' struggles is yet another illustration of how migrants engage in "challenging the limits of the law." Though the nurses did pursue legal action against their recruitment agency, they were confronted with its limits and pursued alternative methods of fighting for justice.

In relation to human rights issues, rather than insisting on international human rights instruments, migrants put transnational political pressure on the Philippine state to intervene extraterritorially on migrants' behalf. According to MI-Middle East, for instance,

> The numerous cases of rights violations resulting to the increase of ran away and stranded OFWs in the Middle East are concrete manifestations to look upon by the Arroyo administration, which has been remiss to its state responsibility protecting OFWs rights and welfare, to come up a policy or link bilateral agreements with host governments advancing and protecting migrant rights and welfare (Monterona 2008).

In the Middle East, run-away migrants, as I discuss earlier in this chapter, are subject to imprisonment if they are found. While in jail, they suffer horrendous treatment. MI contends that the Philippines should step-in to intervene through diplomatic relations with the country of employment. Though we might anticipate that migrants would draw on human rights conventions to assert their rights to humane conditions of detention, they in fact assert their rights as Philippine citizens to protection from foreign states.

While Filipinas are subject to rights violations by their employers or even host governments they can be made vulnerable even when in the custody of Philippine state officials. In 1999, Filipina domestic worker, Glenda Lorio, was murdered at the Philippine Consulate's Filipino Workers' Development Center in Hong Kong. The center is supposed to offer Filipina migrants with temporary shelter if they decide, for whatever reason, to terminate their employment contracts before their official end. Workers stay at the Center temporarily as they await repatriation back to the Philippines. In Lorio's case, she had escaped from an abusive employer and sought refuge at the Center. Yet, due to a lack of security, her employer (the prime suspect in her murder) managed to gain access into the Center where he murdered her.

Lorio's murderer was brought to justice, but MI activists as well as Lorio's family, believed that the Philippine government was irresponsible for not having properly secured the Center. According to a Hong Kong-based MI activist,

> Simply putting the murderer behind bars will not mean justice for Glenda. Justice can only be served if the Philippine government officials who abandoned her are meted corresponding punishment; if the Philippine government will indemnify the family of Glenda, and if the Philippine government will truly provide free, accessible and adequate protection for the rights and welfare of migrant Filipinos (Mission 1999).

MI activists took actions in both Hong Kong and the Philippines calling for Philippine migration officials to launch an official investigation of the consular officers' negligence. Ultimately, the government was forced to provide compensation to Lorio's family including paying the cost of the repatriation of Lorio's remains and personal effects. Other burial costs were provided for by the government. Additionally, the family was promised financial assistance including scholarship for Lorio's children. The transnational organizing efforts of groups like MI offer Filipinas and their family members some measure of justice.

Scholars recognize that the labor-sending state's intervention on behalf of its overseas citizens transnationally can be an important strategy for ensuring that migrants' rights are protected. Labor-sending states, however, rarely do so because they either do not have the power or the interest to intervene (Maher 2004). Successful mobilizations by MI International suggest that when a labor-sending state is pressured transnationally by its citizens, they do intervene and migrants' issues can be successfully addressed.

Conclusion

Through MI, Filipina migrants have challenged the limits of national employment laws and international human rights regimes to fight for their rights. MI International is a transnational migrant movement with an influence that spans the globe, but perhaps more importantly, in the "homeland." MI's organizations include groups in the countries where Filipinas work, as well as groups in the Philippine whose members are not in fact migrants themselves, but migrants' relatives and children. What links these organizations globally, and what accounts for MI's centering in the Philippines, is a shared analysis of the causes and consequences of migration that ultimately displaces Filipinas from their families and therefore, a shared commitment to struggling against the Philippine state. Because the state plays a role in deploying migrants globally, it becomes an immediate target for workers, sometimes even more immediate than their employers or their "host" countries. However, the state is a target for migrants' demand-making also because it has an especially enduring significance for displaced people. The "homeland" continues to be the repository of rights and entitlements for migrants who have no rights in the countries where they work. If migrants' sense of connection to the "homeland" and eventual return becomes the means by which the state is able to sustain the profitability of migration as workers can be trusted to remit their earnings and to come home at the end of a contract, it is also their mooring to the "homeland" that becomes a means by which migrants make demands for particularized rights from the Philippine government.

MI's organizing, as manifested in their struggles for workers' wages and human rights highlights an emergent notion of global Philippine citizenship. This global Philippine citizenship proves to be distinct from "post-national" models of citizenship not merely because it is a model of citizenship that relies on migrants' home states for granting citizens' claims transnationally, but also, because it is a model of citizenship that emerges out of transnational migrant movements "from below."

Finally, despite the fact that migrants are forced to leave their homes and families to join the ranks of the most marginalized sectors of the working class throughout the world, the transnational linkages they form in building a migrant workers' movement in the face of dispersal and displacement is a remarkable example of workers' resistance to the pernicious aspects of neo-liberal globalization. Through organizations like MI, Filipina migrants forge an alternative space of belonging and collective identification, a transnational community that is simultaneously anchored to the nation-state, even as it is constituted outside of and against it.

References

Ball, R.E. (2004), "Divergent Development, Racialised Rights: Globalised Labor Markets and the Trade of Nurses – The Case of the Philippines," *Women's Studies International Forum* 27(2): 119-133.

Ball, R.E. and Piper, N. (2002), "Globalisation and Regulation of Citizenship-- Filipino Migrant Workers in Japan," *Political Geography* 21(8): 1013-1034.

Constable, N. (1997), *Maid to Order in Hong Kong* (Ithaca: Cornell University Press).

MI International (2002), Press Release, "Labor Secretary Sto. Tomas' Wage Cuts for OFWs Sets Bad Precedent for Overseas Filipinos," June 13, 2002.

——(2005), Press Release, "HK Domestic Workers Score Partial Victory with HK$50 Wage Hike; Wage Hike for OFWs Also Needed in Other Countries," May 19, 2005.

——(2005), Press Release, "MI Warns Against RP 'Exporting' Nurses, Caregivers to Japan as Trainees."

MI Sectoral Party–Taiwan Chapter, (Undated), "We Condemn MECO for Selling Out Two of Our Compatriots!" (Hong Kong: Asian Pacific Mission for Migrants).

Mission, G. (1999), "A Death in Hong Kong," *Cyberdyaryo*, <http://gina.ph/Cyberdyaryo/features/cd1999_1014_003.htm>.

Monterona, J.L. (2008), Press Release "'Changed Name' a silly excuse of beleaguered, inept Congen," April 29, 2008.

National Alliance for Filipino Concerns (2007), Press Release.

Parrenas, R.S. (2001), *Servants of Globalization* (Stanford: Stanford University Press).

Santos, M. (2002), *A Matter of Policy or Strategy? The Role of Actors and Institutions in Promoting the Human Rights of Filipina Domestic Workers in Canada* (Toronto: York University).

Chapter 5

Identities, Nation, and Imperialism

Confronting Empire in Filipina American Feminist Thought

Anne E. Lacsamana

Introduction

Recently, while thumbing through a collection of essays by Egyptian feminist Nawal el Saadawi, I stumbled across this passage and was immediately struck by her keen understanding of how one's identity, particularly for the colonized, is always dictated, imposed, and shaped by the colonizer. Her words reminded me of my most recent trip to the Philippines where the imprint of U.S. domination can be found in the fast food restaurants lining the streets, enormous shopping malls perched atop Manila Bay casting long shadows over squatter communities, on the face of the 100-peso bill where the U.S. flag is positioned alongside the Philippine, the ubiquity of the English language, and of course, in the much discussed "colonial mentality" of Filipinos which exalts anything and everything "American." Indeed, el Saadawi's insight into the relationship between imperialism and subaltern subjectivities has a particular resonance for Filipinos.

For second and third generation Filipinos, either born and/or raised in the United States, the issue of identity occupies a privileged position in the scholarship in Filipina–American studies. A prime example is the emerging body of Filipina–American feminist thought referred to as either "pinayism" or "peminism" by its practitioners. Modeled after the pioneering work of U.S. women of color who challenged the white solipsism of feminist thinking, the groundwork for Filipina–American feminism was first outlined in the 1996 essay "Pinayism" by Allyson Goce Tintiangco-Cubales. Since then, a number of articles expanding on the initial working principles set forth in this piece have emerged, resulting in the 2005 anthology *Pinay Power: Theorizing the Filipina/American Experience* edited by Melinda de Jesus.

Having carved out its own niche within the field of U.S. feminist thought, this collection recognizes the contributions of Filipina–American feminist scholarship over the past decade. Situating this development within the intimate and unequal confines of the U.S.–Philippine neo-colonial relationship reveals the unique position Filipina–American feminist theory inhabits a little over a century since the U.S. took up Kipling's "white man's burden" in 1898. With the massacre of over one million Filipinos in the often forgotten Filipino-American War (1899-1902) the United States established itself as an imperialist nation at the dawn of the twentieth century. Today, with U.S. military entanglements in both Iraq and Afghanistan, as part of an unending global "war on terror" in which the Philippines finds itself as the "second front," the early years of the 21st century present an important opportunity for Filipina–American feminist thinkers to center-stage a radical, anti-imperialist, nationalist brand of theorizing that has its historical roots in the revolutionary actions of Filipino foremothers Gabriela Silang, Gregoria de Jesus, and Tandang Sora who bravely fought for Philippine sovereignty in the war against Spain. The nationalist feminism first embodied by these women continues in the collective resistance presently being waged by members of the multi-sectoral Philippine women's movement.

While not intended to be an exhaustive account, this essay will reflect on some of the major theoretical tendencies that have characterized certain aspects of Filipina–American feminism and propose the possibility for future directions. As the largest group of "Asian Americans" in the United States today, the effects of U.S. colonization are manifest in the ongoing marginalization and exploitation of the approximately three million Filipinos living and laboring in the metropolis. Connecting the past with the present, the home with the homeland, is a requirement for Filipina Americans grappling with the inherent contradictions of growing up never truly "Filipina" nor "American."

Filipino–American Feminist Theory and the "Cultural Turn"

One of the earliest attempts to reconcile this paradox can be found in the aforementioned "Pinayism" essay by Tintiangco-Cubales. In explaining what pinayism is *not* she states: "Pinayism is not just a Filipino version of feminism or womanism; Pinayism draws from a potpourri of theories and philosophies, including those that have been silenced and/or suppressed" (2005, 139). Variously described as a "revolutionary action," "self-affirming condition or conduct," and a "peculiarity of language, like anarchism" Tintiangco-Cubales makes clear that the pinayist revolution will remain "localized in the United States" (2005, 140). This insistence on the "local," though, does not mean pinayism can never venture, however fleetingly, into the "global."

For example, Tintiangco-Cubales reminds budding pinayists that it is their responsibility to forge connections with Filipinos living in the diaspora since there is the temptation among Filipina Americans to "neglect the issues of those women who *are* submissive, who *are* mail-order brides, who *are* prostitutes, who *are* maids" (2005, 143). On the one hand, urging Filipina Americans to link their issues with those facing Filipino women in the diaspora to "classism, neocolonialism, and sexism" (Tintiangco-Cubales 2005, 143) is an important and necessary component of pinayist thinking, on the other, Tinitiangco-Cubales's misconception of the diaspora could undermine her well-intentioned attempt at alliance-building. For example, by describing the diaspora to include Filipinos living *outside* the United States in countries such as the "Philippines, Australia, Canada, Kuwait, Japan, and around the world" (Tinitiangco-Cubales 2005, 142). Tintiangco-Cubales has turned the notion of "homeland" completely on its head. In this instance the United States becomes the "homeland" (rather than the colonizer) from which Filipinos have been "dispersed" to live and work in other countries such as the Philippines. This historical rendering could have the unfortunate effect of lulling Filipina Americans into the mistaken belief that they are first and foremost "Americans" with only a tangential connection to their original homeland. Of course, the brutal realities of living as racialized, immigrant subjects in the U.S., best exemplified by the deportation of over 460 Filipinos (some U.S. citizens) shackled with their hands behind their backs, deprived of food and water, during their grueling flight "home" shortly after 9/11 belies this incomplete understanding of the diasporic condition.

Notwithstanding the limitations of this early articulation of Filipina–American feminist thought, Tintiangco-Cubales laid the foundation for the further development of "pinayist" thinking. In fact, her brief discussion concerning the plight of Filipino women working abroad in low-paying service work has now become a central theme in Filipina–American feminist scholarship. Since the Marcos dictatorship institutionalized "migration" as a centerpiece of Philippine economic policy, the economic condition of Filipino women has steadily deteriorated. At present, approximately more than 8 million Filipinos (approximately 70 percent of women) have left their homes and families to find work abroad as overseas Filipino workers (POEA 2004). Each day 3,400 Filipinos leave Ninoy Aquino International Airport with 6-10 returning in coffins, while the Filipino government earns about P25.5 million everyday from various departure charges and fees (De Lara 2008). Scattered across 196 countries, the majority of OFWs find themselves laboring in low-paying, service-oriented occupations as domestic workers, caregivers, and "entertainers." Representing the largest source of foreign exchange, the remittances of OFWs – totaling $12-13 billion a year – keep the Philippine economy afloat. The importance of these remittances has not been lost on Philippine officials, with the past three presidential administrations declaring them to be the "new heroes" of the nation (Aquino), "internationally shared resources" (Ramos), and "overseas Filipino investors" (Arroyo).

Following the 1997 publication of Nicole Constable's *Maid to Order In Hong Kong: Stories of Filipina Workers* a flurry of scholarship focusing on the global dimension of Filipino women's lives has appeared: Rhacel Parrenas's *Servants of Globalization: Women, Migration, and Domestic Work* (2001) and *Children of Global Migration: Transnational Families and Gendered Woes* (2005), Neferti Tadiar's *Fantasy-Production: Sexual Economies and Other Philippine Consequences for the New World Order* (2004), Catherine Choy's *Empire of Care: Nursing and Migration in Filipino American History* (2005), and Emily Ignacio's *Building Diaspora: Filipino Cultural Community Formation on the Internet* (2007) to name a few representative examples. Although each of the aforementioned texts approaches the subject of Filipino women's migration from a specific methodological perspective, what binds the majority of this intellectual work together is their underlying theoretical orientation.

Reflecting the "cultural turn" in feminist scholarship, Foucauldian-inspired discursive analyses emphasizing overseas Filipino women's "agency" and "resistance" has become the prevailing conceptual lens from which to understand their subordinate position in the global economy. For example, coping mechanisms such as "frowning or crying" are recast by theoreticians as performative acts of resistance to elicit "emotions among employers (such as discomfort and guilt) which then makes employers more cooperative" (Parrenas 2001, 252). The "diaries, letters and phone calls" sent by domestic workers to their families serve as examples of the "subjective activity of women" (Tadiar 2004, 131, 136). According to Tadiar, these creative pursuits illustrate that "Filipina domestic helpers are not merely objects of other people's practices, objects of better or worse 'treatment', conservation and regulation; they are active producers and creative mediators of the world in which they move . . ." (2004, 132). Citing the last letter of a domestic worker who died at the hands of her employer, Tadiar explains that her "power" was "enacted through writing to reach beyond the confinements of her bodily labor-time" (2004, 137). For other scholars, such as Catherine Choy, the very act of migration exemplifies an "individual and collective desire for a unique form of social, cultural, and economic success obtainable only outside the national borders of the Philippines" (2003, 7). Together, these accounts portray Filipino women as desiring, laboring, empowered (even in death) subjects in the era of globalization. Often considered cutting edge for their attention to women's subjectivity, these writings mirror the reigning theoretical template in contemporary Filipina–American feminist thought.

Materialist Intervention: Recuperating "Class" and Nation in a Globalized World Order

The current moment of social, economic, and political crisis in the Philippines provides an important opportunity to assess the efficacy of such knowledge production.

My critique of these texts is not meant to minimize the important contributions each has provided to the growth and expansion of Filipina–American feminism. Rather, it is intended to draw attention to the numerous ways U.S. imperialism, masked as "globalization," continues to distort and shape the lives of Filipinos at home and abroad. The postmodern-inspired emphasis on agency, resistance, and representation serves to obscure the fundamentally exploitative neo-colonial relationship between the United States and the Philippines – the very reason the latter finds itself as one of the chief exporters of women's (cheap) labor power in the world. It is difficult, if not impossible, to write about the Philippines and ignore its lengthy history of Spanish and U.S. colonial subjugation. What matters, however, is the manner in which issues of imperialism, capitalism, and globalization are theorized in academic accounts.

If, as I suggest, Filipina–American feminism is reflective of the "cultural" or postmodern turn in Western feminist theory, it would follow that analyses of global capitalism remain confined to the realm of discourse, unhinged from the social relations of production. As Teresa Ebert explained in her groundbreaking work *Ludic Feminism*: "what is at stake in this displacement of the economic by discourse is the elision of issues of exploitation and the substitution of a discursive identity politics for the struggle for full social and economic emancipation" (1996, 42). We see this tendency in Tadiar's work when she discusses the usefulness of Marxism for understanding work and labor, but finds the "obstinate refusal of more orthodox Marxisms to factor in categories of gender, race, and sexuality" limiting (2004, 8). As a result, she turns to the psychoanalytic theory of Slavoj Žižek because he "merges the two theoretical discourses of Marxism and psychoanalysis to arrive at an understanding of ideology as an 'unconscious fantasy structuring our social reality itself'" (2004, 9). In this analytic move Žižek, and by default Tadiar, erase "ideology's relation to a materialist base – the forces and economic relations of production – only to substitute in its place a grounding of all ideology, in fact all reality, on the idealist base of enjoyment" (1996, 61). Thus, any systemic attempt to understand the Philippines and its dependent peripheral status is obscured by the persistent tendency to negate the material (economic) in favor of the cultural (ideological) (1996, 60-61).

The imperative to avoid materialist analyses due to their alleged economic reductionism is largely responsible for the culturalist accounts of Filipino women's identity, labor, and migration. Choy explains that the "desire of Filipino nurses to migrate abroad cannot be reduced to an economic logic" (2003, 7) as so many other studies of migration have suggested. What differentiates Rhacel Parreñas's approach to migration from others is her emphasis on the "level of the subject" which enables her to better understand the "limits and possibilities, of agency" (2003, 250-251). As fragmented subjects attempting to reconcile their contradictory position in their "host" country, they unintentionally end up maintaining "inequalities, particularly the system of global restructuring in which their constitution as subjects is situated" (2003, 253). In an interesting theoretical sleight of hand we discover that the recuperation of power by individual domestic workers makes them unwittingly complicit in their own (as well as others) exploitation by the forces of global capitalism. This diffusion of power, a la Foucault, makes it impossible to ascertain the material realities informing Filipino women's migration or their actions once consigned to living in their "host" country.

As I have written elsewhere, Nicole Constable's study of Filipina domestic workers in Hong Kong is an exemplary model of this particular analytical position. In her conclusion, she maintains that regarding "these women simply as oppressed by those 'with power' is to ignore the subtler and more complex forms of power, discipline, and resistance in their everyday lives" (1997, 202). This attention to the minutiae of Filipino women's lives was repeated in her 2003 comparative study of Filipina and Chinese women's "mail-order marriages," *Romance on A Global Stage*. Again she cautions against viewing "women as simply dominated by men" arguing instead that attention be "paid to more complex and subtle articulations of power" (2003, 5). For Constable, the "more important contemporary feminist concerns with power, ideology, representation and positionality" (2003, 5) prove to be invaluable tools for teasing out the nuances informing Filipino women's decisions to become "pen pals" and/or "mail-order brides."

What our historical moment demands is a return to a systemic analysis that can account for the Philippines peripheral status vis-à-vis the metropole. I realize advocating for a historical materialist framework runs the risk of being dismissed outright as retrograde in certain feminist circles; however it remains the most powerful explanatory tool for understanding and transforming the iniquitous power relations between the West and "the rest." Without such an analysis, some could be misled to believe that the majority of Filipino women working as OFWs are freely choosing to migrate thousands of miles away from their homeland and families to labor and live abroad. This is not to suggest that *all* examples of migration are involuntary, but merely to point out that the international division of labor wrought by capitalist processes underpins the economic crisis currently plaguing the Philippines, prompting today's "warm body" export.

An alternative approach to such issues can be found in the philosophy and work of the multi-sectoral Philippine nationalist feminist movement. In "Filipino American Men: Comrades in the Filipina/o Movement," Frank Samson urges pinayists to move beyond the "womanist" paradigm towards an engagement with Filipino feminists, rightfully acknowledging the importance of a global perspective. However, despite reviewing the works of three prominent Filipino feminists, Sr. Mary John Mananzan, Delia D. Aguilar, and Elizabeth Uy Eviota, Samson's discussion of Philippine nationalist feminism is undermined by historical inaccuracies which produce a flawed and incomplete picture of the struggle for women's liberation in a "Third World" formation. For instance, responding to Tintiangco-Cubales's critique of Filipino-American sexism, Samson attributes this behavior to "conservative, traditionalist, and dogmatic anticolonial nationalism" which is often used to silence "post-colonial third-world feminists" (2005, 153). Because this sexism, apparently best embodied by those involved in anti-imperial nationalist movements, is "rooted in the Filipina/o people's history of colonization" Filipina–American feminists need to "unpack the legacies of the 'colonized mentality'" (Samson 2005, 153). Judging from Samson's assessment, it becomes clear that the primary issue which needs to be cleansed (unpacked, discarded, etc.) from Filipina–American feminism is the "legacy" of Philippine nationalism. Tellingly, Samson does not draw on the work of Philippine feminist theoreticians to support his critique of nationalist movements, preferring instead to gain insight from the more general field of "postcolonial feminisms."

The anti-nationalism present in Samson's essay is echoed by Melinda de Jesus in her introduction to Pinay Power "Toward a Peminist Theory, or Theorizing the Filipina/American Experience." After a particularly unpleasant encounter with a male Filipino colleague in which Filipina–American experiences were being "denigrated by the same tired, sexist, cultural nationalist rhetoric" de Jesus felt compelled to assemble an anthology on Filipina–American feminist theory (2005, 2). The insistence on distancing Filipina–American feminism from nationalism is made explicitly clear when de Jesus explains that peminism "demarcates the space for Filipina–American struggles against the cultural nationalist, patriarchal narratives that seek to squash our collective voice in the name of 'ethnic solidarity'" (2005, 5). This description leaves no doubt that "peminism," as articulated by de Jesus, is imbued with an anti-nationalist character. However, if the "analysis of American imperialism in the Philippines unites peminist discourse" (de Jesus 2005, 6) then an understanding of Philippine nationalism should be a requirement for Filipina–American feminist thought.

Over the years there have been both regressive and progressive forms of nationalism practiced throughout the world. Nationalism in the Philippines, similar to other "Third World" countries, takes on a progressive character due to its explicit anti-imperialist stance. In advocating a materialist perspective, I am aware that some might argue that Marxism and nationalism are fundamentally at odds. However, as Michael Lowy makes clear: "the Marxist distinction between the *nationalism of the oppressors* and of the *oppressed* is more than ever justified. ...[t]he essential point is that the nations and nationalities concerned should freely decide their own future" (1998, 79).

Looking Back, Moving Forward: Nationalism and Philippine Women's Liberation

To understand why foregrounding the political economy is an essential component to comprehending the breadth of U.S. neo-colonialism, a brief history of the intense ideological struggles over the "woman question" that ensued in Philippine Left politics in the late 1960s to early 1980s is necessary. Hopefully, by providing this context, Filipina Americans will come to realize that the sexism de Jesus encountered had a historical precedent, and the challenges to sexism that were waged by Filipino women within nationalist circles resulted in a significant shift in the chauvinistic thinking of various organizations, eventually leading to a flourishing semi-autonomous, multi-sectoral *nationalist* feminist movement. Thus, rather than rejecting nationalism outright, Filipino women made clear that national liberation could never be achieved without women's liberation – the two cannot be divorced in the Philippine context.

In her discussion of Filipino women's organizing against the rapid social, political, and economic changes that were occurring in the Philippines during the latter half of the twentieth century, Elizabeth Uy Eviota notes that within the anti-imperialist movement, "women raised the separate issue of women's liberation from economic exploitation and gender oppression. The material and ideological contradictions of women's position had surfaced and had begun to be expressed in a 'women's movement'" (1992, 96). One of the most important groups to emerge at this time was MAKIBAKA (Malayang Kilusan ng Bagong Kababaihan) or the Free Movement of New Women founded by Ma. Lorena Barros in 1969. Noted Philippine scholar E. San Juan Jr. explains that "MAKIBAKA did not just stress the unity of women with men as oppressed subjects; it also targeted the conservative sexist practices of the whole society" (1998, 161). Reflecting the nationalist sentiments of the time, members of MAKIBAKA believed, however, that "women's liberation could be achieved only in the context of greater social liberation" (West and Kwiatkowski 1997, 152). Although MAKIBAKA can be considered an important organization that eventually helped pave the way for the evolution of nationalist feminism in the Philippines, it is important to stress that MAKIBAKA was not a "feminist" group. This distinction between feminism and women's liberation is a crucial one to make as Filipino feminist theorist Delia D. Aguilar explains, "[f]eminism in revolutionary third world struggles was then anathema. It was considered bourgeois, individualist, and divisive. I understood well that MAKIBAKA...stood for the liberation of women, not feminism" (Aguilar and Aguilar-San Juan 2005, 171). After the declaration of martial law in 1972, MAKIBAKA was driven underground, with Barros eventually being gunned down by government forces.

During this period of intense repression, the "woman question" continued to be debated among Philippine nationalists with the "reaction of men in and outside the struggle [ranging] from ridicule to dismissal" (Eviota 1992, 96). Aguilar, one of the primary authorities on the subject of the nationalist feminist movement, described her feelings at this particular historical moment:

> I was determined to engage the 'woman question' among my revolutionary comrades because, by this point, the limitations of the national democratic platform's stance on women had become apparent to me. The fights I had were angry, fierce, and heated...I questioned what I saw then as the productivist orientation of the movement and its instrumental reckoning of women's participation in it. I wanted conventional gender relations addressed and changed (Aguilar and Aguilar-San Juan 2005, 171-172).

In letters and essays published throughout the 1970s into the early 1980s, Aguilar questioned the stubborn, orthodox view among members of the Philippine left that maintained women's equality was "secondary" in the anti-imperialist struggle. Her research on how traditional gender ideologies informed both the public and private sphere, with particular attention to the reproductive labor women perform at home, resulted in the breakthrough 1988 publication of *The Feminist Challenge*.

Applying the critique Western Marxist feminists launched against the crude economism of traditional Marxism to the situation in the Philippines, Aguilar commented: "just as some Marxist feminists err in giving primacy to ideology in order to call attention to the oppression of women, we have in the main paid little heed to the ideological constructs that both reflect and intensify the concrete conditions of women's subjugation" (1981, 173). Unfortunately, the insistence that women's equality would emerge once national liberation was achieved, prompted her to explain that such a distorted understanding of women's oppression "flies in the face of the experience of existing socialist countries where, despite the very real gains won by women, their subordination persists" (Aguilar 1981, 175). In a semi-feudal country where traditional gender relations were determined by the Catholic Church during the Spanish period and further reified with U.S. colonization, understanding the specific nature of women's oppression was both necessary, if not unsettling, to Filipinos who had grown accustomed to a "female object who [had] been taught to delight in servitude while modestly claiming the 'power behind the throne,' and a male subject whose self-image [derived] from a certain degree of authority at home" (Aguilar 1981, 174).

During this period, it was also not uncommon for Filipino women advocating for the serious treatment of women's oppression to be labeled "divisive." Nonetheless, "throughout the rest of the dictatorial regime, women's groups within or outside the National Democratic Front, including women's religious groups, were engaged in pressure politics" (Eviota 1992, 96). Following the lifting of martial law in 1981 and the assassination of Senator Benigno "Ninoy" Aquino Jr. in 1983, a time many Filipino activists refer to as the opening up of a' democratic space,' women's organizations such as KALAYAAN, PILIPINA, NOW, KABAPA, SAMAKANA, AWARE, and WOMB began to flourish (West and Kwiatkowski 1997, 154). Notably, GABRIELA, founded in 1984 is now considered the largest federation of women's groups in the country with over 200 member organizations. Around the time of its founding, members of GABRIELA began calling themselves "feminists" making "sure to explain that they were appropriating the label for themselves and imbuing it with their own nationalist content" (Aguilar and Aguilar-San Juan 2005, 173). For Filipina–American feminists, the greatest lesson to be learned from this revolutionary history is that despite the intense struggles over sexism that many Filipino women encountered in the progressive movement, their commitment to anti-imperialist nationalism never withered. In fact, the vibrancy and diversity of contemporary Filipino women's groups are the ultimate result of these early engagements.

Imperial Engagements: U.S.–Philippine Relations in the Age of Terror

As the situation in the Philippines continues to deteriorate, with many describing President Gloria Macapagal-Arroyo's regime as far more dangerous and deadly than the Marcos dictatorship, peminism's disavowal of nationalist projects comes at a particularly curious time. There can be no doubt that the murders, intimidation, fraud, and corruption characterizing contemporary Philippine society is directly connected to the U.S.-led "war on terror." The recent mid-May Philippine "elections" is a prime example of how the former "showcase of democracy" has devolved into a virtual killing field to preserve U.S. interests in the region and prop up a presidential administration mired in scandal.

In a June 6, 2007 editorial in the *The Philippine Star* the Philippines earned the dubious distinction of being one of the "least peaceful countries in the world, ranking 100th among 121 in the first-ever Global Peace Index drawn up by the Economic Intelligence Unit." It seems only fitting that a highly corrupt country in the world, would also be one of the most violent places to live in. During the election period, the editorial reported that over "300 people were killed or wounded in violent attacks related to the May 14 elections" (*Philippine Star* 2007). Contrast these observations of the elections with the one made by U.S. Assistant Secretary of State Christopher Hill for East Asia and Pacific Affairs which declared "democracy in the Philippines has already matured" (Lichauco 2007). This incredulous claim prompted Filipino economist Alejandro Lichauco to conclude that "what Hill actually said is the U.S. government is fully backing GMA [Gloria Macapagal-Arroyo] – as it once backed Marcos. Stupid, ugly American" (Lichauco 2007). What is most inspiring, however, amidst a rather bleak situation, is the ongoing collective resistance being waged against U.S. interventionism by Filipinos across all sectors of society. As an Australian member of the People's International Observers' Mission noted: "No one who goes to the Philippines from abroad can fail to be impressed by the people's courage, dynamism, and clarity of understanding of the state and neocolonial forces arrayed against them" (Boeringer 2007). This same clarity of thought and determined sense of purpose is precisely what Filipina–American feminism needs to develop into a potent analytical force that can make linkages between the oppression they face as Filipina Americans living in the heart of empire to the brutal exploitation in their country of origin.

The theme of U.S. domination in the Philippines was at the heart of the recent Permanent People's Tribunal Second Session on the Philippine (PPT) verdict on March 25, 2007 which found both Philippine President Gloria Macapagal-Arroyo and U.S. President George W. Bush guilty of "gross and systemic violation of human rights, economic plunder and transgression of the Filipino people's sovereignty" (<www.philippinetribunal.org>). This damning verdict follows UN Special Rapporteur Philip Alston's indictment of the Arroyo administration and the Armed Forces of the Philippines (AFP) for the extra-judicial killings and "disappearances" of progressive activists, lawyers, journalists, and human rights workers. Since Arroyo assumed office in 2001, over 900 Filipino citizens have been murdered.

This verdict is similar to the one issued when the First Session on the Philippines convened in 1980 in which a panel of experts unequivocally "condemned the dominant economic and political role of the United States of America in the Philippines and in the region, through the implementation of an imperialist policy" (PPT Verdict 2007, 5). Twenty-seven years later, the effects of U.S. intervention in Philippine society is evident in the chronic poverty, hunger, dislocation, and environmental degradation that pervades both the rural and urban areas. Out of a population of 90 million, 67 million exist on less than $2 a day while the "1000 top corporations have increased their annual net income by 325% [with] the top 10% of the population [possessing] incomes 22 times that of the poorest 10%" (PPT Verdict 2007, 6). The incredible disparity in wealth that characterizes the country can be directly traced to the neoliberal economic policies imposed by the Washington consensus coupled with austere "adjustment" programs mandated by the International Monetary Fund and the World Bank. Not surprisingly, those most impacted by these "free trade" schemes are women and children who end up paying the "heavy price of debt repayment and privatization policies where, due to the neglect of the health care system and drastic cuts in public spending, child and maternal mortality has worsened" (PPT Verdict 2007, 7).

Aggravating an already unstable economic and political situation is the ongoing presence of the U.S. military – a key feature of the neocolonial stranglehold the United States continues to exert over the Philippines. Prior to granting formal "independence" on July 4, 1946, the U.S. signed the Military Bases Agreement enabling it to maintain two major military installations in the Philippines: Clark Air Force Base (Angeles City) and Subic Naval Base (Olongapo City) along with several smaller facilities. After being ousted in 1992 by a coalition of progressive, nationalist forces in the country, the United States was able to re-establish its military presence in 1998 with the passage of the Visiting Forces Agreement – enabling the U.S. *unlimited* access to 22 ports of entry throughout the country. Under the guise of "joint" military and training exercises between the two nations, known as *Balikatan*, the U.S. is given a virtual "free pass" to impose its social, political, and military will on its former colony. U.S. militarization of the Philippines has only intensified under the U.S.-led "war on terror" with the passage of the Mutual Logistics Support Agreement in 2002, once again compromising the sovereignty and security of the nation.

Throughout the years, the presence of the U.S. military has had deleterious consequences for Filipino women. Prior to the VFA, the bases were responsible for spawning massive prostitution in their respective communities. During the 1980s there were "9000 'hospitality' girls in Subic Naval Base and 7000 more in Clark Air Field" servicing U.S. military personnel during their "Rest and Recreation" (R&R) (Aguilar 1988, 7). The notorious city of Olongapo was once again making headlines in 2005 as the site of the widely publicized "Subic Rape Case." On November 1, 2005 a 22-year-old Filipina was raped in a moving van by a U.S. Marine as three other soldiers cheered him on. Lance Corporal Daniel Smith was convicted of the crime on December 4, 2006 and sentenced to 40 years in a Philippine jail. Smith's conviction marked the first time a member of the U.S. military had ever been tried, convicted, and sentenced on Philippine soil. Unfortunately, this "victory" would be short-lived: Smith was secretly transferred from the Makati City Jail to the U.S. Embassy on December 29, 2006 while awaiting his appeal. In addition to highlighting critical questions concerning violence against women and sexual assault, the Subic Rape Case has re-ignited protests over U.S. military intervention in the Philippines.

The immiseration, exploitation, and political corruption typifying contemporary Philippine life has galvanized an already well-organized, multi-sectoral, anti-imperialist movement demanding the removal of the U.S.-backed Arroyo regime and an end to U.S. domination. Similar to the women revolutionaries who fought in the war against Spain, Filipino women continue to play a vital role in the struggle for Philippine national liberation. As a testament of their sacrifice, several women from GABRIELA have been murdered by government forces with women leaders being "stripped naked and molested by military personnel. Sexual violence is used both as a form of torture and to create fear among women" (PPT Verdict 2007). The brutal and dehumanizing government response to dissent simultaneously illustrates the effectiveness of the nationalist movement and the willful arrogance of a puppet regime engaged in a murderous spree bolstered by U.S. continuing imperial design in the Philippines.

Confronting Empire from Below: Agency and Resistance in a Nationalist Feminist Framework

Filipino women's collective mobilization challenges the peminist assumption that Filipinas are merely "seen as objects of a sexist, imperial ideology" while "[remaining] invisible as subjects and agents" (de Jesus 2005, 3). I argue that it is precisely the *visibility* of Filipinas' actions, demonstrations, and protests that has caught the attention of both government and military officials hoping to squelch their activities. According to de Jesus, the need for "pinay power" stems from the fact that despite their "ubiquitous presence throughout the diaspora, Filipinas remain contingently visible: as nameless, faceless overseas contract workers, sex workers, and mail-order brides scattered across the globe" (2005, 3). This assessment of Filipino women's invisibility and lack of agency directly contradicts what I witnessed during a January 2007 research trip to the Philippines to meet with several women's organizations. In fact, there was a palpable energy and excitement in the air, as activists shared with me, among other things, their upcoming preparations for the elections, campaigns to aid domestic workers in the Middle East, and daily vigils to bring "Justice for Nicole" and closure to the Subic Rape Case.

When visiting a squatter community in Quezon City, I met over a dozen members of SAMAKANA (an urban poor women's organization) who showed me a school they had recently built for their children and explained their demands for clean water and adequate health care. Despite the constant threat of eviction, government harassment and militarization of the urban centers, this chapter of SAMAKANA demonstrates the breadth and vitality of Filipino women's organizing. On a visit to the headquarters of MIGRANTE International (International Alliance for Filipino Migrant Organizations), I met two young women who had been working as domestic workers in Hong Kong. Both had fled their abusive employers and were seeking refuge at MIGRANTE until their cases were filed. Whilst there, I learned of numerous campaigns to free Filipino women who were being illegally detained in Lebanon, and others who were facing execution on trumped-up charges. At the GABRIELA office I was afforded the opportunity to get a glimpse into what goes into coordinating the tireless rallies and demonstrations being conducted to draw connections between the sexual exploitation of Filipino women, the VFA, and U.S. imperialism. In short, to imagine that "Filipinas are simultaneously everywhere and nowhere" (de Jesus 2005, 3) ignores the struggles of a nation whose only chance of survival against the world's superpower, lies in its collective consciousness of resistance.

In contrast, pinay power or peminism, advocates an entirely different form of "agency" influenced by Western feminism's preoccupation with the postmodern focus on discourse and the micropolitics of everyday life. Thus, for pinayists, their agency and subjectivity is illustrated by incorporating the "Filipino American oppositional politics inscribed by choosing the term *Pilipino* over *Filipino*" (de Jesus 2005, 5). In such a semantic shift, peminism, rather than feminism, "signifies the assertion of a specifically Filipina–American subjectivity" (de Jesus 2005, 5). Aside from the fact that the 1987 Philippine constitution declared the national language of the country to be "*F*ilipino" to be inclusive of other vernaculars (which do have the F sound) besides Tagalog, the decision to make the switch from f to p could be purely for the discursive, exotic, and performative potential such words evoke. However, making such a linguistic substitution, in no way destabilizes, displaces, or transgresses U.S. hegemonic rule of the Philippines nor does it effectively challenge or "repudiate" the institutionalized racism of the feminist movement. In short, while the *structure* of the words might change (peminism/feminism), the *essence* of imperialism, white racism, and U.S. power remain intact.

Conclusion

At a recent Filipino–American conference, keynote speaker E. San Juan Jr. addressed the aforementioned struggles in the Philippines, the importance of history in comprehending the totality of the situation, and the role Filipino Americans can actively play towards grasping the complex processes and contradictions that define our reality.

Unlike today's Filipina–American feminist theorizing which privileges the Filipina–*American* experience above all else, San Juan understands well that "Filipinos in the United States possess their own historical trajectory, one with its own singular profile but always linked in a thousand ways to what is going on in the Philippines" (2007, 111). To make this crucial connection and weave together the histories of Filipinos with those either born and/or residing in the U.S., San Juan warns against "minstrelsy" and "mimicry" represented by the "drive to assume a hybrid 'postcolonial' identity, with all its self-ingratiating exoticism and aura of originality" (2007, 111-112). Perhaps peminism's greatest limitations are the result of its preoccupation with "carving out a distinctive space for the "hybrid Filipina–American experience" (de Jesus 2005, 6). This return to exoticism or nativism is clearly reflected in the deployment of peminism as a way to distinguish Filipina–American feminist theorizing from Chicana, African-American, and Asian American feminisms. In its quest to "invent" an original form of feminist thinking for Filipina Americans, peminism succumbs to a bad case of historical amnesia, resulting in both the suppression of the vibrancy and militancy of the Philippine women's movement, as well as the lengthy history of Philippine opposition to imperial conquest.

As a corrective to these troubling tendencies, I argue that peminism needs a theoretical overhaul which gives primacy to the political economy and the neo-liberal forces now shaping our global order. It is only by placing Filipinas within the international division of labor that we will be able to better understand the specific problems we are confronted with, as well as grasp why and how Filipinos came to live in the United States. So long as peminism retains its parochial character and remains theoretically wedded to Western-influenced feminist formulations that emphasize "micro" rather than "macro" acts of agency, it will be an ineffectual, middle-class, a-historical, identity-based movement.

Situating Filipina Americans within the larger framework of the social relations of production enables one to understand the nationalist impulses that persist in the face of tremendous opposition. Moreover, it is important to emphasize that the history and conditions of Filipina Americans in this country cannot be equated and subsumed under the general "Asian American" category. That is, while Filipinos might share certain similarities with other Asian racial groups, what makes them distinct is the fact that their "country of origin was the object of violent colonization and unmitigated subjugation by U.S. monopoly capital" (San Juan 2000, 13). For this reason, the marginalization and alienation Filipino Americans experience is as much due to this bloody (often sanitized) history as it is to other factors. Therefore, instead of reveling in the hybridity of the colonized Filipino psyche, what James Fallows so famously coined the "damaged culture" of Filipinos, it would be more practical to imagine and implement a collective project of liberation from the excesses of U.S. hegemonic rule. This endeavor of re-imagining and reinventing the future would require confronting and connecting the situation in the "homeland" with the social, economic, and political policies of "home."

References

Aguilar, D.D. (1981), "Some Thoughts on the Oppression of Women." Cited in E. San Juan, "Toward A Socialist Feminism," in *Filipina Insurgency* (Quezon City: Giraffe Books)
—— (1988), *The Feminist Challenge* (Manila: Asian Social Institute).

Aguilar D.D. and Aguilar-San Juan K. (2005), "Feminism Across Our Generations" in Melinda de Jesus (ed.) *Pinay Power: Theorizing the Filipina–American Experience* (New York: Routledge), 167-183.

Boeringer, G. (2007), "Spectacle of a Problematic Election." *Bulatlat*, May 27–June 2, 2007 <http://www.bulatlat.com/2007/05/spectacle-problematic-election>, accessed May 28 2007.

Choy, C. (2003), *Empire of Care: Nursing and Migration in Filipino American History* (Durham: Duke University Press).

Constable, N. (1997), *Maid to Order in Hong Kong: Stories of Filipina Workers* (Ithaca: Cornell University Press).

—— (2003), *Romance on a Global Stage: Pen Pals, Virtual Ethnography, and "Mail Order" Marriages* (Berkeley: University of California Press).

de Jesus, M. (2005), "Introduction: Toward a Peminist Theory, or Theorizing the Filipina/American Experience" in Melinda de Jesus (ed.) *Pinay Power: Theorizing the Filipina–American Experience* (New York: Routledge), 1-15.

De Lara, A. (2008), *Bulatlat* http://bulatlat.com/main/2008/09/20/groups-stage-protest-vs-global-forum-on-migration/, accessed November 12, 2008.

Ebert, T. (1996), *Ludic Feminism and After: Postmodernism, Desire, and Labor in Late Capitalism* (Ann Arbor: The University of Michigan Press).

Eviota, E.U. (1992), *The Political Economy of Gender* (London: Zed Books).

Lowy, M. (1998), *Fatherland or Mother Earth? Essays on the National Question* (London: Pluto Press).

Lichauco, A. (2007), "Ugly, stupid American." *Philippine Daily Tribune*, March 28.<http://yonip.com/Joomla/index.php?option+com_content&task=view&id=58&Itemid=28>, accessed March 28, 2007.

Parrenas, R. (2001), *Servants of Globalization: Women, Migration, and Domestic Work* (California: Stanford University Press).

Permanent People's Tribunal Second Session on the Philippines (2007), "Verdict: Indicting the U.S. Backed Arroyo Regime and its accomplices for Human Rights Violations, Economic Plunder and Transgression of the Filipino People's Sovereignty." <http://philippinetribunal.org/index.php?option=com_docman&Task=cat_view&grid=43&Itemid=53>, accessed March 28, 2007.

Philippine Star (2007), "Editorial: Absence of Violence." June 6. <http://www.abs-cbnnews.com.storypage.aspx?StoryId-79621>, accessed June 6, 2007.

POEA (Philippine Overseas Employment Administration) <http://www.poea.gov.ph/html/statistics.html>, accessed November 17, 2008.

Samson, F. (2005), "Filipino American Men: Comrades in the Filipina/o Movement." In Melinda de Jesus (ed.) *Pinay Power: Theorizing the Filipina–American Experience* (New York: Routledge), 149-166

San Juan, E. (1998), *Filipina Insurgency* (Quezon City: Giraffe Books).

—— (2000), *After Postcolonialism* (New York: Rowman and Littlefield Publishers).

—— (2007), *On The Presence of Filipinos in the United States* (California: SRMNK Publishers).

Tadiar, N. (2004), *Fantasy-Production: Sexual Economies and Other Philippine Consequences For the New World Order* (Hong Kong: Hong Kong University Press).

Tintiangco-Cubales, A. (2005), "Pinayism," in Melinda de Jesus (ed.) *Pinay Power: Theorizing the Filipina–American Experience* (New York: Routledge), 137-148.

West, L.A and Kwiatkowski L.M. (1997), "Feminist Struggles for Feminist Nationalism in the Philippines," in Lois A. West (ed.) *Feminist Nationalism* (New York: Routledge), 147-168.

Chapter 6

The Struggle for Land and Food Sovereignty

Feminism in the Mau Mau Resurgence

Leigh Brownhill and Terisa E. Turner

Introduction

A new series of battles is being fought at the Jubilee of the anti-colonial Mau Mau war in Kenya. In the period 2000 to 2003, a new social movement has been involved in over 50 land occupations and instances of armed and unarmed defences of land from enclosure. The struggle for land and freedom now involves the same social forces and some of the same individuals who were engaged in the war which brought Kenya's national independence in 1963.[1] At the 50th anniversary of Mau Mau, the "jubilation"[2] participates in the worldwide groundswell which is affirming a life-centred political economy against a profit-centred death economy. The front line protagonists of the new Mau Mau are peasant and landless women. They demand communal land titles; universal, free education and producer control of trade.

The Mau Mau of the 1950s was a composite of social forces including peasants, the landless, squatters, waged laborers, prostitutes, rural and urban women, hawkers, *ahoi* (tenants with customary land rights), those exiled from the Rift Valley, ex-WWII soldiers and some ex-chiefs (Odhiambo and Lonsdale 2003; Robertson 1997; Rosberg and Nottingham 1966; wa Kinyatti 1986; wa Wanjau 1983, 1988, 213). The multi-class features of the 1950s Mau Mau along with regional distinctions in oaths and organization, indicate that there were in fact "many Mau Maus" with many origins and class aspirations. Similarly, there are many new Mau Maus. The new Mau Mau includes peasants, the landless,

---

1 Padmore (1953, 254) described the Mau Mau war as "a full-scale military operation – the biggest colonial war in Africa since the Boer war. Over thirty thousand British troops have been assembled to assist the local police force, the Kenya Regiment recruited exclusively from among the European male population, the Kikuyu Home Guards, and the King's African Rifles are in open warfare against what the Africans call the Kenya Land Liberation Army."

2 The biblical concept of jubilee contains six elements: "First, jubilee happened every fifty years. Second it restored land to its original owners. Third, it canceled debt. Fourth, it freed slaves and bond servants. Fifth, it was a year of fallow. Sixth, it was a year of no work" (Linebaugh and Redicker 2000, 290).

squatters, touts, *jua kali* (informal sector) artisans, waged laborers, prostitutes, rural and urban women, traders, refugees from the 1990s land clearances, students, retrenched workers, street children, hawkers, ex-Mau Mau elders, the unemployed, forest dwellers, pastoralists, revolutionary intellectuals, exiles, prisoners, settlement scheme tenants, professionals, human rights and faith-based activists and members of non-governmental organizations. This study focuses especially on the actions of landless women.[3]

We examine resistance to enclosure in Africa using a theoretical framework called "gendered class analysis," which includes seven concepts: commodification, subsistence, globalization from above, globalization from below, fight for fertility, male deal, and gendered class alliance (Turner 1994).

This theory expands the definition of the working class to embrace both the *waged* and the *unwaged.* Capital encloses and commodifies nature, unwaged work, social services and built space (Turner and Benjamin 1995). Women and other unwaged people rely for their daily production and reproduction upon these same "goods." In their struggle with capital, the social power of the unwaged is precisely that they possess and stand on the very ground of subsistence which capital seeks to enclose, commodify and destroy.

The life-centred or "subsistence" political economy is defined by Bennholdt-Thomsen and Mies (1999, 19) as

> freedom, happiness, self-determination within the limits of necessity - not in some other world but here; furthermore persistence, stamina, willingness to resist, the view from below, a world of plenty. The concept of self-provisioning is, in our opinion, far too limiting because it refers only to the economical dimension. 'Subsistence' encompasses concepts like 'moral economy,' a new way of life in all its dimensions: economy, culture, society, politics, language etcetera, dimensions which can no longer be separated from each other.

In the commodified or "death economy" of the "corporate male gang" (McMurtry 2001) profit is central and "life is, so to speak, only a coincidental side-effect. It is typical of the capitalist industrial system that it declares everything that it wants to exploit free of charge to be part of nature, a natural resource. To this belongs the housework of women as well as the work of peasants in the Third World, but also the productivity of all of nature" (Bennholdt-Thomsen and Mies 1999, 20-21)

"Globalization from below" is the process by which the capacities of local "civil commons"[4] are strengthened and linked to their counterparts elsewhere in the world. As corporate "globalization from above" proceeded in the 1990s,

---

3   An estimated 75 percent of Kenya's population of 37 million is engaged in agriculture, mainly subsistence farming in both rural and peri-urban areas.

4   McMurtry defines civil commons as any social construct which enables universal access of members of a community to a life good (2001). For a critique of globalization from below, see Laxer (2003).

popular social forces united to resist. Marx tied the centralization of capital in ever fewer global corporations to the expansion and revolt of the global exploited class, members of which are "disciplined, united, organized by the very mechanism of the process of capitalist production itself" (Marx (1887) 1967, 763).

One way to conceptualize capital's attempt to assert a "new world order" and popular resistance to it is as a "fight for fertility." Fertility is the capacity to reproduce and sustain life in all its forms, principally people, their labor power and their food. Land and labor, as well as the knowledge, bodies and time of women, are major sources of fertility. Women therefore have a special stake in exercising control over their own fertility. They contend for control with their own menfolk and with capital, foreign and local. In the fight for control over fertility, capitalists make "male deals" with many men, and in particular kinsmen, who elicit, coerce, supervise and regulate the exploitation of women's labor. "Male dealers" serve as intermediaries to channel resources and women's paid and unpaid labor into the commodified realm to make profits for capital and minor earnings for themselves. In contrast, some men break with the male deals and join women in "gendered class alliances" for the defense and elaboration of the subsistence political economy, against the incursion of capitalist commodified relations (Turner 1994, 20-21).

Three "moments" in the analysis of gendered class struggle are (1) subsistence: the insurgents' program to foster a life-centered society for the well-being of all; (2) enclosure: the commodifying impacts on communities of neo-colonial "development" of corporate globalization through structural adjustment programs; and in the 2000s, of Empire and (3) resistance: through a fight for fertility.

The study is presented in three parts. Part 1 examines precursors to the emergence of a new Mau Mau from the 1940s to the 1990s. Part 2 analyses the resurgence of Mau Mau in the period 2000 to 2003. Part 3 addresses counterinsurgency against the new Mau Mau and concludes with a consideration of feminism in the movement.

Part One: Subsistence, Enclosure and Resistance: the 1940s to the 1990s

Squatter women in the Rift Valley and small farming women in the reserves extended and defended the subsistence political economy during the 1940s (Brownhill 1994). The British responded with restrictions on the numbers of animals squatters could keep and the number of acres squatters could cultivate on the white settler farms (Throup 1987). In the Central Province reserves, the British demanded that women provide unwaged labor for "soil conservation" campaigns, which were designed to concentrate African settlement and "free" land for European appropriation (MacKenzie 1990, 1998).

The British were able to enforce the eviction of over 100,000 squatters from the Rift Valley and impose the privatization of clan land in the reserves during the 1950s. What African resistance had prevented the colonists from doing in the 1940s, they did at the point of a gun during the state of emergency from October 1952 to

January 1960. They virtually obliterated women's customary entitlements to land by giving European title deeds to their African male "loyalist" allies (Tamarkin 1978). The British strengthened capitalist relations in the reserves while creating a largely female landless population that could provide cheap labor on the new African export-oriented farms and on the white settler plantations.

In the 1960s the majority of women were landless because they were married to men who got no land or because they were widows, single mothers, abandoned wives, unmarried or orphans. These women became plantation workers or moved to the forests, crown holdings or cities to squat on public land. Some were able to join together with other women, pool resources and buy ex-white settler land in the Rift Valley. Tens of thousands of families collectively purchased land in the highlands. By the 1970s squatter women, "coffee wives"[5] and Rift Valley collective land owners channelled much of their time and resources into strengthening the subsistence political economy in ways reminiscent of the 1940s. Coffee wives re-established women's work groups to expand their collective well-being. Some 23,000 women's groups raised money to put tin roofs on houses, bring piped water to villages, build schools and clinics and send children abroad to university. Coffee wives established autonomous trade with urban and Rift Valley women. Squatter women innovated by planting thousands of gardens in urban areas to feed their families, build trade networks and sustain life through marketing their produce and prepared foods.

In the 1980s the World Bank imposed structural adjustment, a new set of enclosures (Palast 2001). Politicians from KANU (Kenya African National Union), the party which had ruled since independence, grabbed urban public land. Women who had squatted on public space found their gardens destroyed. The markets, kiosks and residential sites of the landless were increasingly under attack as corrupt politicians sold off public spaces. In response the landless organized to defend themselves. At the same time, rural coffee wives rejected the failing commodified economy, took back the resources that their husbands sought to direct into coffee and focussed on subsistence production of crops such as bananas, maize and tomatoes (Brownhill, Kaara and Turner 1997).

The World Bank policies of privatization, increased export crop production and "user fees" were weapons against Africans' subsistence alternatives to low waged labor (Federici 2001). The 1990s featured an intensification of the conflict between privatizers and the landless. In May 1990 Nairobi's Muruoto slum was the site of a pitched battle between landless residents and demolition crews sent to clear the land in preparation for its sale. Old Mau Mau women were crucial to the successful defence. The brutality of the state's armed forces in Muruoto engendered widespread resistance, which erupted on July 7, 1990 in the Saba Saba (Kiswahili = Seven Seven) general strike. Traders, subsistence farmers and transport workers organized the strike by stopping traffic and closing markets throughout the country for three days. They demanded an end to police brutality,

---

5   We use the term "coffee wives" elsewhere to refer to all women producing export crops.

evictions and slum demolitions. Structural adjustment policies had created conditions within which the dispossessed joined forces to resist the dictatorship and defend subsistence entitlements. The actions of coffee wives and landless urban slumdwellers threatened debt repayment and the profits of investors in Kenya (Turner, Kaara and Brownhill 1997). Their spokesmen in the Paris Club of Euro-American governments held up aid to pressure the Moi government to moderate dictatorship by re-introducing multi-party politics in 1991.

In the 1990s state functionaries were increasingly violent in their attempts to enclose public land and to grab private land from rural subsistence producers and opponents of the dictatorship. By this time a low-intensity land war had emerged which directly pitted subsistence women against "male dealers" in league with government land grabbers. Elderly Mau Mau women were at the forefront of the direct action politics which broke the land grabbers' single party hold on the Kenyan state.

At Freedom Corner in February 1992 a hunger strike by mothers of political prisoners provided a platform for a cross section of Kenyans to speak out against the draconian policies of the Moi regime. Many of the mothers had fought in the Mau Mau war. A brutal police attack on the old women and thousands of supporters in March 1992 set the stage for a much wider, more militant coming together of disparate popular forces. One elderly Mau Mau fighter, Ruth Wangari wa Thungu threw off her clothes (Gikuyu = *kutura nguo*), thereby exercising a customary form of women's power to drive off police who were aiming to shoot at the protestors. In the pitched battle she stripped naked and cursed the police and the head of state by exposing her vagina.[6] The power of women over fertility was recalled in the most remote peasant households as major newspapers gave this deep customary curse frontpage coverage. After the police attack the women occupied a nearby cathedral to carry on their hunger strike and vigil. The protestors remained there for one year and secured the release of 51 men from jail (First Woman 16 July 1994; 24 April 1997).

The actions of the Freedom Corner women crystallized into a new movement for the defence of the commons. Thousands joined Mungiki (Gikuyu = the Multitudes), Muungano wa Wanavijiji (Kiswahili = Organization of Villagers) and other organizations to resist rural and urban land clearances.[7] The rest of the 1990s

---

6 Wangari Maathi (cited in Zwartz 23 May 1992) offered her explanation of the meaning of the women's use of the curse of nakedness: "They were showing disgust and contempt for sons who never had the nerve to come and beat their own mothers. In Kikuyu tradition, they were cursing the men saying, 'I have no respect for you. I wish I had never given birth to you.'" See also Miring'uh (1992) on Kenya and Turner (1994, 140-141) and Turner et al. (2001) for analyses of West African women's use of this curse to confer "social death" on personnel of foreign oil companies and other "male dealers."

7 For a gendered critique and comparison of Mungiki and Muungano wa Wanavijiji, see Turner and Brownhill 2001. See also CESNUR 2001; Harris 2000; Wamue 2001 and World History Archive 2000.

was characterized by the explosion of popular forces who were increasingly bold in their confrontations with police and armed forces. The KANU regime was on the defensive but it continued massive landgrabbing and violent enclosures which it mislabeled as "ethnic clashes." By the end of the 1990s, KANU landgrabs were challenged by militant resistance from Muungano wa Wanavijiji, Mungiki and a host of autonomous organizations of the dispossessed. Land defences of the 1990s escalated into outright land occupations in 2000.

The new Mau Mau in Kenya has emerged in four organizational stages. The first period, 1975 to 1984, was characterized by the coalescence and dispersion of underground political organizing (MwaKenya 1987). This was followed by the democracy struggle of 1985 to 1992. By 1992, Mau Mau women elders and their allies had re-established open politics. This created the preconditions for stage three, 1993 to 1999, in which a proliferation of new organizations arose to both challenge corporate globalization and to institute a subsistence life economy. The land occupation movement of stage four, 2000 to 2003, ousted KANU from power, challenged corporate rule, expanded "commoning" and integrated Kenyan activists more closely into the global movement against capitalism and imperial war.

Part Two: The Mau Mau Resurgence, 2000 to 2003

The land occupation movement reversed enclosures, stopped land grabbing, seized and repossessed land, changed the government, re-instituted free universal primary education and curtailed export production which in effect repudiated the debt. Transnational groups within the movement pursued reparations from the British for three types of alleged criminality: death and injury due to army land mines, soldiers' rapes of pastoralist women in the vicinity of Dol Dol in the 1980s (Walter 2003, 23) and atrocities during the 1950s Mau Mau war (McGhie 2003, 8; Mulama 17 September 2003).

As the numbers of activist organizations grew, so too did the range of actions they undertook. Organizations began to relate to one another in what became, by 2000, a multi-centred movement. It extended abroad through a network of refugees, exiles and immigrants, such as Njoki Njoroge Njehu who headed the international 50 Years is Enough campaign in Washington D.C. (Osoro 2001). Massive demonstrations against corporate globalization in the Americas, Europe and worldwide signalled to social movements in Kenya that they were not alone in their dispossession or in their resistance (Bassey 2002). Kenyans joined demonstrations in Seattle in 1999 against the World Trade Organization, in Genoa in 2001 against the Group of Eight and in South Africa at the United Nations anti-racism and sustainability conferences in 2001 and 2002. They hosted the World Social Forum in Nairobi in January 2007. "Land for the landless" was the theme that brought Kenyans together with international activists in these fora.

By 2000 it was apparent that the new Mau Mau was both national and international. This decentralized and global network of organizations pursued a new strategy as of January 2000. It moved from defence to re-appropriation of land. This shift accompanied a sharp increase in hunger and desperation between 2000 and 2003.[8]

Muungano wa Wanavijiji and Mungiki had been important to the shaping of these direct action strategies. In 2000, a diverse array of organizations occupied private land, defended public land from enclosure and re-appropriated enclosed land in rural and urban areas. A few examples follow from the two years up to the December 2002 election (Turner and Brownhill 2001b, 1064-1066). The movement began with pastoralists' successful occupation of private ranches in October 1999, when drought threatened their herds. By February 2000, when the Zimbabwe government initiated occupations of white settler farms, the anti-state Kenyan movement had already erupted (Brown 2000). In April 2000 workers and squatters autonomously organized themselves into the Taveta Welfare Society. They occupied a Greek-owned plantation seized from them by force during the colonial era. The Society's chairperson, Ruth Lelewu said land theft was "a matter of life and death. Depriving thousands of people of their birth-right is not something to play with ... The solution to the matter is for the government to buy the land and settle thousands of Taveta squatters. The community will not allow any other individual to buy the land" (Mutonya 8 June 2001). The British high commissioner in Nairobi, Jeffrey James, warned in May 2000 that foreign investors were being scared off by the calls to take over white owned land (*Daily Nation*, hereafter D.N., 17 May 2000).

Tenants of the state-run Mwea irrigated rice settlement scheme asserted control and succeeded in ousting one set of corrupt officials. In May 2000 Marakwet squatters occupied the 14,500-acre Cherangany state agricultural experiment station on learning that it had been grabbed by a senior government official. Ogiek traditional forest dwellers went to court to protect their forest land from enclosure and destruction. Squatters repeatedly attacked ex-Cabinet Minister Nicholas Biwott's farm and burned his crops after he "hived off" 1,000 acres of clan land from the Kaptagat Forest. In the fourth attack, in June 2003, nine people, including two elderly women, were arrested for pulling down a fence moments after it had been erected around the disputed land (D.N. 21 June 2003).

8　The economy was in a slump and the European Union banned agricultural imports from Kenya because test results showed that they contained higher than the acceptable quantity of toxic substances and hence violated consumer and labor safety standards (Tomlinson 2003; Njeru 2003). Food and cash crop production fell significantly while child labor increased (Kimenyi 2002, 11, 22). Poor performance in tourism in 2000 worsened after the November 2002 attack on an Israeli hotel in Mombasa. When the new government refused to join Bush's "coalition of the willing" in its war on Iraq and pursued "anti-terrorism" with less than the requisite fervour, Britain and the United States announced travel bans in May and June 2003 (Nyagah 2000; Onyango-Obbo 2003).

By the December 2002 general election the organizations involved in these actions had gained enough strength to remove the corrupt KANU government from power. In the new coalition government were champions of the resurgent Mau Mau, including Wangari Maathai as assistant minister for the environment. She had since 1977 been organizing with rural women to assert women's customary claim to land through tree planting. Her participation in the 1992 Freedom Corner hunger strike was a lightening rod for the international media. Kiraitu Murungi was a lawyer for the political prisoners freed by the Freedom Corner Mau Mau women. He became minister of justice. The National Rainbow Coalition (NARC) of a dozen political parties won the 2002 election by promising justice, punishment of corruption and the return of free, universal primary education. Land invasions escalated even more after NARC's leader Mwai Kibaki took office in 2003.

Kibaki's election was a major victory for the many organizations that had for decades challenged KANU and its policies. The landless had high expectations. It was a double victory for women who had fought for the re-institution of free universal primary education. In January 2003, on the first day of the new school year, thousands of mothers and grandmothers accompanied their children to primary schools and demanded that they too be enrolled. Access to schools was won by a gendered class alliance between women, who have demanded education for girls since the 1930s, and those men who worked to achieve this goal. Second, the school fees imposed by the World Bank were the equivalent of the colonial hut and poll taxes. School fees were women's largest cash expense and the major mechanism forcing them into the commodified market. The demand for free education was analogous to an anti-tax struggle. Women's double repudiation of coffee and school fees was a tremendous victory over the World Bank's subversion of subsistence.

The first six months of 2003 were dominated by labor rebellion, land take overs and opposition to foreign corporate-military intervention. In the mobilization of the multitudes, all exploitations were excoriated. Land take-backs took precedence.

2003 opened with an explicitly feminist uprising against sexual and economic exploitation. On 20 January, 10,000 women workers in the Athi River Export Processing Zone destroyed 16 textile factories, raided Kitengela shopping centre, looted shops and battled contingents of anti-riot police. Teargas prevented them from trashing a second shopping centre. The women strikers "broke gates and smashed windows at Alltex EPZ, Nodor and Tri Star EPZ to flush out the workers who had not joined the strike and moved from factory to factory in the expansive garments manufacturing zone to ensure all the [24 factories'] operations were paralysed" (Mulaa and Githaiga 21 January 2003). The strikers demanded an end to sexual exploitation and harassment, a medical scheme, transport at night, compensation for over-work, remittance of their statutory deductions to the National Social Security Fund and the National Hospital Insurance Fund, sick leave and no termination for illness (Mulaa and Githaiga 21 January 2003).

All sectors experienced labor insurgency in the first six weeks of 2003. Trade union bureaucrats had lost control over waged workers and an incipient revolutionary situation was on hand.[9]

On 3 February in the Mungiki stronghold of Thika, 2,000 oil workers staged a sit-in at Bidco, a refinery owned by ex-president Moi and his cabinet minister Nicholas Biwott. The strikers demanded permanent status after working for ten years as casual laborers in the strategic oil industry. They demanded an end to 13 hour shifts at U.S. $2.60 a day with no overtime pay and no medical coverage (D.N., 4 February 2003).

The land occupation movement of 2003 was different from the pre-election movement in two ways. First, the scale of occupations increased dramatically in 2003. While dozens of cases were recorded in the *Daily Nation* in the two years prior to the December 2002 election, in the post-election period there was a virtual "jubilation" of land reappropriations. There were vastly more territories, incidents and people involved. Second, the new Mau Mau moved from defence to offense. There was a qualitative shift on the part of the movement to outright occupation of new terrain. This shift had two facets. From 2000 to 2002 some resisted eviction by land grabbers while others converted from export to subsistence crops. After 2003 the landless began a massive move to expand onto new ground. Complimenting this facet was a deeper transformation. The 2000 to 2002 period involved women and their allies defending subsistence social relations in gardening, transport, marketing, collective work and collective savings. The 2003 expansion of the movement impelled the parallel expansion of subsistence relations into larger territories, collectivities and networks.

The quantitative and qualitative expansion of the land occupation movement was made possible by the increased control that workers and traders extended over transport and marketing between 2000 and 2003 (East African Standard 18 November 2001). The capacity to move produce from farm to market called for an increase in land under subsistence production. Urban and regional demand for low-priced, indigenous foods grew stronger as foreign corporate imports monopolized commodified markets which were inaccessible to the half of the population that survived on less than one U.S. dollar a day (Inter-Church Coalition on Africa 2000).

By ousting KANU, militants put sections of the police on hold. They now moved forward in large numbers with great speed to refashion property relations. Some examples follow. On 21 January 2003, demonstrators invaded and repossessed a state-owned Kenya Agricultural Research Institute (KARI) farm in Kiambu said to have been grabbed by private developers in 1993, only to be foiled by

---

9   One editorialist observed that the economy was "more and more vulnerable to wildcat stoppages and a climate of chaos and uncertainly in the industrial sector. ... In this climate of high expectation, the impoverished classes start demanding radical changes. ... And, sooner or later, the narrow economic grievances by the protesting workers will transform into broad political demands" (Kisero, 19 February, 2003).

police. Another KARI farm in Kitale was invaded on 25 January, when 13 houses were burnt and property destroyed on the public land which had been allocated to individuals (D.N. 22, 27 January 2003). On 27 January, 1,700 students from Nakuru's Kenyatta Secondary School destroyed 60 mud-walled rental houses and a church under construction on land belonging to their school (Agutu 28 January 2003). On 7 February 300 squatters invaded 322 acres in Kilifi and sub-divided it amongst themselves. Police drove them away (Oketch 9 February 2003). A month later, 5,000 squatters returned and occupied some 2,700 acres. A spokesperson said the take-over was autonomous, with "no politician behind it." The squatters denied having leaders. They "had a committee since July 2002 to coordinate the land occupation" (Kithi and Mwandoto 18 March 2003).

On 10 February 500 traders stormed the Soko-Huru market in Nyeri and reconstructed their stalls on the spot where two people were shot dead in 2002 during a forced eviction. "The traders sub-divided the plots amongst themselves and prepared to start selling their wares" (Ogutu 11 February 2003). On the same day, the government repossessed the Kenyatta International Conference Centre (KICC) from KANU and de-privatized the Kenya Cooperative Creameries.

Between 21 January and 2 July 2003, Kenya's *Daily Nation* reported some 30 instances of land occupation and repossession of property from land-grabbers.[10] Occupiers were from many ethnic groups and were concerned with access to many different kinds of land. Seventeen of the 30 cases were organized by school children, parents and teachers, herders, squatters, neighborhood watch committees, traders, community groups, landless farmers, women and men, young and old. The remaining 13 cases involved the government revoking title deeds to irregularly allocated land, buildings and houses.

The reported cases encompassed more than 50,000 acres of land. In a single action the government reclaimed 300 irregularly allocated plots. The cases have occurred throughout the country, from the coast to the borders with Uganda, Tanzania, Somalia, Ethiopia and Sudan. By June 2003 the land occupation movement had re-appropriated the following types of property: playgrounds, settlement schemes, forests, stadiums, urban neighborhood land, a cemetery, public farm research centres, public utility plots, markets, private ranches, game reserves, dump grounds, bus terminals and road reserves. Under re-appropriation were: school grounds, the National Cereals and Produce Board property, hospital compounds, parking areas, fire stations, council clinics, weather stations, loading zones, open air markets, public gardens, social halls, public toilets, housing estates, open spaces, parks, alms houses for the old and the poor, rivers, lakes, the grounds of courthouses and government houses. The scope of the

---

10   In the two year period 2000 to 2002, the *Daily Nation* reported some 20 land occupations and defences. It is estimated that the *Daily Nation* documented, in the first six months of 2003, only from 1 percent to 25 percent of the total number of strikes, uprisings, land defences and invasions. There was a six-fold increase in reported cases from approximately one to six per month.

"liberation" was all-encompassing. The new Mau Mau was taking back the whole of the society, environment and polity.

In March 2003 the lands and settlement minister Amos Kimunya announced that all land owners were to be issued with new title deeds. He was reported to have stated that

> second-generation title deeds would be introduced to weed out those which were issued fraudulently. The move is aimed at undoing the damage of fake title deeds which have been blamed for double registration of land. ... Well-connected people in the former government, assisted by professionals in the ministry, had also used the fake titles to grab public utility land. The current titles in use were misused by the former government to obtain land fraudulently and can no longer be considered sacrosanct (Muriuki 14 March 2003).

In Kenya, multiple competing land tenure systems are in force (Okoth-Ogendo 1989). The land occupation movement justified take-overs with reference to at least three potentially contradictory and overlapping "bundles of land entitlements:" British legal, customary and moral claims (Turner and Brownhill 2001b; *Africa* 1989). A *Daily Nation* editorialist conceded a "fact" that landless Kenyans had long asserted: that the British colonial legal system was an inadequate tool for the resolution of conflict over land:

> What about the helter-skelter which our land ownership system has become? It is extraordinary that, legally, the colonial land tenure situation is what still obtains. The post-independence governments have merely misused an already unjust law to allocate land to suit their narrowest political interests. *Almost all public land and property have been grabbed* by undeserving individuals. The web is widespread and intricate. With a myriad of social, political, economic, legal and even cultural strands, how can it be undone by an approach as legalistic as the Njonjo team took? (D.N. 2 July 2003, emphasis added)[11]

In July 2003 after six months in power, the new government made the remarkable revelation that "[a]lmost all public land and property have been grabbed by undeserving individuals." This grabbing of public property was life-threatening to landless women. By 1985, a hundred thousand people constituted an army of urban gardeners in Nairobi. Two thirds of them were women. Almost all occupied public, open spaces of the city (Freeman 1991, xiii, 82). This autonomous "army" cultivated

---

11   The Njonjo Commission on Land Law was set up in November 1999 by the Moi government to address matters related to land: registration, documentation, tenure and legislation. "How," the editorialist asked, "could that inquiry be trusted when it was beholden to a Government which had been the primary cause of the problem, one whose other commissions of inquiry have been but a cynical way of avoiding a solution?" (D.N. 2 July 2003)

thousands of gardens which fed families, supplied markets and contributed to Nairobi's reputation as the "green city in the sun." When politicians and developers grabbed "almost all public land," they evicted the occupants and destroyed their subsistence livelihoods. The Nairobi pattern prevailed nationwide. This explains much of why women initiated and are the majority in the new Mau Mau.

The activism of a resurgent Mau Mau forced the government to disband corrupt land boards and land tribunals which for over twenty years had been instrumental in the misappropriation of land (Otieno 5 July 2003). Kibaki set up an official land theft inquiry on 30 June 2003 to ascertain "exactly who has what and where, how he/she acquired it, and whether it can be reclaimed justly" (D.N. 2 July 2003). This inquiry cannot possibly resolve millions of individual counter-claims especially because it is limited to the British legal system, the very tool used by thieves to steal the commons. Nor is state ownership a solution. The new Mau Mau land occupiers have claimed state land and sought collective titles. Elderly Mau Mau women in Muungano wa Wanavijiji have long fought for specifically communal title deeds for residential and market sites, with equal access and tenure rights for women and men. In 1998 they asserted that any just resolution of the land crisis must take into account the principle that everyone has a right to land (First Woman 25 July 1998). The Lands Ministry countered the call for collective title deeds with a promise to develop a comprehensive slum land tenure policy (D.N. 14 June 2003). Will the new policy build on Muungano members' initiatives at collectivity or will it entrench individualized private property relations?[12]

Part Three: Counterinsurgency

Corporate globalizers, the imperial U.S. regime and elements within the Kenyan state responded to the multitudes with counterinsurgency. A "good cop, bad cop" routine was played out in Kenya through the velvet glove of "poverty alleviation reforms" and the mailed fist of "anti-terrorist" repression. Factions of the coalition government and civil service in conjunction with corporate rulers scrambled to throw some palliative reforms at the insurgents and to coopt the compliant.[13] In the meantime, they attempted to retool the relations of global commodification.

---

12   See Table, "Difference between World Bank corporate "land reform" and popular redistributive land reform" in Turner and Brownhill (2001b, 1044). See also Rosset (2001).

13   The cooptation of sections of Mungiki began in 2000. Some "leaders" were reaping private profits from Mungiki's control over *matatu* (minibus) routes. Divisions between "leaders" and ordinary members signified the move of some men into male deals with local capitalists. The involvement in 2001 of several Mungiki in the killing of rivals on *matatu* routes and in the slum community of Kariobangi caused a further division in the organization. When in 2002 Mungiki founders ran for political office on a KANU ticket, many members decamped. Part of the fall out of the cooptation of sections of Mungiki is the growing strength of other organizations to which people turned as an alternative to the

Forty years of KANU rule had come to an end, but many "homeguard-loyalists" were still in office. They and their class allies continued to own huge farms, plantations, ranches and city properties. Class factionalism appeared early in the coalition government as male dealers worked to protect their ill-gotten wealth. While some members of parliament such as Murungi and Maathai sought social and environmental justice, others courted the World Bank and IMF as had KANU. These others introduced counter-insurgent strategies in the arenas of property rights, agricultural production, mining and militarism.

As political space opened, elderly Mau Mau veterans called for substantive not symbolic recognition and justice. A faction in the government claimed that the demands of the Mau Mau had been met. Presidential aide Dzoro announced that no land will go to the 1950s freedom fighters (D.N. 26 March 2003). Within three months of taking office members of parliament and police warned the landless to halt invasions and allow the government to repossess public land.

Kibaki reinstated subsidies and price supports for export agriculture. Export crops had been destroyed by most farmers and especially by women. The agriculture ministry's official emphasis on reviving exports was part of a reinstatement of the male deal in agriculture (Ronald 2003). The refusal by coffee wives to grow the crop was met by a new effort to reimpose commodified agricultural relations.

Despite opposition Kibaki approved "foreign aid," titanium exploitation and oil exploration (Makokha 2003). On 15 February 2003 Kenyans took part in the 50 million strong global demonstrations against the U.S. war on Iraq (Museka 2003). In mid 2003 the *Daily Nation* reported "rising public protests at what is seen as Washington's bullying tactics against Kenya" (Gatheru 23 June 2003).

On an international level in the 2000 to 2003 period, dominant capital shifted its strategy from corporate globalization to neo-imperialism. U.S. oil and military corporations funded a neo-conservative "coup" in Washington D.C. and the Bush regime launched a "world war without end" (White House 2002). Unipolar imperial militarism trumped multi-polar corporate globalization. U.S. military interventions are a response to failure and factionalism within the World Trade Organization and to the growing international coordination of popular struggles against corporate rule (Bichler and Nitzan 2004; Laxer 2003; Klein 2003, 7).

U.S. capital responded to challenges to its rule in Kenya with policies that reduce the country to the status of a province in the empire. First, a made-in-the-USA anti-terrorism bill allows United States police full access to information, persons and physical space in Kenya. American agents can enter Kenya and arrest anyone at any time for actions as innocuous as using the internet.[14] The

---

discredited Mungiki. A further split was evident in 2005, when most Mungiki opposed a government sponsored constitutional referendum, while a small minority split to support the government's position.

14 "The Bill creates a general climate of fear and suspicion in which the State is invested with coercive, intrusive, and intimidating powers. No area of private activity is spared. The Bill makes it criminal, for example, to surf the Internet and collect or transmit

anti-terrorism bill is an attempt to close the openings for direct action and was hotly contested.[15] Second, the U.S. government pressured its Kenyan counterpart to pledge never to seek prosecution of United States military personnel before the International Criminal Court. Third, the United States announced plans to build at least seven military bases in Africa, including a "forward base" in Kenya.[16] In June 2003 one opponent commented in the *Nation* that "As the official corporate voice, the U.S. government will try to twist our Cabinet's arm by tying the military pressure to "aid" resumption by the IMF and the World Bank" (Ochieng 22 June 2003). U.S. militarization and a version of the U.S. Patriot Act are direct threats to the implementation of collective land entitlements. A central objective of imperial repression is to undermine and break up the world movement towards commoning.

Conclusion: Feminism in the Mau Mau Resurgence

Each of the cycles of struggle in Kenya between 1940 and 2003 contain three approximately decade-long phases: (1) subsistence, (2) enclosure and (3) resistance. The initial cycle examined here extended from the 1940s to the 1960s. First, in the 1940s women elaborated their subsistence activities and relations. Second, when the 1950s Mau Mau war is considered from the point of view of women's land rights, it can be seen as a period of enclosure (Kershaw 1997, 335). Third, during the 1960s women began a period of resistance expressed in at least three modes. Landless women squatted all kinds of public land; those landless women who could, joined women's groups or "buying companies" to purchase farms and finally, coffee wives channelled resources into the community and the domestic economy.

By the 1970s a subsequent cycle of struggle had begun, first with women's elaboration of an integrated subsistence political economy. Markets and transport systems united them and forged a closer union with pastoralists still established on the commons. Second, in the 1980s, with structural adjustment, the landless lost access to public space which was enclosed by corrupt politicians. Coffee wives found their food crops sacrificed by husbands who wanted to increase cash crop production. Third, in the 1990s landless women's resistance erupted in the Muruoto, Saba Saba and Freedom Corner insurgencies and continued in a multiplying array of community organizations and political associations.

---

by email information that is likely [in the judgement of the U.S. and Kenyan states] to be useful to a person committing or preparing an act of terrorism" (Mutua 2 July 2003).

15   In August 1998 there were attacks on the U.S. embassies in Nairobi and Dar es Salaam. In November 2002 there were two further incidents. One commentator opposed U.S. presence in Kenya on the grounds that it attracted terrorists and subjected Kenyans to U.S. pressure to curtail Kenyans' civil liberties and national sovereignty (Mutua 2 July 2003).

16   U.S. military bases were planned for Kenya, Mali, Ghana, Senegal, Tunisia, Morocco and Algeria (Mugonyi and Kelly 17 June 2003; *The Economist* 22 May 2003).

In 2000 the multitudes moved to occupy land and defend public space from land grabbers. This third cycle began with their assertion of subsistence over the death economy of commodification.

In 2003 the Kenyan land occupation movement was nascent, especially compared to, for example, the landless workers' movement in Brazil (Veltmeyer and Petras 2002, 86-87). Thousands of organizations involving millions of Kenyans demonstrated their intention to re-establish a producer-controlled life-centred society. They wanted an end to corporate theft of Kenya's fertile farmland. They did not want to be exploited on plantations or in factories. They wanted their own land for their own production. Their direct actions to take land constituted a radical step that went far beyond declarations and demonstrations with demands written on banners. Kenyans voted with their feet in a march back onto the land.

The commodification of Kenya's economy led to impoverishment, starvation and environmental ruin. Millions of Kenyans made it known, through direct action, that their solution was the defence and revitalization of the commons. More commodified production and unfair "free trade" could not solve the crisis caused by those very capitalist relations. This applied equally to land redistribution. A refurbished private land tenure regime could not resolve the inequities caused by the expansion of the private tenure system imposed by the British. Kenyans were not driven to defying death because their subsistence political economy was incapable of sustaining them. They were defiant because the global corporate regime had for more than a century been parasitic upon the subsistence political economy. Solutions to Kenya's social, economic and environmental crises were prefigured in the direct actions taken by the new, feminist Mau Mau in Nairobi, Dol Dol and Kilifi. There, respectively, the multitudes realized in practice collective title deeds to common land, reparations for rape and autonomous organization of the commons by villagers.

Feminism can be defined as the recognition that women are exploited and the fight against that exploitation. In this sense, the Mau Mau resurgence is feminist in at least five ways. First, since the 1940s and before, women have fought for control over fertility. The fight for fertility continued in the 2000 to 2003 period in an expanded set of struggles. Women and men in gendered class alliances counterattacked against those who had dispossessed them of almost all means of survival. Women's struggle in the new Mau Mau was a life and death struggle between, on the one hand; starvation, HIV AIDS and illiteracy and on the other hand; good nutrition and health, literacy and community well-being. Second, women never surrendered in the Mau Mau war nor subsequently (Turner and Brownhill 2001a). Their demand for land has not yet been met (Africa Watch 1991; Walsh in Human Rights Watch 2003). They were dispossessed of customary land rights in the 1950s. In the 1980s, their subsistence commoning on family land and in public spaces was curtailed by the new enclosures of structural adjustment. The new Mau Mau has arisen in particular to challenge these second enclosures.

Third, landless women's demands for land for all, education and autonomous trade were taken up by the movement as a whole. The momentum of the land occupation movement has forced a recognition that any land redistribution must go beyond the narrow legalistic framework of British law. A fundamental resolution of the struggle for "land and freedom" must take into account the moral and customary claims asserted by the subsistence forces within the new Mau Mau. Fourth, the Mau Mau resurgence actively engaged in repossessing "values' which especially women produce and on which they depend. These include the common life goods of nature, social services, built space and time itself. Fifth, women resisted rape, beating and genital mutilation not as individuals but in common and in alliance with men. This resistance was inextricable from the struggle for land. Maasai women were able to collectively prosecute rape by British soldiers because their communities were strengthened by the transnational organizing which won them compensation for the devastation caused by land mines. Women textile workers struck and rioted against sexual exploitation. Their capacity to confront their exploiters was enhanced by land occupations which opened alternatives to waged work.

The "fight for fertility" was earlier defined as a struggle in which women contend with their own menfolk and with foreign and local capital for control over land, labor, knowledge, time and the use of their bodies. In this fight, capitalists make "male deals" with those men who regulate the exploitation of female labor necessary to realize all other aspects of fertility. The new Mau Mau is feminist in the degree to which these relations of exploitation were negated. Women's strike against cash crop production was the negation most costly to capital and its local allies. This, taken together with the five initiatives listed above, constitutes an immense gain for women in the three-way gendered class struggle to control fertility. The women and men of the Mau Mau resurgence broke male deals. Together in gendered class alliances, they began to re-invent the commons and re-assert their autonomy from capital. This is the feminist content in the resurgence of Mau Mau.

Postscript: Kenya's December 2007 Election Disaster, Persistent Struggle, and Challenges Ahead

Mwai Kibaki was elected president of Kenya in December 2002 in large measure because he promised to enact a new constitution within 100 days of his inauguration. More than a year's worth of meetings were held at the Bomas conference center, which gave rise to what was known as the Bomas Draft constitution. The draft came to be dubbed the "Wanjiku" constitution. Wanjiku is a common Kikuyu woman's name, and the name indicated that the draft reflected the views and interests of the ordinary Kenyan woman.

The Wanjiku constitution brought the needs and demands of the landless into the legal framework governing the society as a whole. It abolished the colonial system of government-appointed "chiefs." It included provisions for the devolution (or shift to the bottom) of power by establishing local community committees with the power to decide on development priorities in their areas. The ten members of the committees were to be elected, and three seats were reserved for women. The Wanjiku constitution specified that Parliament had the power to decide on the acceptance of any loans from external sources. This opened the way for a repudiation of Kenya's odious debts and for reparations. In sum, the Wanjiku constitution facilitated the redistribution of land, resources and power. It redefined Kenya's weak, representative democracy as a robust, participatory democracy. And in March 2004, every clause of the Wanjiku constitution was passed by a majority of the members of the constitutional conference.

But President Kibaki refused to enact it. He could not or would not break his long-standing commitments to local and foreign corporations by enacting a constitution that prioritized Kenyans' utilization of Kenya's resources. His regime, like those before, has provided favourable legal, property, tariff, regulatory and wage policies to attract private foreign investors. Kibaki rejected the Wanjiku Constitution in large part because Washington opposed.

World Bank and IMF advisors "helped" Kibaki write another constitution, known as the Wako Draft. The Wako Draft watered down the transformational aspects of the Wanjiku constitution, removed clauses protecting women's rights to inherit land and erased the clauses which provided for the devolution of power.

It was at this point that Raila Odinga broke with Mwai Kibaki and started the "Orange Democratic Movement" (ODM). The ODM campaigned against this Wako draft in the run-up to a Referendum on the constitution in November 2005. Kenyan voters rejected the Wako Draft in the referendum. Citizens had in mind the far-reaching changes promised by the Wanjiku constitution, and the Wako Draft paled in comparison. Since rejecting this World Bank authorized draft, the old tattered colonial-era constitution has provided the legal framework within which the violence of the 2007 election unfolded.

The struggle for a new constitution in Kenya marked a shift in social movement activism towards the fundamental transformation of the society. When Kibaki failed to deliver on the promise of a new constitution, tremendous momentum built towards the 2007 election. This was the ordinary citizen's next opportunity to put in place a government responsive to the demands of the dispossessed majority.

Mwai Kibaki's reign has coincided with the rapid militarization of international relations in the wake of 11 September and the Bush regime's "endless war on terror." After rejecting the popular Bomas or Wanjiku draft constitution in 2004, and finding his watered down version in turn rejected by the citizenry in 2005, Kibaki turned his attention to bolstering relations with imperial powers. He joined a U.S.-led regional Anti-Terror Taskforce, set up an Anti-Terror Police Unit and extended agreements giving the United States full access to military sites in Kenya. Volman (2008) observed that "The Bush administration has built a close military relationship with the government of Mwai Kibaki and has played a central role in the creation of his internal security apparatus, now being deployed with such bloody results throughout Kenya."

The Anti-Terror Police Unit has been accused of participating in the extraordinary rendition of Kenyan citizens to jails in Ethiopia. A vicious onslaught by another special police unit against the outlawed Mungiki group was launched in June 2007 in Mathare. The Minster for Internal Security, Michuki, reportedly issued a shoot-to-kill order against suspected Mungiki members. Police shot dead at least 30 suspects in Mathare within the first two weeks of their crackdown. Over 500 young women and men simply suspected of being members of Mungiki were summarily executed between May and August 2007. Their bodies were dumped in forests and at various police stations around the country. Most had been shot through the head and showed signs of torture and mutilation. Many were last seen alive in the custody of policemen.

The killing of hundreds of Mungiki members was just one sign of trouble to come in the 27 December 2007 general election. Increasingly hostile campaign tactics were employed by members of all the major parties. In playing the ethnic card, parties were promising land-hungry Kenyans respite through evictions of other ethnic groups from so-called "ancestral lands." Hundreds of rural peoples were violently evicted from their homes and found themselves camped in police and church compounds in the weeks before the election. The race-based electioneering stoked the fires of violence and division while diverting attention from the elites' own land thefts and corruption.

The 27 December 2007 general election saw a huge voter turn-out. Voting was peaceful and orderly, but a delay in the announcement of the results of the presidential race spurred a descent into chaos. Between 28 December 2007 and the end of February 2008, some 1,500 people were killed and 500,000 people were evicted from their homes. Those evicted from their homes crowded into police station compounds, churches, mosques, schools as well as beside roads, at the edges of forests and on the corners of relatives' small rural plots.

The post-election chaos in Kenya was the culmination of years of state repression against ordinary people. It was an expression of elites' competition for control over the state.

The post-2007 election chaos in Kenya was especially disastrous for women. Nairobi doctors who treated some 500 rape survivors within the first weeks after the election, said that 95 percent were gang raped. Scores of women were feared to have been infected with HIV (Mwai 29 January 2008). Dr Kanyenje Gakombe, of Metropolitan Hospital, Nairobi, protested to the Daily Nation, "We ... are the ones treating the injured and performing post mortems on the dead. ... I know that our membership [in Kenya Medical Association] comes from across the political divide. I know that many of us campaigned for, funded and in many ways supported and voted for different candidates. I also know that each of us had a right to support whomever we did and should not be killed, raped or have our property destroyed for making the choices we made" (Nyabiage and Kumba 5 January 2008). Dr. Gakombe was among the many ordinary citizens to raise their voices for peace. Those most visible were women, from every walk of life.

In Kibera in early January 2008, two hundred women joined together across party and ethnic lines to march through the Nairobi slum calling for peace and reconciliation. One elderly founder of the group said she needed peace in order to begin selling her vegetables again. The area District Officer, Kepha Maribe, who was responsible for distribution of food aid to the evicted slumdwellers, recognized the women as the custodians of peace: "I will give food to the women from various villages in Kibera for distribution because they know their neighbors well" (Kumba 20 January 2008).

Journalist Mildred Ngesa used her newspaper column to plead for the armed men to return home from the battlefield: "On my knees every Saturday at the Nairobi Pentecostal Church where daughters of Zion like me will meet to seek your deliverance from this power of darkness, I shall attempt to grab back that man that I knew so well — that man that you ought to be. I shall join my sisters from all faiths, tribe and status to plead and cry for your redemption" (Ngesa 4 February 2008, emphasis added).

Wahu Kaara, who came in third in the parliamentary race in the Nairobi constituency of Starehe, intensified the pace of her peace-building activism in the slum communities there. She reported that a young woman in Huruma began a youth soccer league to help build peace in and between Nairobi's urban villages. The Huruma sportswoman planned dozens of soccer matches to be held over the month of February 2008 between teams across the city, so that youth could talk and play together to diffuse tensions and build camaraderie (Kaara 3 February 2008).

In January 2008 a coalition of women's organizations formed the Kenyan Women's Consultation Group on the Current Crisis in Kenya. In a petition to mediators Kofi Annan, Graca Machel and Benjamin Mkapa, these women drew attention to the fact that during the crisis, "Kenyan women have been at the forefront in community peace building and mediation efforts in the North Rift and other areas." They recommended, among other steps, comprehensive constitutional reform that would "ensure equitable distribution of national resources, gender equality, affirmative action, equal rights for minorities and persons with disabilities including rights to political participation" (Kenyan Women's Consultation Group 2008).

A Kenyan politician led healing circles at a camp for internally displaced people in the Rift Valley in January 2008. Women refugees said that peace prevailed "when they are able to provide food, shelter and health to their families, including being able to educate their children" (Ringera 31 January 2008). These are among the hundreds of peace initiatives that ordinary Kenyans have launched in early 2008. Behind these initiatives are thousands of long-standing, multi-ethnic, social, cultural, economic, spiritual and political organizations, both formal and informal, many founded by women.

Peace is more than the absence of violence. To restore peace is to facilitate the provision of "food, shelter, health and education" for all, which in turn requires that everyone has secure access to the necessities of life, including a healthy environment. This chapter has considered how Kenya's commoners' movements have addressed these very concerns. It has argued that in the success of the commoners' movements, in particular in the struggle for a new constitution, lies the best hope for the construction of a just and lasting peace in Kenya.

For Kenyans, the question of how to bring about peace has already been largely answered: in the "Wanjiku Constitution" of 2004. The Coalition government that resulted from the flawed 2007 election in Kenya has proven unable to gain the confidence of the citizenry or the world. Politicians in the coalition have rejected the results of an inquiry into the election violence. It implicated many high-ranking officials in inciting attacks. The coalition's efforts to introduce a new constitution promise to re-open the question of the progressive Wanjiku draft.

While most Kenyans support the Wanjiku draft, the Bush regime strongly opposed it. Will the new government of Barack Obama back the Kenyan peoples' desires for a new constitutional dispensation? With or without his support, or the support of the Kenyan government, the women-led social movements analysed here are going ahead to implement popular power through their efforts to regain control over land, to hold their government accountable and to turn their attention and energy towards food production for the well-being of the Kenyan people.

Acknowledgement

This chapter is a slightly revised and updated version of an article which appeared in the *Journal of Asian and African Studies* (Vol. 39, No. 1-2, March 2004, pp. 95-117), under the title, "Feminism in the Mau Mau Resurgence." With thanks to Sage for permission to reprint.

The authors wish to acknowledge funding for field work in Kenya from the Canadian International Development Research Centre (IDRC) and from the Canadian Social Science and Humanities Research Council.

References

Africa (1989), Vol. 59, No. 1, Special Issue on land tenure in Africa.

Africa Watch. (1991), *Kenya: Taking Liberties* (New York: Africa Watch).

Agutu, M. (2003), "70 families made homeless," *Daily Nation* (Nairobi), 28 January.

Akolo, J. (2003), "Kanu loses KICC to Narc government," *Daily Nation* (Nairobi), 11 February.

Bassey, N. (2002), "What Peace in the World Today?" International Day of Peace Solidarity, Kenule Saro-Wiwa Gallery, ERA Headquarters, Benin City, Nigeria, 21 September, eraction@infoweb.abs.net.

Bennholdt-Thompsen, V. and Mies, M. (1999), *The Subsistence Perspective: Beyond the Globalised Economy* (London: Zed Books).

Bichler, S. and Nitzan, J. (2004), *Journal of World-Systems Research*, Vol. 10. No. 2. August. pp. 254-327.

Brown, D. (2000), "Kenyan farm take-overs spotlight plight of landless poor," Pacific News Service, 7 June, <http://www.ncmonline.com/in-depth/2000-06-09/kenyan.html>.

Brownhill, L.S. (1994), "Struggle for the soil: Mau Mau and the British war against women 1939-1956," unpublished MA thesis, Department of Sociology and Anthropology, University of Guelph, Ontario, Canada.

Brownhill, L.S., et al. (1997), "Gender relations and sustainable agriculture: Rural women's resistance to structural adjustment in Kenya," *Canadian Woman Studies/Les Cahiers de la Femme*, Vol. 17, No. 2, Spring, pp. 40-44.

CESNUR: Centre for Study of New Religions, "Mungiki Movement (Kenya): 2001 Updates," <http://www.cesnur.org/testi/mungiki_001.htm>.

Daily Nation, "Invasion calls scare investors, says envoy," 17 May 2000; "Police foil bid to repossess," 22 January 2003; "17 arrested after houses are burnt on disputed farm," 27 January 2003; "300 city EPZ workers sacked as row persists," 4 February 2003; "Dzoro rules out land for Mau Mau kin," 26 March 2003; "Slum dwellers merit titles," 14 June 2003; "Nine seized in row over Biwott farm," 21 June 2003; "Yes, probe land allocations," 2 July 2003; "Anti-Terrorism Bill," Reprinted in full, online in PDF, 3 July 2003, www.nationaudio.com/News/DailyNation.

East African Standard. (2001), "The battle for matatu turf in the city," Special Report, *East African Standard* (Nairobi), 18 November.

Federici, S. (2001), "Women, Globalization and the International Women's Movement," *Gender, Feminism and the Civil Commons*, Special Issue of the *Canadian Journal of Development Studies*, Vol. XXII, pp.1025-1036.

First Woman, Interviews with Njeri Kabeberi and Ruth Wangari wa Thungu, Nairobi, 16 July 1994; Wahu Kaara, Nairobi, 24 April 1997; *Muungano wa Wanavijiji*: Caroline Atieno, Livingstone Gichamo, Sabina Wanjiku, Nairobi, 25 July 1998.

Freeman, D.B. (1991), *A City of Farmers: Informal Urban Agriculture in the Open Spaces of Nairobi, Kenya* (Montreal: McGill-Queen's University Press).

Gatheru, C. (2003), "Reject U.S. demands, leaders urge Kibaki," *Daily Nation* (Nairobi), 23 June.

Harris, P. (2000), "Mau Mau Returns to Kenya," *Sydney Morning Herald*, 17 January, <http://www.hartford-hwp.com/archives/36/260.html>.

Inter-Church Coalition on Africa. (2000), "Kenya in 1999: A human rights report, 'Which way forward?,'" Inter-Church Coalition on Africa, Toronto, March, www.web.net/~iccaf.

Kaara, Wahu, interview with Leigh Brownhill and Terisa Turner, Ottawa, 3 February 2008.

Kenyan Women's Consultation Group on the Current Crisis in Kenya, "Women's memorandum to the mediation team," released 25 January 2008, republished in *Pambazuka News* , Issue 340, 30 January 2008.

Kershaw, G. (1997), *Mau Mau from Below* (Athens: Ohio University Press).

Kimenyi, M. S. (2002), "Agriculture, economic growth and poverty reduction," Kenya Institute for Public Policy Research and Analysis (KIPPRA), Occassional Paper No. 3, June.

Kisero, J. (2003), "Unrest reflects desire for change," *Daily Nation* (Nairobi), 19 February.

Kithi, N. and Mwandoto, W. (2003), "Squatter fury on MPs: Leaders ejected from meeting and asked to free suspects," *Daily Nation* (Nairobi), 18 March.

Klein, N. (2003), "After pulverizing Iraq, the U.S. is now busy privatizing it," The Canadian Centre for Policy Alternatives *Monitor*, June, p.7.

Kumba, Samwel, "Kibera women in campaign to restore peace," *Daily Nation*, 20 January 2008.

Laxer, G. (2003), "Radical transformative nationalisms confront the U.S. empire," *Current Sociology*, Vol. 51, No. 2, March, pp.133-152.

Linebaugh, P. and Redicker, M. (2000), *The Many-Headed Hydra: Sailors, Slaves, Commoners, and the Hidden History of the Revolutionary Atlantic* (Boston: Beacon).

MacKenzie, A. F. D. (1990), "'Without a woman there is no land:' Marriage and land rights in small-holder agriculture, Kenya," *Resources for Feminist Research*, 19, 3/4, p. 68-73.

_____ (1998), *Land, Ecology and Resistance in Kenya, 1880-1952* (Portsmouth, N.H.: Heinemann).

Makokha, K. (2003), "Kenya should never discover oil," *Daily Nation* (Nairobi), 21 March.

Marx, K. ([1887] 1967), *Capital, Vol I* (New York: International Publishers).

McGhie, J. (2003), "Mau Mau war crime inquiry," *Guardian Weekly*, 22-28 May, p. 8.

McMurtry, J. (2001), "The Life-ground, the civil commons and the corporate male gang," *Gender, Feminism and the Civil Commons*, Special Issue of the *Canadian Journal of Development Studies*, Vol. XXII, pp. 819-854.

Miring'uh, E. and Masai, M. (1992), "Pastor denounces women's stripping," *East African Standard* (Nairobi), 5 March, pp 1 and 13.

Mugonyi, D. and Kelly, K. (2003), "Mystery of U.S. base plea to Kenya," *Daily Nation* (Nairobi), 17 June.

Mulaa, A. and Githaiga, P. (2003), "Chaos rocks EPZ firms: Textile companies forced to close as workers damage property and battle anti-riot police in wave of strikes," *Daily Nation* (Nairobi), 21 January.

Mulama, J. (2003), "Former freedom fighters to sue britain for compensation," Inter Press Service News Agency, <http://www.ipsnews.net/africa/interna.asp?idnews=20175>, 17 September.

Muriuki, M. (2003), "All land owners to get new title deeds," *Daily Nation* (Nairobi), 14 March.

Museka, L. (2003), "Anti-war demonstrators seek poverty alleviation," *Daily Nation* (Nairobi), 17 February.

Mutonya, N. (2001), "Row over Criticos land sale," *Daily Nation* (Nairobi), 8 June.

Mutua, M. (2003), "Kenyans must reject anti-terrorism bill," *Daily Nation* (Nairobi), 2 July.

Mwai, Elizabeth, "1000 new HIV infections," *The Standard Online*, 29 January 2008.

MwaKenya (1987), *The Draft Minimum Programme of MwaKenya*, Nairobi: Union of Patriots for the Liberation of Kenya, September.

Ngesa, Mildred, "I plead that my man returns home soon," *Daily Nation*, 4 February 2008.

Nyagah, R. (2000), "Slump in tourism blamed on marketing," *Daily Nation* (Nairobi), 25 April.

Njeru, M and Aduda, D. (2003), "World Bank $5b aid to fight hunger," *Daily Nation* (Nairobi), 5 February.

Nyabiage, J. and Kumba, S. (2008), "Teachers union wants peace restored before schools reopen," *Daily Nation*, 5 January 2008.

Ochieng, P. (2003), "A U.S. base would be suicidal," *Sunday Nation* (Nairobi), 22 June.

Odhiambo, E.A.A. and Lonsdale, J. (eds) (2003), *Mau Mau and Nationhood: Arms, Authority and Narration* (Oxford: James Currey).

Ogutu, E. (2003), "Traders storm disputed Soko-Huru," *Daily Nation* (Nairobi), 11 February.

Oketch, W. and Ringa M. (2003), "Squatters invade Kilifi farm at dawn," *Sunday Nation* (Nairobi), 9 February.

Okoth-Ogendo, H.W.O. (1989), "Some issues of theory in the study of tenure relations in African agriculture," *Africa*, Vol. 59, No. 1, pp. 6-17.

Onyango-Obbo, C. (2003), "'Secrets' behind U.S., UK anti-terror war in Kenya," *Sunday Nation* (Nairobi), 22 June.

Osoro, J. (2001), "The Kenyan anti-debt crusader in the U.S.," *Sunday Nation* (Nairobi), 24 June.

Otieno, J. (2003), "Land boards will be ready in two months," *Daily Nation* (Nairobi), 5 July.

Padmore, G. (1953), *Pan-Africanism or Communism* (London: Dobson).

Palast, G. (2001), "The globalizer who came in from the cold: Joe Stiglitz, today's winner of the Nobel Prize in Economics," *The Observer* (United Kingdom), 10 October, <http://www.gregpalast.com>.

Ringera, Karambu, "The heart of the Kenya violence and peace," *Pambazuka News*, Issue 341, 31 January 2008.

Robertson, C.C. (1997), *Trouble Showed the Way: Women, Men, and Trade in the Nairobi Area, 1890-1990* (Bloomington: Indiana University Press).

Ronald, K.A. (2003), "Africa must say NO to GM foods," *Daily Nation* (Nairobi), 17 June.

Rosberg, C. and Nottingham, J. (1996), *The Myth of "Mau Mau": Nationalism in Kenya* (Nairobi: East African Publishing House).

Rosset, P. (2001), "Tides shift on agrarian reform: New movements show the way," *Third World Resurgence*, 129/130, May/June, p. 43-48.

Shiva, V. (2003), "The causes and implications of the failure of W.T.O. Ministerial in Cancun," Press Statement, Diverse Women for Diversity, divwomen@vsnl.com, 18 September.

Starhawk (2003), "Cancun Update 9/12/03 We did it!" www.starhawk.org and www.utne.com, 12 September.

Tamarkin, M. (1978), "The Loyalists in Nakuru during the Mau Mau revolt," *Asian and African Studies*, Vol. 12, No. 2, July, pp. 247-261.

The Economist (2003), "The global menace of local strife," *The Economist*, 22 May, www.economist.com/printedition.

Throup, D. W. (1987), *Economic and Social Origins of Mau Mau 1945-1953* (London: James Currey).

Tomlinson, C. (2003), "Africa faces hunger, why can't the continent feed itself?" *East African Standard* (Nairobi), February 10-16.

Turner, T.E. (1994), "Rastafari and the new society: East African and Caribbean feminist roots of a popular movement to reclaim the earthly commons," in T. E. Turner (ed.), *Arise Ye Mighty People! Gender, Class and Race in Popular Struggles* (Trenton, New Jersey: Africa World Press), pp.9-58.

Turner, T.E. and Benjamin, C.S. (1995), "Not in our nature: The male deal and corporate solutions to the debt-nature crisis," *Review: Journal of the Fernand Braudel Center*, State University of New York, Binghamton, XVIII, 2, Spring, pp. 209-258.

Turner, T.E. et al. (1997), "Social reconstruction in rural Africa: A gendered class analysis of women's resistance to cash crop production in Kenya," *Canadian Journal of Development Studies*, XVIII, 2, p. 213-238.

Turner, T.E. and Brownhill, L.S. (2001a), "'Women never surrendered:' The Mau Mau and globalization from below in Kenya, 1980-2000," in Bennholdt-Thomsen, Nicholas Faraclas and Claudia Von Werlhof, (eds) *There is An Alternative: Subsistence and Worldwide Resistance to Corporate Globalization* (London: Zed), pp. 106-132.

_____. (2001b), "African Jubilee: Mau Mau resurgence and the fight for fertility in Kenya, 1986-2002," in *Gender, Feminism and the Civil Commons*, Special Issue of the *Canadian Journal of Development Studies*, Vol. XXII, pp. 1037-1088.

Turner, T.E., et al. (2001), "Fightback from the Commons: Petroleum industry and environmental racism," paper presented at the *United Nations World Conference Against Racism, Racial Discrimination, Xenophobia and Related Intolerance*, Durban, South Africa, 31 August – 7 September,www.uoguelph.ca/~terisatu.

Truglia, E. (2003), "Africa Is not for sale: The resistance continues in Cancun," Indymedia, Mexico, <http://cancun.mediosindependientes.org/newswire/display/664/index.php?, 13 September.

Veltmeyer, H. and Petras, J. (2002), "The social dynamics of Brazil's rural landless workers' movement: Ten hypotheses on successful leadership," *The Canadian Review of Sociology and Anthropology*, Vol. 39, No. 1, February, pp. 79-96.

Volman, Daniel, "U.S. Military activities in Kenya," *Concerned Africa Scholars*, 5 January 2008.

wa Kinyatti, M. (ed.) (1986), *Kimathi's Letters: A Profile of Patriotic Courage* (Nairobi: Heinemann, London: Zed).

wa Wanjau, G. (1983,1988), *Mau Mau Author in Detention* (Nairobi: Heinemann Kenya).

Walsh, J. (2003), "Double standards: Women's property rights violations in Kenya," *Human Rights Watch*, Vol. 15, No. 5 (A), March.

Walter, N. (2003), "Terror at Dol Dol," *Guardian Weekly*, May 29-June 4, p. 23.

Wamue, G.N. (2001), "Revisiting our indigenous shrines through *Mungiki, African Affairs*, 100, 400, July, p. 453-467.

White House. (2002), *The National Security Strategy of the United States of America*, September, <http://www.whitehouse.gov/nsc>.

Women's Edge Coalition. (2003), "WTO talks collapse as poor nations unite against rich nations to resist unfair trade rules," <http://www.womensedge.org/pages/newsandevents/news.jsp?id=152>, September 15.

World History Archives. (2000), *History of the Mungiki Movement of Kenya* January – December, http://www.hartford-hwp.com/archives/36/index-bfba.html.

Writers Bloc. (2003), "Report from Cancun: We are winning," *Counterpunch*, <http://www.counterpunch.org/cancun09152003.html>, 15 September.

Zwartz, H. (1992), "Mothers try to free political sons," *The Dominion* (New Zealand), 23 May.

Chapter 7

Alternative Economies
Mexican Women Left Behind: Organizing Solidarity Economy in Response

Ann Ferguson

Introduction

In 1994 the US Congress approved the NAFTA Free Trade treaty with Mexico and Canada and a new stage of neo-liberal globalization was put in play that has contributed to increasing poverty both in the US and Mexico. It has particularly harmed the popular classes in Mexico, including farmers, industrial workers and small business owners. In this chapter I will briefly review the increasing structural inequalities that have been caused by this free trade policy, in conjunction with harsh US immigration laws and decreased social spending by the neo-liberal Mexican and US governments. My particular focus will be on neo-liberalism's effects on the women and families left behind by male migrants to the US from Mexico, looking at an ethnographic case study of four rural women in the film documentary *Letters from the Other Side* (Courtney 2006). I shall outline a particular strategy of resistance by women in these migrant families to corporate capitalist globalization's negative effects, namely their formation of women's producers' cooperatives. Their cooperatives are just one example of alternative economic practices to capitalist economies as a part what has been called the "solidarity political economy" (cf. Allard, Davidson and Matthaei 2008; Ferguson 2007, 2008a, 2008b; Bowman and Stone 2006). As in other cases of such anti-capitalist globalization projects, such efforts require support by national and global networks. Cooperatives need equipment and training and loans to deal with start up costs, as well as markets to sustain them. They also need markets of consumers and political activists willing to pay a bit more for their products which often are competing with lower cost capitalist corporate products. This requires a globalization from below, including a transnational solidarity culture and alternative cooperative economy which resists local self-interested individualist consumer and workers' mere profit-oriented approaches. There must be created a collective interest in global cooperative-based economic networks which can alter the neo-liberal priorities of nation states.

The Structural Inequalities of NAFTA

The NAFTA treaty requires the member governments to open up their borders to imports from other members without imposing tariffs on them, and to allow the free flow of capital across borders. Its infamous Chapter 11 provisions restrict member governments from protecting workers' rights, e.g. to unionize, or from subjecting multinational corporations to national penalties if they create toxic environmental effects. Almost a decade and a half into NAFTA the result is that unlike the continental integration meticulously underway in Europe, market imperfections are producing stunning market failures in both the United States and Mexico: without an end to American subsidies to its farmers, below-market products, particularly corn, have flooded Mexico, bankrupting millions of rural farmers, and sending several million undocumented workers into the United States, exacerbating an immigration crisis that is infuriating the American electorate. After the passage of NAFTA, the number of Mexican farmers has fallen by 1.3 million while US exports of corn to Mexico have grown by 240 percent, corn prices in Mexico have fallen by 70 percent, and the average hourly income has decreased by 40 percent there.[1]

Without the restructuring of Mexico's oil and electrical industries, current Mexican President Felipe Calderon is confronting a looming energy crisis; only the sharp rise in the price of oil has buffered Mexico's antiquated oil and electrical industries. Without higher taxes on the most privileged, and through the systematic failure to control monopolies, the United States government has allowed the emergence of oligopolies the size of which the robber barons of the Gilded Age could not have dreamed, and the failure of the Mexican Congress to support small businesses has also allowed for oligopolies there.

It is often said in defense of NAFTA free trade policies that allowing capitalist multinational corporations to move their production to Mexico because of a cheaper labor force there and other cheaper production costs will create more jobs, e.g. in the maquiladora factories, for Mexican workers, and thus will "grow" the Mexican economy. There might have been a short term effect that allowed some, particularly young women, to have increasing job opportunities in US-based corporate maquilas in Mexico for a time. However, the capitalist corporate globalization "race to the bottom" process (Brecher and Costello 1994) has now involved the move of many of those corporate industries who first re-located to Mexico from the US, to even cheaper labor markets in places like China and Singapore, so the advantage to the Mexican work force has been a very temporary one.

It is not only poor industrial and agricultural Mexican workers who suffer the loss of jobs and income due to the corporate globalization processes fostered by NAFTA: middle class professional workers, particularly women workers, are

---

1   Cf. *Letters from the Other Side*, video produced by Heather Courtney (2006), www.lettersfromtheotherside.com.

increasing at risk for job layoffs or pay cuts as the results of so-called SAPs or "structural adjustment policies" of the IMF and World Bank lending policies. These policies are sometimes called "neo-liberal" because they aim for a smaller government economic sector and a larger private sector which is governed by capitalist market principles (Friedman 1962). They require cutbacks in state spending and privatization of any nationally-owned resources, such as land and utilities, as preconditions for loans to governments. This has meant that in order to receive loans from these bodies, Mexico has had to reduce spending on state services such as education, health and welfare. These are just those areas which have traditionally employed more women than men, and whose family services are used more by women than men in fulfilling their traditional gender duties of caretaking for the education and health of children and elder family members. In 2006 the teachers in the city of Oaxaca struck for a pay raise and for more material resources for public schools. The subsequent city-wide strike and occupation of the city center were signs of local resistance to these policies, but unfortunately these democratic protests were met with police repression and a refusal to change the conservative educational policy under attack.

Not only have Mexican male farmers been forced out of the market by US subsidized agriculture. Also Mexican women workers who were engaged in home production of crafts such as clothing, baskets and pottery find themselves in a similar position of being put out of work as low cost mass-produced plastic goods of the multinational corporations undercut their ability to sell their traditional products for a fair price. Furthermore Mexican population growth is outpacing economic and job growth, and although there are some non-governmental organizations which are doing popular sex education and distributing contraception, their efforts reach a relatively small proportion of the population since they are not supported or funded to any great extent by the Mexican government.

Ironically, as Mexican workers, male and female, are under pressure to migrate to the North for low paid jobs that will replace their subsistence economy jobs lost through NAFTA supposed "free trade" in goods, US and Mexican government policy do not allow free trade in workers, so possibilities for legal migration are sparse compared to the demand for opportunities to migrate or for low paid migrant workers in the US. This situation forces many Mexicans to consider illegal immigration which is dangerous for them and disruptive to their families, particularly for the women left behind, who now must be the chief breadwinners for children. The wide-scale emigration has left many villages with decaying infrastructures such as schools, roads, irrigation, flood control and loss of farming productivity, hence local food, due to loss of labor. This lack of people power has also made it much more difficult to maintain valuable social, political, and cultural institutions. Those Mexican workers who try to get better working conditions at home through unionization and demands for higher pay and benefits are either laid off or abused by corrupt nationally-controlled labor unions in collusion with the government.

Meanwhile the Mexican economy is surviving importantly on the remittances of undocumented Mexican immigrants in the US to their Mexican families: in 2004 there were $1.3 billion USD in remittances from migrants, which is a greater source of revenue in Mexico than tourism and second only to income from oil. These remittances have grown by 300 percent since the 1994 NAFTA Treaty's negative effects on the average Mexican family, forcing nearly 400,000 undocumented immigrants a year to come to the US in search of work to feed their families back home (Courtney 2006).

In part the failure of President Bush and the Congress to alter US immigration policy to adjust to the increased supply of Mexicans as cheap laborers and the increased US demand for their services is due to the frustration of American workers whose own salaries have not kept up with inflation and whose lives have worsened due to the obscene differential between low paid workers and the very wealthy US oligarchy. This latter group has been made much richer by the Bush administration's neo-liberal tax cuts and resultant cuts or increased costs of welfare state services like education, health and mass transportation, which primarily benefit the working and middle classes. Meanwhile in the US the hysteria caused by the bombing of the World Trade Center in New York City on September, 2001, has allowed for a huge increase in funds for US border patrols who now exceed 11,000 officers. Increased fencing and more patrols to try to avoid make illegal border crossing even more dangerous: in 2004 461 Mexican migrants were killed trying to cross the US border, mostly by deaths in the deserts (Courtney 2006).

Gendered Effects on Women and Families

NAFTA and other neo-liberal policies, such as cuts in state spending, have disproportionately affected women of the popular classes for the worse. Major effects on women have been

- Major family disruption, including deaths of family members who have tried to emigrate, and emotional costs to themselves and remaining children of the absence of husbands and teenage children who have migrated. Many migrant husbands, unable to return for years, form other families in the US, and reduce their emotional contact and remittances to their family of origin, leaving the women at home to pick up the emotional and economic consequences for the rest of the family.
- The formation of female-headed households, with women forced to take on the additional role of sole breadwinner for the family in addition to unpaid domestic tasks for the family's welfare. Women are now working much harder, usually with less to show for their work in achieving the family's welfare.
- The two above effects create serious health effects due to grief, stress, overwork, poverty, and lack of adequate health care.

Case Study of Mexican Women of Migrant Families in the State of Guanajuato, Mexico, as Documented in *Letters from the Other Side*

I want to sketch the situation of the women in four Mexican families affected by migration due to the NAFTA treaty's globalization effects. These are case studies presented by Heather Courtney in her film *Letters from the Other Side* (2006). She is an independent filmmaker who interviewed women involved with a network of rural women cooperatives called Mujeres Productoras in small towns in Guanajuato, Mexico. All the women have male relatives who have migrated to the US because of economic pressures. In the case of Eugenia González, her husband Hector first migrated to the US to try to increase the economic situation of his family with five children, but when he got there, found that the costs of living in the US didn't allow him to send much money home. He was afraid to return due to the dangers of the border crossing (several men had died in the group he came over with). In time, out of loneliness, he found another woman to live with in the US and stopped sending money to his Mexican family. His first son, worried about his father who had been out of touch, emigrated to the US to find him, and the second son went to try to get money to build himself a house in Mexico, but never returned, out of fear of the passage back, although he does send money regularly. Eugenia, initially left with five children to support, became a member of a women's cactus-growing cooperative which makes soap, jam and candies out of nopal. This has made her much more independent, but still bitter about the loss of her husband and two sons. One of her daughters has left high school to live with her boyfriend who is going to emigrate to the US. She may as well, since there is not sufficient money to pay for her to complete her high school education.

Carmela Rico is a single mother whose husband and brother-in-law died with 16 others in a smuggler's truck emigrating to the US. He had emigrated to try to get money to pay a debt the family incurred when his young son hurt his eye in an accident. The death was so upsetting to the family that the son suffered a nervous breakdown, and has only slowly recovered. Carmela has started a bakery cooperative with Laura Almanza Cruz. The government did give them assistance to get a scale, an industrial mixer and an oven. However, they are not able to use the latter two items, since they run on gas and require gas hookups and money for gas which is very expensive which the women cannot afford. So the equipment sits unused, while they make do with their small ovens and hand-mixing. In spite of this, they are making a modest living with their cakes and pastries.

Maria Yañez is 58 years old, and has done heavy farm work with her husband all her adult life. They have three sons in the US who left because they could not make a living with farm work. Their remaining son, Julio, is now helping them with the farm work they are getting too old to do alone, but he doesn't want to do this all his life. As Maria acknowledges, they cannot really make ends meet now without her work in the women's sewing collective she is a part of, and Julio would like to get an education and do something else. For awhile he thought of joining the military to get educated by them, but his hopes were dashed when he failed to pass their minimum height requirements for service. He doesn't want to migrate since it is so dangerous, so he will be looking for work in Mexico but realizes it will be hard to find anything where he can make a living. If he decides not to farm, the farm will just be abandoned, and Maria and her husband will have the problem in their old age of who will care for them.

Guanajuato Women's Production Cooperatives

The four women interviewed in the film are all part of women's production cooperatives in the Mujeres Productoras network coordinated by Yolanda Millán, a social worker from San Miguel de Allende who also works with the new Center for Global Justice there. This is a center created by progressive retired North Americans concerned, among other things, with promoting an alternative solidarity economy to combat corporate globalization. With the Center and Yolanda's help, these women's cooperatives now have a store in San Miguel from which to market their products to tourists, mostly from the US, as well as their regular vending at street markets and fairs in the state of Guanajuato. In addition, commitment to solidarity economy values, to attempt to meet the material needs of individuals in the network in a committed cooperative fashion, has led the Center to begin a revolving loan fund to aid these and other cooperatives to form and acquire working capital.[2] The problem is, that even with this help, the cheaper products available from mass produced goods and low paid workers are more competitive than theirs to the average Mexican family, and their markets in the solidarity economy are not sufficiently large to guarantee that their cooperatives will make enough money to offset the loss in income their families have sustained through the forces of globalization and migration. Furthermore, the neo-liberal state policies of the Mexican government have not provided them with sufficient capital or equipment to produce on a larger scale that would allow them to compete very well with these capitalist-produced products. Nonetheless, there is the hope that the growing examples in Latin America of nations who are resisting neo-liberal financial agreements and supporting local cooperatives, such as Cuba, Bolivia, Venezuela and Nicaragua, and the radical social movements opposing the neo-liberal policies of the disputed Mexican PAN government of Felipe Calderón such as AMLO (the 2006 PRD candidate for president Lopez Obrador's social movement) and APPO (the Oaxacan social movement including the teachers on strike opposed to the Oaxacan governor Ruiz) will create the possibility of a progressive change in Mexican national policy to eliminate neo-liberalism in favor of these people-centered alternative globalization economic sectors.

---

2 For more information on the Center for Global Justice's activities, cf. www.globaljusticecenter.org

Resistances to Neo-Liberal Corporate Globalization: Solidarity Economies and Politics

In what remains of this chapter I would like to brainstorm some ideas and problems of the new solidarity economies and politics that are developing in Mexico, the US and elsewhere by first, giving a characterization of solidarity economies, second, discussing how they connect to solidarity politics, and finally, sketch a few ongoing problems such anti-corporate globalization networks face in achieving their goals.

First, how is a solidarity economy defined? The concept of the "Solidarity Economy" as an oppositional economic and political network against neo-liberalism as an economic and political strategy of capitalist globalization developed in the 1990s. The term "solidarity economy" was created by a Brazilian professor Luis Razeto who referred to "Factor C: cooperation, co-responsibility, communication, and community" as a form of alternative economy (Allard, Davidson and Matthaei 2008, p. 5). The idea of a solidarity economy global network was launched globally at the World Social Forum in Puerto Alegre, Brazil in 2001 and drew 55,000 participants representing many social movements and NGOs. The goal of that conference was to bring people and movements together to form a new vision and new political networks based on a shared set of principles which include opposition to neo-liberalism, commitment to nonviolence, and "respect for Human Rights, the practices of real democracy, participatory democracy, peaceful relations, equality and solidarity, among people, ethnicity, genders and condemns all forms of domination and all subjection of one person by another."[3]

The Social Forum movement has spread to many countries: in 2005 there were 2,560 Social Forum activities in the world at the regional, national and local level.

At the US Social Forum in Atlanta this past June 2007, the US Solidarity Economy Network was formed.[4] This network has as its expressed aim to offer "an alternative economic framework to that of neoliberal globalization—one that is grounded in solidarity and cooperation rather than the pursuit of narrow, individual self-interest." (Kawano 2007). I have claimed elsewhere (Ferguson 2007, 2008a, 2008b) that such a network attempts to operate on a Solidarity Principle of Social Justice similar to that referred to by Marx in the *Critique of the Gotha Program* as one which demands "From each according to their ability, to each according to their needs" (Marx 1877/1977), a principle which is not achievable in a capitalist economy. When such economic alternative networks operate in a political context where social movements are pushing for participatory democracy and sustainable

---

3 World Social Forum Principle 11, quoted in Allard, Davidson and Matthaei 2008, p. 3.

4 For more information about this network, which has a coordinating committee and a list serve, contact Emily Kawano at the Center for Popular Economics, University of Massachusetts Amherst (www.populareconomics.org) or subscribe to the list serve by sending a message to sen-subscribe@lists.riseup.net.

development, the networks also explicitly promote social and economic democracy and equity in all dimensions, which can include attention to race, class, gender and LGBT inequalities. Examples of projects in solidarity economic networks include:

- cooperatives of all sorts, whether worker, producer, consumer, or housing;
- transnational trade union solidarity actions;
- complementary currencies that insure local re-circulation of capital;
- fair trade and solidarity financial projects;
- anti-privatization and "reclaim the commons" movements;
- worker-controlled pension funds;
- land trusts;
- co-housing and eco villages;
- consumer-supported agriculture or CISAs;
- green technology and development;
- open source movement for intellectual property products, such as Linux software and Wikipedia; and
- participatory budgeting processes, such as those operating in Saõ Paulo, Brazil and in many communities in Venezuela (Kawano 2007).[5]

Gar Alperowitz (2006) has called this set of alternative economic networks in the US the "commonwealth tier" of the economy. With its more than 11,000 cooperatives and increasing attention to localism, due to environmental concerns about global warming, there are increasing opportunities for anti-corporate globalization movements to find root in political and economic projects which expand this sector and politicize it so as to widen its scope beyond the local niches

---

5   Complementary currencies are often locally based credit for services based on an estimated money equivalent, which entitles the bearer to comparable services from others in the network. "Fair trade" refers to products which are bought a higher than market value price in order to ensure that the producers get a living income from the sale. "Land trusts" involve land which is not individually owned and therefore cannot be sold, although individuals can purchase the right to use of the land, similar to those who rent. The intent is to guarantee that the land continues to be available for use by members of the community rather than being controlled by the profit motive. The "open source" movement involves inventors or producers of intellectual tools like software or an encyclopedia who renounce any right to income from a copyright in the interest of making it available to all. Participatory budgeting by a community involves opening meetings of workers, government officials and citizens in town councils deciding together what to produce or have as services, based on expressed needs rather than by employers or by politicians acting from self-interest. Community-supported agriculture (CISAs) are arrangements between farmers and consumers (who become members of the CISA associated with a particular farm) that the latter will pay a fixed rate for a certain quantity of seasonal goods that will provide a sustainable income for the farm. All of these arrangements have in common that they are not based merely on the logic of profit for individuals, but on what is seen to benefit the community.

in which such cooperatives and other solidarity projects operate. Indeed if this does not occur, it is clear that isolated attempts to form producer cooperatives such as that happening in Guanajuato will not be successful against the relentless political and economic forces of multinational corporate globalization, given the incredible power of their control of capital and political clout to shape markets and trade policies.

Fortunately there are important new models of solidarity economic and political networks emerging in governmental and social movement political practice in Latin American. One example is what Hugo Chavez, president of Venezuela, calls "Bolivarian socialism," which aims to challenge the neoliberal corporate capitalist logic that otherwise undermines small local cooperative solidarity networks. Venezuela under Chavez is a nation state pursuing a mixed economy with capitalist firms as one sector, nationally owned enterprise such as the oil industry as a second sector, and as a third sector, worker-owned cooperatives. Government land reform has been strengthening this latter sector by appropriating some private property for worker cooperatives and these latter have also given financial and technical help by the state.

Chavez has been diverting profits from the national oil sector to social programs to benefit the poor, creating a new sector which the government calls "the social economy" (Hahnel 2007, Allard, Davidson and Matthaei 2008). The Chavez government has created a massive program to create worker-owned cooperatives, which established a Vuelvan Caras cooperative job-training program in 2004 and gives graduates of the program who want to start up their own cooperatives zero-interest loans for start-up costs. As a result 8,000 cooperatives have been formed by the graduates of this program and 181,000 cooperatives are now officially registered in the country, up from only 800 officially listed coops when Chavez took office in 1998 (Fox 2007). Many of these cooperatives are owned by poor women, a number of whom took part in a government free literacy program started by Chavez and were then recruited into the Vuelvan Caras program. This has allowed poor women, many of whom are single mothers like Estrella Ramirez, to open baking, sewing and other production cooperatives funded and given on-going technical support by the government. Ramirez, a disabled woman who lost an arm, was not able to get a waged job before this program because of job discrimination, and now is able to support her family because of the government training and the textile cooperative, Manos Amigas, in which she is one of the hardest workers (Fox 2007). Venezuela is also developing an alternative popular tier of local political decision-making centered in the creation of communal councils and social missions which are involved in participatory budget-making with the elected political officials such as mayors and city councils. The aim is to bypass often corrupt local party officials and encourage participatory democracy through separate money funneled to the neighborhood communal councils which must establish local spending priorities based on a participatory democratic process (Hahnel 2007).

Other Latin American leftist governments such as Bolivia, Ecuador and the returned-to-power Sandinista government in Nicaragua are struggling to implement aspects of a new type of mixed-economy socialism similar to that in Venezuela which does not center all decision-making power in a central state, but attempts to channel some of profits gained by national or corporate capitalist firms toward decentralized alternative social and economic projects aiming to foster a new type of participatory democracy (Fuentes 2007). These leftist governments are aided by the Venezuelan Latin American inter-state solidarity initiative called MercoSur, which creates national trade agreements geared toward meeting popular class needs rather than simply building GNP. Examples include the trade of oil to Cuba at cheap prices by Venezuela in exchange for Cuban doctors to staff free health clinics for the poor in Venezuela, and the Venezuelan–Nicaraguan trade of beef for oil to stimulate jobs in the rural sector in Nicaragua.

What is to be Done?

What is needed in the US is continued organization to create the transnational solidarity networks that can change neo-liberal and present immigration policy in the US. This requires a broad front of activism that includes organizing against multinationals like Walmart stores which buy non-union goods abroad, now mostly from China, and sell cheap in the US, including in Mexico where they illegally have so-called "volunteers" bagging goods that are not paid anything except the tips they receive from customers. Walmart eliminates many small businesses in its wake and makes it difficult for small cooperatives of all sorts to compete with it, so the political commitment of solidarity is needed for these small businesses to survive.

Another necessary political solidarity action includes struggles to raise the minimum wage to a living wage in the US so that citizens of color in the US, particularly African Americans, are not undercut by immigrant workers for jobs, which fosters anti-immigrant attitudes. However, as well, solidarity political-economic networks between Mexico and the US must take as a key political issue challenging the draconian Mexican and US immigration policies which, in tandem with NAFTA, create economic conditions which force Mexicans to leave Mexico in search of work in the US but continue to make them undocumented persons with no citizen rights here, and allows them to be easily exploited by US corporate agriculture and other businesses. Amnesty is a bare minimum change to deal with this injustice, and increasing the number of legal visas allowed, but there must also be a change in the US farm subsidies that flood the Mexican markets with cheap corn. Taking the big picture into account would be to demand a change in all the neo-liberal policies in both Mexico and the US that support multinational corporate profits over local sustainable development. For example, in Guanajuato the Mexican government could be providing real ongoing help to alleviating the start-up costs for producer cooperatives, and could aid in promoting tourist consumption of their product as well as finding fair trade markets in the US for them.

More fair trade marketing of Mexican cooperatively produced goods to the US is very important. None of the Guanajuato cooperatives at present have a marketing partner in the US who is selling their goods here, as this is being done for coffee and for other cooperatives. This would make a big difference in their ability to survive. For example, the Nueva Vida cooperative clothes production factory in Nicaragua, the first of its kind in the free trade zone there, has a marketing partner in Maggie's Wear in the US, who buys and markets their goods here. It remains to be seen if the solidarity cooperative movement can produce the political solidarity and economies of scale to compete with the large multinational corporations and financial institutions like the World Bank and IMF with their neo-liberal policies. Another world is possible, but it will take a lot of consciousness-raising, value-changing, and organizing to get there.

In conclusion, I wanted to give a few inspiring examples of movements for social justice which are now involved in creating alternative cooperative economic networks that are empowering women in Latin America. I will mention three examples: the landless farmworkers' movement in Brazil, the Zapatista movement in Chiapas, Mexico, and the autonomous unemployed movement in Argentina. In the first, which is now nearly 2.5-million-people-strong, farmworkers are setting up cooperative communities on land that is not presently being farmed, owned by wealthy landowners, and beginning to farm the land cooperatively. They are demanding that the land be given to them under Brazilian law which requires that land be serving a social use or else the government has the right to expropriate it. They have very strong women leadership and have formed separate women's caucuses which demanded equal participation by women in leadership positions in the movement. They have also raised consciousness against violence against women by male partners of women involved in these new communities, and have a rule in place that requires any men guilty of this to leave the communities.

My second example involves the Zapatista movement in Chiapas, Mexico. They have been involved since 1994 in opposing changes in the Mexican Constitution that have benefited outside investors in land at their expense. They aim to create autonomous indigenous communities who control the land communally and make decisions by participatory democracy, women's human rights to marriage of choice, education, freedom from male violence, reproductive rights, and equal say with husbands have been acknowledged by the Zapatista list of 10 Revolutionary Laws for Women. Women organized in production cooperatives are equally involved in decision making.

My final example involves the Autonomous Unemployed Worker movement in La Matanza, a barrio in Buenos Aires, Argentina, where women are in the leadership of various worker cooperatives that have formed since worker takeovers there of factories which had closed down in the economic crisis in 2001. Some of them are also involved in creating their own free school for children based on cooperative anarchist principles that children should learn to think critically for themselves and learn to be involved democratically in education decisions in the school. The school is run by a collective of parents and teachers seeking to create self-respect in unemployed workers, both women and men, and help facilitate the creation of community cooperative small businesses that can help those without salaries find a way to make a living and buy food at prices they can afford.

These three examples show that there are developing various practical forms of resistance to the economic hardships suffered by poor families whose livelihoods and family ties have been undermined by neo-liberalism and free trade practices benefiting large multi-national corporations at their expense, and that these forms of resistance are part of growing solidarity networks that may succeed in achieving greater economic justice for them.

Hopefully the idea that justice requires solidarity with these efforts on the part of those of us who are more privileged in our globalizing world will create the kind of political and economic support they require from us, as consumers purchasing their products, and as citizens of the world who can give political support to their demands for an end to the economic injustice that neo-liberal policies have brought them. To the extent that world solidarity movements based in the alternative solidarity political economy gain political clout, nearly all of us stand to benefit from the struggle against neoliberal governmental foreign and domestic politics and anti-immigrant policies, as well as against the neo-liberal policies of the International Monetary Fund, the World Bank and the World Trade Organization. What is needed is not a few paternalistic gestures of charity, but the mutual aid that allies offer each other who see that their enlightened interests are bound up with struggles for social justice for those least well off. When and if this happens for the majority of people our solidarity struggles can develop into the mutual aid networks necessary to bring about a better world.

References

Alperovitz, G. (2006), "Another World Is Possible," *Mother Jones* (January/ February 2006).

Brecher, J. and Costello, T. (1994), *Global Village or Global Pillage: Economic Reconstruction from the Bottom Up* (Cambridge: South End Press).

Bowman, B. and Stone B. (2006), *Latin America's Solidarity Economy* (in 3 parts): "Argentina's Crisis"; "Venezuela and Argentina" and "The Meek Want the Earth Now: the Solidarity Economies of Brazil and Mexico," <www. globaljusticecenter.org/news.htm>.

Center for Global Justice, San Miguel de Allende, Mexico. www.globaljusticecenter. org>.

Courtney, H. (2006), "Letters from the Other Side," DVD available from <www. lettersfromtheotherside.com>.

Ferguson, A. (2007), "Iris Young, Global Responsibility and Solidarity: A Theory of Global Justice," <http://www.umass.edu/wost/events/ferguson.pdf>.

—— (2009), "Women, Corporate Globalization, and Global Justice," in Lisa Tessman, (ed.) *Feminist Ethics and Social and Political Philosophy: Theorizing the Non-Ideal* (Dordrecht: Kluwer/Springer).

Kawano, E. (2007), "US Solidarity Economy Network Launched," Center for Popular Economics, *The Popular Economist Newletter,* Fall 2007. www. populareconomics.org.

Chapter 8

Towards a Global Economy of Commoning
A "Gift to Humanity": Third World Women's Global Action to Keep the Oil in the Ground

Terisa E. Turner and Leigh Brownhill

> We demand that the world takes the example of Ecuador and join with one voice to demand the revolutionary step of keeping the oil in the ground in order to rescue the world from the destructive path mapped and propelled by the fossil fuel mode of civilization. This major move makes both moral and economic sense and every nation that takes it should be adequately compensated for the positive contribution.
>
> Nnimmo Bassey, Environmental Rights Action, Nigeria, 2007

Introduction

Production shut-downs and calls for moratoria on fossil fuel production multiplied in the first years of the 21st century.[1] Keeping the oil in the ground is clearly the only way to achieve the 90 percent reduction in hydrocarbon use by 2050 that is minimally required to restrict global warming to under two degrees centigrade (Monbiot 4 December 2007). Citizens of countries across the world have become increasingly aware of the links between extreme weather events, carbon emissions, Big Oil and US militarism (Khosrave 2007). This awareness has helped create the enabling environment for the proliferation of coordinated direct actions against the global warming activities of the corporations exploiting hydrocarbons. This chapter examines the convergence of these actions. First, we review a few of the many calls for fossil fuel moratoria made in the past decade. Second, we consider in more depth three successful movements to keep the oil in the ground – those of Nigeria, Costa Rica and Ecuador. Third, we suggest that new relations of

---

1 In June 2008, climate change campaigners stopped a coal train outside of Drax, the biggest power station in Britain, and shoveled its contents on to the only rail line into the plant. They hung a banner on the train that read "Leave it in the Ground," chained themselves to the engine car and mounted a day-long stand-off with police. The protesters promised more actions in the coming months (Wainwright 2008).

energy exchange are emerging to support "commoning"[2] understood as a feminist ecosocialist alternative to capitalist-driven ecocide.

Calls to End Oil, Gas and Coal Production

Five of many demands that hydrocarbons be left in the ground are considered here. One of the first was made in 1998 by aboriginal peoples in the Americas organized in the Indigenous Environmental Network (IEN). The IEN passed a pioneering declaration to fight climate change by targeting the perpetrators.

A second moratorium demand focused on firms in Canada's Athabasca tarsands that produce the dirtiest oil in the world. Several national organizations led by the Council of Canadians have demanded a moratorium. In 2007 even that servant of Big Oil, Alberta's ex-premier Lougheed, called for a moratorium. Confronted with toxic water, depleted rivers and rare cancers, the indigenous Chipewyan people of northern Alberta have also called for a shut-down and commenced legal action to keep the bitumen in situ.

A third example responds to the fragility of the fast-warming Arctic. The usually-oil company friendly World Wildlife Fund in February 2008 called for a moratorium on all oil and gas developments in the Arctic. This entails opposition to the building of any new pipelines, including the proposed MacKenzie Valley gas pipeline. The oil companies working in the Athabasca tarsands want this pipeline to transport natural gas from the Arctic to Fort McMurray to boil the oil out of the sand.

A fourth instance of the campaign to cut fossil fuel emissions brought together all the indigenous peoples of the Americas to defend the ecology on which depend the Inuit communities around the North Pole. Ecocide feeds ethnocide. A 2008 report spells out the urgency of the Inuit case. The study's authors have calculated that the Arctic sea ice "will go into irreversible decline once temperatures rise between 0.5C to 2C above those at the beginning of the century, a threshold that may already have been crossed" (Sample 2008). In 2005 the Inuit Circumpolar Conference (ICC) petitioned the Inter-American Commission on Human Rights

---

2   This chapter draws on Linebaugh's definition of "commons" as "the theory that vests all property in the community and organizes labor for the common benefit of all" (Linebaugh 2008:6). We have also employed the term "civil commons" to refer to social constructs which enable universal access of all members of a community to life goods. It is within the civil commons that women create and socialize human beings, the most critical "product" of human labor from the perspective both of capital and citizenry. (Turner and Brownhill 2001; McMurtry 1998). The commons, the subsistence political economy (Bennholt-Thompsen and Mies, 1999, Shiva 23 January 2007) and feminist ecosocialism are used interchangeably to designate a life-centered organization of world society (Turner 1994a; Turner and Brownhill 2006; and see the entire issue of *Capitalism Nature Socialism*, Vol. 17, No. 4, containing one part of a symposium on feminist ecosocialism, edited by Ariel Salleh).

of the Organization of American States to take action against the US government for human rights abuses due to climate change. This petition on behalf of 150,000 Inuit and other indigenous peoples of the Americas charged the US government with responsibility for failing to curb emissions by "third parties," that is, oil and other corporations (ICC, 7 December, 2005).

A final example of calls for hydrocarbon moratoria is the demand by Nigerian villagers that Shell stop burning the gas that is produced with crude oil. The Niger Delta communities won a litigation victory in 2006 in their campaign to force Shell to stop flaring natural gas (Turner and Brownhill 2007). In the face of Shell's refusal to honour the court order to douse the flares, insurgency in the Delta has increased to the point of cutting as much as a fifth of total oil production or almost half a million barrels a day (Reuters, 23 June 2008).

Supplementing these demands that fossil fuel oil production be stopped is the December 2007 call from Oil Change International to end "oil aid," or massive use of tax payer money to subsidize the oil and gas industry. Since 2000, at least $61.3 billion in international money has gone to subsidizing the oil and gas industry worldwide and an additional estimated $150-$250 billion in domestic subsidies have been provided by national governments to their oil and gas industries annually.[3]

While many activists demand that oil production be shut down and no new reserves be developed, global production is being further reduced by three additional forces: (1) war (Zahller 2008), (2) the exhaustion of deposits (Citi 4 February 2008; Monbiot 12 February 2008) and (3) flagging demand due to high prices (Hopkins 2008).

The five moratoria noted above illustrate demands that corporations and governments leave hydrocarbons in the ground. In contrast, some of the struggles to block oil production have been successful. They are, in effect, production strikes. We now turn to a consideration of three campaigns that have actually blocked fossil fuel production and suppressed emissions underground.

---

3 Oil Change International (2007) pointed out the irony that "While the world's governments are negotiating a complex system to reduce carbon emissions, they are subsidizing the very emissions that must be curtailed, and they are often doing so in the name of development." With respect to these subsidies Klein (2007) observed that "the idea that capitalism can save us from climate catastrophe has powerful appeal. It gives politicians an excuse to subsidize corporations rather than regulate them, and it neatly avoids a discussion about how the core market logic of endless growth landed us here in the first place."

Enforcing a Halt to Oil Production

Costa Rica

In 2002 Costa Rica became the first country in the world to declare the entire territory a no-go zone for oil exploration and production. The struggle was led by indigenous people and a broad alliance within which women were prominent. The government terminated concessions held by Harken oil, formerly owned by George W. Bush. The US retaliated with heavy-handed efforts to impose a Central American Free Trade Agreement (CAFTA) that would force open Costa Rica's "services" sector, including oil (ADELA 2002).

The US extended the end February 2008 deadline for passage of CAFTA's enabling legislation, giving Costa Rica until end October 2008. Environmentalists denounced the December 2007 signing of a pact by the Arias government with the Chinese state oil corporation to rebuild the Limon-Moin refinery (2008 throughput of 20,000 b/d) to process 100,000 b/d, and explore for oil offshore in the Caribbean. Massive opposition to the Central American Free Trade Agreement may succeed in retaining the oil exploration ban (Anon. 2007).

Nigeria

A second instance of popular mobilization to stop oil and gas production in practice is the on-going campaigns of peasants and fishing peoples of the Niger Delta, site of Nigeria's massive petroleum industry. Women-led shut-downs of oil activity achieved international prominence as of the early 1980s (Turner and Oshare 1994b). Shell was expelled from the territories occupied by Ogoni peoples as of 1993. Through 2008 the Ogoni-enforced moratorium on any oil and gas exploration or production in licenses on Ogoni territory was maintained, largely as a result of efforts by peasant women. This tremendous achievement led to action by the Nigerian government[4] to terminate Shell's licenses to operate in Ogoniland due to the super-major's inactivity for more than a decade (Wiwa 23 September 2006 quoted in Turner and Brownhill 2007).

In 1999 Nigerian women and their allied menfolk shut down a quarter of oil and gas production in a monumental action distinguished by two features: (1) the campaign was explicitly aimed at suppressing toxic emissions underground as indicated by its names, "Operation Climate Change" and "A Gift to Humanity" (Anon. 1999); and (2) the campaign was international in that it coordinated direct action by parties in Nigeria and London, UK, shut down part of Shell's Niger Delta operations while simultaneously occupying the London head office of Shell (Turner and Brownhill 2007).

---

4   Olusegun Obasanjo was president of Nigeria from 1999 to 2007. He ruled over a population of some 141 million people, 91 percent of whom lived on less than $2 a day. A majority of the people live in rural areas (53 percent).

As Shell and the Nigerian government repressed anti-oil activists in the Delta in response to their "Operation Climate Change of 1999, over a hundred international organizations protested by circulating a declaration of solidarity that proclaimed that "The world is watching," – a chant that was taken up a few months later in December 1999 by demonstrators against the World Trade Organization meeting in the "Battle of Seattle" (Drillbits and Tailings 1999).

In July 2002 some 600 Nigerian women again sparked a global explosion of protest, but now at a much expanded scale. The women took over ChevronTexaco's Escravos oil export terminal for eleven days. They negotiated 27 concessions but also demanded that ChevronTexaco leave Nigeria (Turner and Brownhill 2004). Just as Nigerian women blocked the production and export of significant quantities of crude oil, their allies pursued a successful international consumption boycott against major oil companies including ChevronTexaco and Exxon (Osouka, Martinez and Salazar 2002). Big Oil was under attack both at the point of production and the point of consumption.

In Nigeria, when soldiers unleashed repression, Niger Delta women threatened to confront collaborators with the state and Big Oil with the dreaded "curse of nakedness." This ultimate curse announces the revocation of life by those who give birth. As a last resort, women expose their vaginas to remind their opponents who threaten them with death of where, quite literally, they come from. The curse launches social ostracization that is believed to lead to madness and even death (IOWG 2003 cited in Turner and Brownhill 2004).

Explicitly inspired by the Nigerian women, California women protested ChevronTexaco's actions in Nigeria and the threatening US war for oil in Iraq. They also went naked, spelling out with their bodies the word "Peace," photographs of which circulated in cyberspace and sparked hundreds of women's naked protests against Big Oil. Soon men joined in. These naked protests were closely linked to what is possibly the world's first global use of drama against war. By 3 March, 2003 on the eve of the US attack on Iraq, the organizers website had recorded over one thousand performances of Lysistrata – the 411 BC Greek play by Aristophanes in which prostitutes and wives unite to deny warring men sex until they make peace. Remarkably, in less than a year, a virtual strike by women refusing to support men who made life unlivable had swept the world. Corporations and governments, bent on war for oil while destroying the environment and climate, were confronted by a wave of coordinated direct actions by women worldwide. The women affirmed the commons and dramatized the threat to life itself constituted by Big Oil. Most significantly (and apart from cutting oil production), they symbolically and actually withdrew life-supporting personal and domestic services, thus exercising the special power of the unwaged and of women within capitalist relations. This special power, the capacity to stop creating and supporting life on a generational and day-to-day basis, both (1) undermined capital's access to labor power and the profits from its exploitation and (2) gave notice that women and their allies had found the means and global reach to affirm that "there is an alternative" to neoliberal disaster – the alternative of common, universal sovereignty over nature, resources and all dimensions of life.

The pioneering actions of Nigerian women in shutting in Shell and other oil companies' operations escalated into global, coordinated strike-like refusals in a matter of a few weeks. The 15 February, 2003 worldwide demonstration against the US war on Iraq involved from 12 to 50 million people in an historically unprecedented panoply of coordinated opposition to imperial war. Resistance to war, not least by citizens of Iraq and the US, doomed to failure Bush's aggression in war and economic imperialism as the 2003 "collapse at Cancun" relegated the agenda of the World Trade Organization and the Free Trade Area of the Americas to the defensive margins of corporate fantasy, soon to flounder in global financial crisis and capitalist meltdown. We return to the Nigerian shut-downs in the concluding discussion of moratoria, after examining our third instance of successful action to keep the oil under the soil.

Ecuador

A significant move in 2007 by Ecuador took the drive for "no new oil" to a higher level (Baird, et al. 2008). In September 2007, Ecuador's President Rafael Correa[5] announced at the United Nations that Ecuador would not allow production of oil that had been discovered in Yasuni National Park in the Amazon. The oil was to be left in the ground. In exchange the international community was asked to compensate the government with $4.6 billion, the equivalent of $5 per barrel of oil not produced. The government has sovereignty over the oil-rich territories and is using this sovereignty to defend the life-centered economy of virtually-uncontacted indigenous peoples.

In his speech to the United Nations, President Correa noted that Ecuador has worked, "with justice and creativity" to resist global warming. By keeping the oil underground, Ecuador will conserve one of the most bio-diverse areas of the world; but it will also forego hundreds of millions of dollars of investments. While asserting the country's commitment to making "this immense sacrifice," Correa also requested "co-responsibility from the international community and a minimum compensation for the environmental goods that we generate and from which all the planet benefits" (Correa 24 September 2007).

He argued that the proposal "will prevent the emission of around 111 million tons of carbon." Ecuador's opportunity cost "for not exploiting the crude" is at least $10 to $15 per barrel (at September 2007 prices, and about $20-$30 per barrel in 2008). As such, Correa requested that the international community contribute "5 dollars per barrel, to conserve the biodiversity, to protect the indigenous population who lives in the area [in] voluntary isolation and to prevent carbon

---

5   Rafael Correa was elected Ecuador's president in December 2006 and took office in January 2007.

dioxide emissions. The total amount we request is approximately 4.6 billion dollars" (Correa 2007).

The background to Ecuador's proposal lay in a position paper written by activists within OilWatch, an international southern non-governmental organization, based at the time in Quito, Ecuador. The OilWatch paper, presented at Kyoto in 1997, called for carbon credits to permanently keep underground some 920 million barrels of very dirty, heavy oil in the Ishpingo-Tambococha-Tiputini (ITT) homeland in Ecuador's Yasuni National Park (Alier and Temper 2007).

During a ten year interval, as awareness about the climate impacts of oil production rose, the activists' Yasuni-ITT proposal was taken up by the Ecuadorian government. Energy Minister Alberto Acosta lent his support to the project in early 2007. President Correa formalized the moratorium in September 2007. By 2008, Acosta was president of the National Assembly, elected to write a new Ecuadorian constitution. This is significant because the keep-the-oil-underground proposal would be immeasurably strengthened by constitutional provisions, especially if Ecuadorians ensure that their constitution takes precedence over international trade and investment rules.[6]

The Ecuadorian proposal has been met with contradictory responses. Support came from Niger Delta social movements as the call from Nnimmo Bassey reproduced at the beginning of this chapter indicates. Other advocates have pointed out that "this project, if successful, could be copied elsewhere – for instance in the U'Wa territory in Colombia, in the Niger Delta, [and] in some of the worst coal mines in the world" (Alier and Temper 2007).

The BBC reported that the proposal "has been favourably received in several quarters: Germany says it is taking the idea seriously. Norway is to send a delegation to Ecuador in the next few months. The World Bank is consulting with other international organizations. Italy's parliament is about to vote on whether to give official approval to the project."[7] In contrast, the Arab Group's Algerian

---

6   Ecuador's president Correa may well side, ultimately, with the anti-commoners. A confrontation between the president and Conaie (Confederation of Ecuadorian Indigenous Nationalities) emerged in June 2008 (Declas 13 June 2008:11). Indigenous Ecuadorians (a third of the country's 14 million people) demand "a local veto on mining and oil drilling on their land. The current constitution simply requires the authorities to consult the Indians before issuing licenses." President Correa acknowledged that "Conaie can overthrow a government" but threatened to resign rather than "yield to pressure from special interests, whether they are Indians, public sector unions or employers. ... A minority cannot impose its views on the majority. ...The radical left and naive ecologists are turning into our worst enemies."

7   "Paolo Cacciari, one of the Italian MPs in favour, says the motion before parliament already has the support of more than 50 of his colleagues from both left and right. None of them appears worried by the idea of reducing potential global oil supplies in this way. "We've extracted more oil than we were ever meant to," he says. "We have an ecological debt to pay back, and this suggestion by Ecuador is an intelligent solution. It's the responsibility of all of us to look after these reserves'" (Gordon 2007).

representative at the December 2007 Bali United Nations Framework Convention on Climate Change Kyoto II meeting expressed concern about measures to cut oil production, claiming it would negatively impact major oil exporters.[8]

In 2007 Yvonne Yanez of OilWatch argued for giving the highest priority to cutting climate change emissions at the source. In contrast the World Bank is promoting profitable market-centered pseudo-solutions, including "clean" development mechanisms (CDMs), direct foreign investment, official development assistance, technology transfer and public and private loans for technological changes, energy conversions, gas projects and agro-fuels.[9]

Most industry and northern consumers "do not want to accept the uncomfortable reality that the only way of mitigating climate change is through not burning more fossil fuels." The Ecuadorian proposal is presented as the only measurable way of cutting CO_2 emissions and simultaneously avoiding the loss of natural forests. "It is not about looking for the best business offers to save the planet and its people, but rather about taking revolutionary measures" (Yanez 2007:59).

Analysis of Initiatives to Keep Hydrocarbons in the Ground

We have reviewed declaratory and practical initiatives to keep hydrocarbons in the ground as means of averting global climate disaster. In Costa Rica, Nigeria and Ecuador these initiatives have been realized to a greater degree than elsewhere, although all cases are still highly contended. A number of observations can be made regarding the global move towards moratoria on oil, gas and coal.

Moratoria clearly aim to reduce hydrocarbon production and also contribute to reducing the amount of oil available on the market and therefore reducing fossil fuel combustion and consumption. Moratoria may also raise the price of oil, causing further reductions in use. Measures to stop oil production and the necessarily entailed cut in oil consumption are, in effect, production-consumption strikes. The simultaneous, global refusal to produce and refusal to consume was expressed

---

8   This controversy within OPEC was heightened on 18 November 2007 in Riyadh when Ecuadorian President Rafael Correa proposed a new eco-tax on oil exports by OPEC countries to lower demand for oil and thereby cut emissions. The proceeds would go for poverty reduction, including energy-poverty reduction, and alternative energies (geo-thermal, wind, solar). This economic and climate justice proposal would begin with a tax of 3 percent on the price of oil (Alier and Temper 2007).

9   With respect to the "clean development mechanism" (CDM), Vidal (30 May-5 June, 2008:1-2) reported on two 2008 studies that demonstrated the billions of dollars "are being wasted in paying industries in developing countries to reduce climate change emissions," under the United Nations' carbon offsetting programme. The UN's offset fund "is being routinely abused by chemical, wind, gas and hydro companies who are claiming emission reduction credits for projects that should not qualify" with the result that "no genuine pollution cuts are being made...." The studies show that "Judging additionality has turned out to be unknowable and unworkable."

dramatically by the 2002 Nigerian women's shut-down of ChevronTexaco's oil production and export at the same time as consumers boycotted ChevronTexaco's products. These strikes deprive oil companies of their special commodity and its market. Therefore these strikes undermine the power of the most strategically central corporations in the world capitalist system: oil companies, weapons and military contractors and financial institutions ("the weapon-dollar-petro-dollar coalition" analyzed by Nitzan and Bichler in 2002).

Moratoria work by placing a higher value on the preservation of nature and of the very lives and cultures of the inhabitants than on the short term profits accrued from oil sales. In this way, moratoria raise awareness about the negative impact of oil on the immediate environment and on the global climate. In addition, they express a new kind of valuation which places life before profit and celebrates the ecological benefits of moving from a regime of exchange values to one of intrinsic and use values.

The recognition of the actual trans-national or global scope and reach of the actors in the instances analyzed here underlines the inaccuracy of both left and capitalist characterizations of oil and energy protests as initiatives that are *merely local* or at best as initiatives that are circumscribed by parochialism but pieced together by agents with an overarching reach such as the big international NGOs. Our analysis shows that the global character of local struggle in oil is an unavoidable and inherent consequence of the global character of energy capital. It is not spontaneous. It is structured. And this structure is not mechanical; it is dynamic and constituted by social relations of exploitation and their transformation through struggle into social relations of commoning. The concrete moment of the transformation is the moment of negotiation, an on-going process, of new bases of interaction between and among producers and consumers in different parts of the globe. These negotiations center on re-valuing energy, air, all of nature and all that is needed for the maintenance and full flowering of all life.

Let us consider more closely the actors involved in these "value wars" (McMurtry 2002). Production-consumption strikes are premised on the fact that parties refusing to produce oil and declining to burn it are in charge of their resources and capacities. This control or sovereignty has always been the focus of struggle, which in some instances (for example, Costa Rica, Ecuador, Venezuela, Cuba) is reflected through the actors shaping state policy. To the extent that parties to the production-consumption strike have this control, this sovereignty, they can use it to establish new relations with each other as in the case of the Venezuela-Cuba direct oil for doctors deal.

These new relations of direct deals have a very special revolutionary potential in that the *value* of the transaction is decided through negotiation by the parties to the deal rather than by profit-seeking actors gambling in hedge funds in the capitalist market (Abuja Declaration 2006). In the Ecuadorian case, the direct deal is between a section of the Ecuadorian people, through the government; on the one hand, and any parties in the global arena, who agree to compensate or transfer values to Ecuador in response to that country's commitment to suppress emissions underground.

The ongoing discussion in Ecuador about the value of not producing Yasuni oil has generated a long list of benefits to indigenous peoples and to non-indigenous Ecuadorians as well as to citizens of the region and the world. These values embrace the Amazon rainforest, bio-diversity, climate health, eco-tourism (controversial), social services expansion and relief from ecological and "odious" debts. In sum, Ecuadorians value the protection of the commons by blocking pollutants at source and by committing to use compensation to elaborate the life-centered political economy.

The discussion has now begun outside Ecuador about the values to be secured through paying the government to keep the oil in the ground (Baird et al. 2008). Most immediate is the major value of a huge cut in deadly emissions that would otherwise be produced, combined with helping to retain the Amazon rainforest as the functioning "lungs of the world." The crucial point here is that Ecuador is offering to all comers an opportunity to imagine and determine the value each places on Ecuador's "zero exploitation" offer.

What is gained through joint valuation between Ecuador and its supporters, beyond the values mentioned, is a partnership of cooperation, sharing and solidarity. "This," declared Ecuador's President Correa in September 2007, "would be an extraordinary example of worldwide action to reduce the global warming in benefit of the entire planet" (Correa 2007). This partnership places producers and consumers in a cooperative dynamic of mutuality with the potential to underpin expanded collaboration in the support of life. Such expanded collaboration for energy sovereignty supports the Via Campesina goal of food sovereignty and makes more possible the achievement of global people's sovereignty over all natural resources (Demarais 2007).

Ecuador's President Correa has characterized this direct deal as "the recognition of the values of use and service, of the non-market values of a safe environment and the maintenance of planetary diversity." Correa told the United Nations that "the Ecuador proposal seeks to transform the old conceptions of the economy and the concept of value." Climate change, he pointed out, "forces us to a serious reflection on the actual model of development," where, in a borderless world the US emits 23.6 tonnes of CO_2 per capita per year compared to a world average of 3.58 tonnes,[10] thus "establishing with clarity where the major responsibilities reside with respect to affecting the environment and the life of the planet. This situation ... demonstrates that the present model of growth, based on the intensive use of fossil fuel and over consumption, is an untenable model whose benefits reach a privileged minority but enormously harm us all." For Correa the Yasuni oil moratorium produces use values that "inaugurate a new economic logic for the 21st century" (Correa 24 September 2007).

---

10   Monbiot, 4 December 2007. Monbiot's figures are based on global CO_2 production in 2000 and a 2007 world population of 6,635 million.

Also of importance in considering Ecuador's moratorium are the paths not taken. In prioritizing the use values of the commons, Ecuador is rejecting capitalist market "pseudo-solutions" to climate change (carbon tax, cap and trade, cap and auction, clean development mechanism). It is also exposing these "for-profit" diversions for what they are – neo-colonial and ecocidal steps towards the tipping point of climate Armageddon. In contrast to capitalist market carbon approaches, in the Ecuador instance, no land is being bought or sold, no title deeds are transferred and no additional carbon release is being authorized.

The Ecuador initiative stands against the "corporate rule" trajectory of the Washington consensus and the logic of corporate profit taking. The proposal levers a transition from capitalism to global commoning. It deprives both Big Oil and emissions traders of their commodity. By drastically decommodifying in this way, Ecuador strengthens the world's commoning alternatives. It short circuits and blocks efforts to privatize the remaining commons, especially indigenous territories. It is anti-enclosure and pro-commons.

We have suggested that production-consumption strikes are leading to direct deals. In this we see the beginnings (and pre-figuring of) of a transition from a capitalist political economy to a commoning political economy. That is, we see an erosion of the power of capital and the strengthening of a pre-existing (and constantly re-configured) commoning, life-centered or subsistence political economy (Bennholt-Thompsen and Mies 1999; Shiva 2006, January 2007).

It is widely recognized that the many opponents of climate change are linked by the organization of corporations within the energy system. At the same time, opponents also rely on their own unique culturally inherited social forms which they combine with the organization that is the corporate form (Brownhill 2009). We have seen how subordinated actors involved in the capitalist energy system have asserted control over parts of that system and used this control to turn this global organization away from profits and towards commoning.

It is crucial to emphasize the feminist content of the revolutionary transition now underway. It is feminist insofar as it overcomes dispossession by enclosure and hence some of the exploitation of women under capitalism. It is feminist in that protagonists as self-aware life-givers employ "the curse of nakedness" to actually and symbolically announce the withdrawal of life support – a women's strike against agents of death.

The central actors in this challenge to capital are the multitudes of unwaged people, including indigenous people and small farmers. Because the unwaged are intensely engaged with nature in the course of supporting life, they and especially the women amongst them, are crucially and most immediately impacted by "the curse of oil" including climate change.[11] Those who occupy territory under which

---

11 Inuk climate activist Sheila Watts-Cloutier (2005), in her legal brief on climate change and human rights, observed that "As the Inter-American Court of Human Rights has noted, "the close ties of indigenous people with the land must be recognized and understood as the fundamental basis of their cultures, their spiritual life, their integrity, and

oil and gas reserves are located have repeatedly mobilized the global petroleum system within which they are incorporated to halt oil production. This mobilization has escalated in scale. From the 1999 "Gift to Humanity" organized by Niger Delta women in coordination with allies who occupied Shell's head office in London, there has been a great leap by Ecuadorian indigenous people, their allies and government onto the global plane to enlist, as of 2007, everyone in a collectivity to keep oil in situ and build carbon-neutral alternatives. This universalization of coordinated, direct action to keep hydrocarbons in the ground is mirrored in the call to all the world's people and institutions to compensate the non-producers and expand the commons.

This chapter has reviewed global direct actions against climate change, oil and war, undertaken by the unwaged and, in particular by peasant and indigenous women, in "gendered and ethnicized class alliances" (Turner and Brownhill 2006; Brownhill 2009) with men within their own communities and with women and men on a global scale. Three features of these direct actions can be highlighted.

First, unwaged peoples and especially the women among them, are identified as historic actors against global capital. This is significant because the actions of these social forces suggest that the "way forward" towards a post-capitalist, post-climate change and post-oil world is not (only) about workers taking over factories, but instead it is about the much broader conception of commoners taking over the commons.

Second, the mobilizations that these commoners have pursued; especially global, coordinated direct action to stop the production and consumption of oil, are effective challenges to corporate rule and suggest strategies for expanded campaigns.

Third, peasant commoners, like much of the poorest half of the world's population, already live in a largely non-oil age. The subsistence political economies within which many 21st century commoners live provide actually existing low-oil, carbon-balanced alternatives to the capitalist political economy. When commoners (peasants, indigenous peoples, others) say "No!" to capitalist exploitation of oil, they already have a "Yes!" in mind, for they are often acting against oil exploitation in order to defend their subsistence political economies that sustain them, the earth and the earth's climate.

According to Vandana Shiva, village commoning in India has long provided non-oil sources of fuel. "The ecological biodiverse farm is not just a source of food; it is a source of energy. Energy for cooking the food comes from the inedible biomass like cow dung cakes, stalks of millets and pulses, agro-forestry species

---

their economic survival.'" The 2007 People's Protocol on Climate Change recognizes that "there are large parts of humanity who are more dependent [than others] for their survival on their access to and use of natural resources, as well as on the state of the climate and the natural environment. We then stress that the specific needs of farming communities, indigenous peoples, coastal communities, fisherfolk, and other marginalized, poor and rural producers need to be given special attention in all adaptation efforts."

on village wood lots. Managed sustainably, village commons have been a source of decentralized energy for centuries." Further, she states that ecological, organic agriculture reduces emissions both by (a) reducing dependence on fossil fuels, chemical fertilizers and intensive feed, and by (b) absorbing more carbon in the soil. Shiva's studies show an increase of carbon sequestration of up to 200 percent in biodiverse organic systems.[12]

Conclusion

What can be done to facilitate the recognition and emergence of the commons? With respect to recognition, this means, concretely, that we need to understand the production-consumption strikes and initiatives towards direct deals as a pivotal core of the transition to a world of commoners. This "actually existing" movement of commoners is the result of the exploited taking over elements of the organizations of the capitalist core (the petro-dollar-weapon-dollar coalition) and using them to (a) undermine profit, private property and imperial power while at the same time (b) negotiate, reaffirm and construct means for satisfying universal needs.

Backed by their imperial home states, corporations have long asserted sovereignty over natural resources, via imperialism, colonialism, neo-colonialism, neo-liberalism and trade regimes such as NAFTA, EPAs, and WTO trade and investment rules. These assertions are always contended and are sometimes defeated as in the July 2008 success of third world governments in affirming "food sovereignty" and refusing at the Geneva meeting of the WTO to further "open" their societies to food imports. Moratoria and other actions by commoners in defense of the commons (that is the "alternative" global, feminist, ecosocialist society for a post-oil carbon-balanced age) are repressed by the institutional framework of capitalism, notably the hegemonic legal, property and trade regimes; all backed by force. Commoners assert and establish a degree of sovereignty over resources first by blocking capital from using those resources.

Some peoples' struggles for such control over resources have found degrees of support at the level of the state (Cuba, Venezuela, Ecuador, Costa Rica, others).

---

12 According to Shiva (13 December 2007), "When 'ecological and organic' is combined with 'direct and local,' emissions are further reduced by reducing energy use for 'food miles,' packaging and refrigeration of food. And local food systems will reduce the pressure to expand agriculture in the rainforests of Brazil and Indonesia. We could, with a timely transition reduce emissions, increase food security and food quality and improve the resilience of rural communities to deal with the impact of climate change. The transition from the industrial globalised food system being imposed by WTO, the World Bank and Global Agribusinesses to ecological and local food systems is both a mitigation and adaption strategy. It protects the poor and it protects the planet. The post-Kyoto framework must include ecological agriculture as a climate solution."

These states have moved to over-ride corporate bids for sovereignty over natural resources. They have engaged in direct deals and moratoria. In other cases citizens' class-based organizations relate directly to one another across national boundaries, such as in the 1999 and 2002-2003 Nigerian peasant women's actions.

State or national sovereignty over natural resources can be[13] a step in a process of reconfiguring the commons and asserting *peoples'* sovereignty over natural resources on a global scale. This involves the move from *national* to *peoples'* sovereignty.

The 2007 People's Protocol on Climate Change develops this perspective: "We declare that in order to address the climate crisis, the people must have real stewardship, access and control over the natural resources on which they depend rather than TNCs, international financial institutions or even governments which represent the narrow private interests of a global elite and their local collaborators. In so-doing we assert people's sovereignty over natural resources."

Esperanza Martinez of OilWatch argues for the sovereignty of the entire planet: "This [carbon trading] colonization of both political space and environmental policy threatens not just the sovereignty of the ecosystems and cultures of the inhabitants of the global south, but the concept of a shared responsibility for reclaiming the sovereignty of the planet. Sovereignty as a concept and practice, both in terms of the ecosystems and cultures of indigenous people, cannot be turned into a commodity to be sold on the market of political policies or quick-fix carbon-shifting "solutions." Sovereignty is at the root of resistance to the commodification of land and life" (Martinez 2007).

An international mobilization for popular sovereignty will congregate at a congress parallel to the December 2009 United Nations (post-Kyoto) climate change meeting in Copenhagen. The organizers anticipate more than a million people ratifying and planning the implementation of a People's Protocol on Climate Change focused on global action to keep fossil fuels in the ground. This congress holds the promise of enshrining in an institutional context the demands and interests of "third world" women whose central concerns, as expressed in the actions analyzed above, prioritize planetary survival and the elaboration of a life-centered political economy of commoning.

---

13   In June 2008 James Petras warned against the claim of rightist, pro-imperial separatism: "...because the class, race and national content of that claim is antithetical to an even more important principle – popular sovereignty based on the democratic principles of majority rule and equal access to public wealth.... In Ecuador, the Mayor of Guayaquil, backed by the right wing mass media and the discredited traditional political parties have proposed "autonomy" from the central government of President Rafael Correa. ... The lessons of failed governance in Bolivia stand as a grim reminder to Chavez in Venezuela and Correa in Ecuador: Unless they act with full force of the constitution to crush the embryonic separatist movements before they gain a power base, they will also face the break-up of their countries. ..."

References

Abuja Declaration (2006), Resolution of Friends of the Earth International Conference on Climate Change, Abuja, Nigeria, 28-29 September, 2006, <http://www.eraction.org/index.php?option=com_content&task=view&id=14&Itemid=12>, accessed 26 June 2008.

ADELA (2002), (Accion de Lucha Antipetrolera - Action of Anti-Petroleum Struggle) <http://www.cosmovisiones.com/adela2002/somos.html>, accessed 26 June 2008.

Alier, J. M. and Temper L. (2007), "Oil Politics from the South," in Boedt, Piet and Esperanza Martinez, *Keep Oil Underground: The Only Way to Fight Climate Change*, OilWatch, presented at the UNFCCC COP13, Bali, December 2007, pp. 64-65.

Anonymous (1999), "Office Politics," *Weekly Schnews*, Issue 197, Friday 15 January 1999, <http://Schnews.org.uk/archive/news197.htm>, accessed 26 June 2008.

Anonymous (2007), "Costa Rica: Big plans, but Cafta-DR Still Faces Opposition," *Latin American Carribean and Central American Review*, 13 December 2007 <http://global.factiva.com.Cerberus.lib.uoguelph.ca/ha/default.aspx>, accessed 26 June 2008.

Baird, V. et al. (2008), "Viva Yasuni!," *New Internationalist*, Issue 413, July 2008, pp. 4-20.

Bennholt-Thompsen, V. and Mies M. (1999), *The Subsistence Perspective: Beyond the Globalised Economy* (London: Zed).

Bichler, S. and Nitzan J. (2002), *The Global Political Economy of Israel* (London: Pluto).

Brownhill, L. (2009), *Land, Food, Freedom: Struggles for the Gendered Commons in Kenya, 1870-2010* (Trenton, New Jersey: Africa World Press).

Citi (2008), "Industry Focus," 4 February 2008, Citigroup Global Markets Equity Research, <http://peakoil.solarhorizons.com/reports/Citi-Oil-Report.pdf>, accessed 26 June 2008.

Correa, R. (2007), "Speech of the President of the Republic of Ecuador," High Level Dialogue on Climate Change of the 62 Period of Sessions of the General Assembly of the United Nations, New York, 24 September 2007.

Declas, M. (2008), "Ecuador's Indians Defy Powerful President," *The Guardian Weekly* (London) 13 June 2008, p.11.

Demarais, A. (2007), *La Via Campesina: Globalization and the Power of Peasants* (London: Pluto Press; Halifax: Fernwood).

Drillbits and Tailings (1999), "Vital Statistics: A Sampling of Shell's Activity in Nigeria Over the Last Four Years," *Drillbits & Tailings*, Volume 4, Number 18, November 9, 1999, <http://www.moles.org/ProjectUnderground/drillbits/4_18/vs.html>, accessed 22 Sept 2006.

Gordon, D. (2008), "Ecuador seeks oil 'compensation,'" *BBC News*, 21 September 2007, <http://news.bbc.co.uk/go/pr/fr/-/2/hi/americas/7000345.stm>, accessed 26 June 2008.

Hopkins, K. (2008), "UK Joins Global Watchdogs in Oil Price Probe," *The Guardian Weekly*, June 6, 2008, p. 41.

ICC (2005), Inuit Circumpolar Conference Petition to the Inter American Commission on Human Rights Seeking Relief from Violations Resulting from Global Warming Caused by Acts and Omissions of the United States," December 7, 2005. <http://www/inuitcircumpolar.com/index.php?ID=316&Lang=En>, accessed 26 June 2008.

IOWG (2003), International Oil Working Group, Interview #2 with Nigerian source, 2 August 2003.

Khosrave, C. A. (2007), "A Really Inconvenient Truth – A Critical Essay on Al Gore's An Inconvenient Truth with Joel Kovel" <www.areallyinconvenienttruth. com>.

Klein, N. (2008), "Guns Beat Green: The Market Has Spoken," 29 November 2007, <http://www.naomiklein.org/articles/2007/11/guns-beat-green-market-has-spoken>, accessed 26 June 2008.

Linebaugh, P. (2008), *The Magna Carta Manifesto: Liberties and Commons for All* (Los Angeles: University of California Press).

Martinez, E. (2007), "Esperanza Martinez on Yasuni and the ITT proposal" Retrieved 6 February 2008, from <http://colonos.wordpress.com/2007/11/22/ esperanza-martinez-on-yasuni-and-the-itt-proposal/>.

McMurtry, J. (1999), *Unequal Freedoms : The Global Market as an Ethical System* (Toronto: Garamond Press, 1998 and Westport, Conn: Kumarian).

McMurtry, J. (2002), *Value Wars: The Global Market Versus the Life Economy* (London: Pluto).

Monbiot, G. (2007), "What Is Progress?" *The Guardian*, 4 December 2007, <http://www.monbiot.com/archives/2007/12/04/what-is-progress/>, accessed 26 June 2008.

—— (2008), "Apart from Used Chip Fat, There is no Such Thing as a Sustainable Biofuel," *The Guardian*, 12 February 2008, <http://www.guardian.co.uk/ commentisfree/2008/feb/12/biofuels.energy>, accessed 26 June 2008.

Oil Change International (2007), *Aiding Oil, Harming the Climate: A Database of Public Funds for Fossil Fuels*, Oil Change International, December 2007, <http://oilaid.priceofoil.org/>, accessed 26 June 2008.

Osouka, Asume, Esperanza Martnez and Leila Salazar (2002) "Boycott Chevron-Texaco," *OilWatch*, 26 September 2002, <www.corpwatch.org>, accessed 26 June 2008.

Petras, J. (2008), "Separatism and Empire Building in the 21st Century," *Global Research*, 8 June 2008, <http://globalresearch.ca/index.php?context=va&aid= 9246>, accessed 26 June 2008.

Reuters (2008), "Nigeria's oil saboteurs agree to ceasefire," *Globe and Mail* (Toronto), 23 June 2008, p. A13.

Sample, I. (2008), "Global meltdown: scientists isolate areas most at risk of climate change," *Guardian Weekly*, 5 February 2008, p. 1,<http://www.guardian.co.uk/environment/2008/feb/05/climatechange/print>, accessed 26 June 2008.

Shiva, V. (2006), Interview with Terisa Turner, New Delhi, India, 15 December 2006, recorded by Terisa Turner, transcribed by Terran Giacomini.

―― (2007), "What Kind of Post-Oil Civilization Can We Build?" presentation on the Oil Watch Panel, World Social Forum, Nairobi, Kenya, 23 January 2007, recorded by Terisa Turner, transcribed by Terran Giacomini..

―― (2007), "Food, Forests and Fuel : From False to Real Solutions for the Climate Change," *Z-Net*, 13 December, 2007, <http://www.zmag.org/sustainers/content/2007-12/13shiva.cfm>, accessed 26 June 2008.

Turner, T.E. (1994), "Rastafari and the New Society: Caribbean and East African Feminist Roots of A Popular Movement to Reclaim the Earthly Commons," in Terisa E. Turner (ed.), *Arise Ye Mighty People: Gender, Class and Race in Popular Struggles* (Trenton, New Jersey: Africa World Press).

Turner, T.E. and Oshare M.O. (1994), "Women's Uprisings Against the Nigerian Oil Industry in the 1980s," in Terisa E. Turner (ed.), *Arise Ye Mighty People: Gender, Class and Race in Popular Struggles* (Trenton, New Jersey: Africa World Press).

Turner, T.E. and Brownhill L. (2001), "Introduction: Gender, Feminism and the Civil Commons: Women and the Anti-Corporate, Anti-War Movement for Globalization from Below," Gender, Feminism and the Civil Commons, *Canadian Journal of Development Studies*, Special Issue XXII, 2001, pp. 805-818.

―― (2004), "'Why Women are at War with Chevron:' Nigerian Subsistence Struggles Against the International Oil Industry," *Journal of Asian and African Studies*, Special Issue on Africa and Globalization, Vol. 39, No. 1-2, March 2004, pp. 63-93.

―― (2006), "Ecofeminism as Gendered, Ethnicized Class Struggle: A Rejoinder to Stuart Rosewarne," *Capitalism Nature Socialism*, Vol. 17, No. 4, December 2006, pp. 87-95.

―― (2007), "Climate Justice and Nigerian Women's Gift to Humanity," *Women and Environments International*, Special Double Issue on Women and Global Climate Change, No. 74/75, Spring 2007, pp. 47-48.

Vidal, J. (2008), "Billions Wasted on UN Climate Programme," *The Guardian Weekly*, 30 May – June 5, 2008, pp. 1-2.

Wainwright, M. (2008), "Coal Train Ambushed," *The Guardian Weekly*, June 20-26, 2008, p. 17.

Watts-Cloutier, S. (2008), "Global Warming and Climate Change," EarthJustice and Centre for International Environmental Law, 2005, <http://earthjustice.org/library/references/Background-for-IAHRC.pdf>, accessed 26 June 2008.

Wiwa, O. interview with Terisa Turner, Toronto, 23 September 2006.

Yanez, Y. (2007), "Mitigating Emissions or Mitigating Impacts," in Boedt, Piet and Esperanza Martinez, *Keep Oil Underground: The Only Way to Fight Climate*

Change, OilWatch, presented at the UNFCCC COP13, Bali, December 2007, pp. 58-59.

Zahller, T. (2008), "International Day of Solidarity to say NO to the Iraq Oil Law," 12 February 2008, <http://priceofoil.org/2008/02/12/international-day-of-solidarity-to-say-no-to-the-iraq-oil-law/>, accessed 26 June 2008.

Chapter 9

Neo-liberalism in Women in Development Discourse

Using ICTs for Gender and Development in Africa: The Case of UNIFEM

Christobel Asiedu

If we accept that the access and use of ICTs is a powerful driving force towards economic growth and poverty alleviation then it must be imperative that women gain equal opportunities to access the technologies and exploit them for their own economic empowerment.[1]

Introduction

As indicated in the above statement, technology is often seen as the panacea to the problems of development. The statement also links economic empowerment with Information Communication Technologies (ICTs). Development organizations have proclaimed how ICTs are supposed to transform societies and bring about social justice and gender equity, especially in the field of women's rights (Tandon 1999). As a result, the number of development programs designed to address the information technology gap between rich and poor countries (also known as the digital divide) has grown tremendously. Third world women especially are a strong focus of these programs because it is believed that ICTs can aid them to leapfrog over other development stages missed (Knight 1995). Since Africa lags behind the other continents in terms of access to ICTs, (especially Internet users as shown by Table 9.1), attempts have been made to assist African countries, especially women, to empower them technologically. Given that major development organizations such as the United Nations and women's Non-governmental Organizations (NGOs) have devoted resources into using ICTs for gender and development in Africa, it is important to examine how the issues and problems are constructed to determine the effectiveness of the solutions and alternative strategies to address existing inequalities.

As pointed out previously, there have been arguments made about the importance of ICT to the development of Africa. However, the counter arguments point to

---

1   UNIFEM's Vision for ICT in Africa. Speech by Grace Okonji, UNIFEM African Program Specialist at the WSIS preparatory meeting in 2002 at Accra, Ghana.

Table 9.1 Measures of poverty and the availability of infrastructure averaged 2000-2006 for selected regions

Description of Variable	East Asia and Pacific	Europe and Central Asia	Latin America and Caribbean	Sub-Saharan Africa	South Asia	Middle East and North Africa
Personal computers (per 1,000 people)	27	74	68	12	7	35
Mobile phone subscribers (per 1,000 people)	168	302	243	55	27	95
Internet users (per 1,000 people)	52	96	91	14	21	40
Telephone mainlines (per 1,000 people)	161	249	167	15	34	122
Telephone faults (per 100 mainlines)	NA	21	7	55	24	25
GDP per capita (constant 2000 US$)	1,134	2,227	3,860	536	496	1,681
Life expectancy at birth, total (years)	70	69	72	46	63	69
Mortality rate, under-5 (per 1,000)	39	36	34	167	92	57
Literacy rate, adult total (% of people ages 15 and above)	91	97	90	61	58	71

Source: 2007 World Development Indicators CD-Rom, published by the World Bank.

other more pressing issues such as low life expectancy, high mortality and low GDP per capita rates (as shown in Table 9.1) that needs to be addressed to improve the development status of individual countries in sub-Saharan Africa. Also, other issues such as low literacy rate, and infrastructural problems, especially in rural areas where about 67 percent of the population in Africa reside, pose challenges to the use of ICT for development.

This chapter gives an account of the conceptualization of gender and ICTs by examining the activities of the United Nations Development Fund for Women (UNIFEM) in Africa. According to Escobar (1995b) and Crush (1995), as a discourse, development articulates knowledge and power through the construction of social problems and institutional interventions. Institutional discourse represents the interpretations of development institutions working in their global context, rather than the interpretations of individual practitioners. Escobar notes that through institutional practices, the nature of social problems, social change, and beneficiaries are categorized and enacted in development programs. Development texts, such as reports, evaluations, and speeches, constitute assembled knowledge of the development industry (Crush 1995). Staudt (1990) adds that policies and programs of central development agencies constitute official program intentions, which may not correspond with actual practice, but reflect institutional discourse. Consequently, development discourse creates knowledge about women, which is then processed into institutional justifications and intervention strategies. Organizations not only select the issues to be addressed through mediated campaigns, but also define the problem they hope to resolve through their interpretation and characterization of the issue. The ICT discourse of UNIFEM mirrors the Women-in-Development (WID) framework by privileging the importance of the individual in social change, the role of experts as well as the importance of economic growth.

Although the rhetoric of ICTs by UNIFEM addresses the use of ICTs for economic, political and social empowerment, the actual practices of the organization, reflected in projects and programs, mirrors a WID framework. It shows an ICT discourse centered on economic empowerment and private partnerships. Using ICTs for economic empowerment include activities such as giving women access to local and international markets for women producers and traders and obtaining information on prices. Positioning ICT interventions within the private sector accentuates this tendency to frame the programs within economic parameters. Like the WID approach, the ICT discourse by UNIFEM does not appear to question but rather to expand upon an economic emphasis on development by illuminating women's contributions and potential for economic empowerment. ICTs are touted to offer new opportunities for women to be employed in innovative and non-traditional sectors such as e-commerce and Internet services. However, there is no mention of how employment in the ICT industry has exploited and rendered women in some cases as a source of cheap labor.

The focus on economic empowerment in the ICT discourse frames social change as a set of economic conditions and choices realized at the individual level. This reflects a neoliberal discourse that emphasizes self-reliance and entrepreneurship. Focusing on individuals draws attention away from critical structural influences. Wilkins criticizes WID projects as follows:

> Few projects...attempt to promote social change as a gradual, macro level process. Instead, the dominant discourse targets women as individuals who need to change their actions to achieve development goals... (1999, 63).

The issue of private and corporate interests in ICT projects is linked to the economic empowerment of ICTs. According to Marcelle (2002),[2] ICT policy is frequently driven by the politics of the ICT sector, often impelled by commercial interests. Not surprisingly, multinational firms are not very interested in the social analysis of how products will impact people, nor in distributive goals and objectives to address gender and other social inequalities. In the case of ICTs, local communities are not given the opportunity to appropriate ICTs to fit their needs, but rather the interests and agenda of external groups are fulfilled. UNIFEM's adoption of the Results-based Management (RBM) approach (explained in detail later) which attracts donors and sponsors, is an example of the influence of corporate interests.

Lastly the ICT discourse of UNIFEM creates a top-down approach to development. The focus on women entrepreneurs in mostly urban areas and middle-class and the educated excludes rural and poor women who form the majority of the population in Africa. Isserles (2002) documents in a study examples of how UNIFEM projects that were set to integrate women into certain positions of power said little about who these women were and how they were represented. This mimics the WID discourse that treats third world women as a coherent group and renders class inequalities invisible.

As stated by Main:[3]

> It is difficult...to see how market-driven Internet development can go beyond the small groups that constitute the professional classes. Do we need to take care that the Internet revolution does not create a knowledge caste system? Such a system could further widen the gap between the well-educated elite and the poorly educated masses..." (2001, 83-97).

Since the input and ideas of the rural and illiterate women are missing in the discourse, the knowledge created by the latter is overlooked. This approach reflects the WID discourse of privileging expert knowledge.

---

2   Marcelle, G. (2002), 'Gender Equality & ICT Policy,' Presentation at the World Bank Digital Divide Seminar Series, Washington, D.C Available at: <http://www.worldbank.org/gender/digitaldivide/workdbankpresentation.ppt> accessed 11 March 2007.

3   *Third World Quarterly*, 22:1, 83-97.

ICTs and Economic Empowerment

Although the definition of empowerment in the ICT for development literature remains undefined, the focus is almost always on economic empowerment, which assumes that power comes automatically through economic strength (Everts 1998; Sweetman 1998). UNIFEM's rationale for the focus on economic empowerment is that women represent the main economic force in most developing countries. Women produce 60-80 percent of food and comprise 70 percent of entrepreneurs in the informal sector of developing countries (Snyder 1995). Recent figures show that more than three quarters of women are agricultural producers, and 55-65 percent of informal sector business owners and operators are women.[4] ICTs play an important role in the economic empowerment of women who find themselves isolated in their access to knowledge.[5]

UNIFEM also states the following, as the rationale for economic empowerment:

> In a world economy undergoing major transformations as a result of the technological revolution, having the capacity to take advantage of the opportunities generated by Information and Communication Technologies (ICTs) is particularly critical in order for businesses to remain competitive. Women must be positioned to take advantage of these opportunities given the explosive growth in women's entrepreneurship around the world in the past twenty years.[6]

The argument then is that ICTs have the potential to assist poor women by providing information and training on technologies to improve their productivity and their quality of life. Moreover, ICTs could offer new opportunities for women to be employed in innovative and non-traditional sectors.[7]

Also, excerpts from a speech by the Executive Director of UNIFEM at a WSIS panel note the following:

> UNIFEM is committed to ensuring that women, particularly poor women are not excluded from the benefits of ICTs...those who remain excluded from the digital revolution will also be excluded from an increasingly globalized and IT-based job, trade and production market, thereby missing out on many possibilities to lift themselves out of poverty, enhance their economic security and contribute to

---

4   Address by UNIFEM Chief to Africa, Laketch Dirasse at the World Bank Gender and Digital Divide Seminar Series, Washington, D.C.: 21 May, 2002.

5   Interview with UNIFEM Programme Officer to Africa on ICTs, June 2005.

6   Fact Sheet on "Women into the New Network for Entrepreneurial Reinforcement" prepared for WSIS, Geneva 2003 and Tunis 2005.

7   "Bridging the Gender Digital Divide in Africa through Strategic Partnerships" prepared for the WSIS, Geneva 2003 and Tunis 2005.

the overall development of their communities, regions and countries. ICTs have the potential to help women increase their productivity and efficiency, building of their existing income-generating activities and enabling them access to new employment and entrepreneurship opportunities in the information economy. Thus, ICTs offer not only email, e-commerce and e-jobs but 'E-quality.'[8]

The topic for the WSIS panel was on an action plan for an equitable information society. The paragraph above reflects a clear link between economic empowerment and ICTs.

Again, UNIFEM states the benefits of ICTs as follows:

The new information and communication technologies (ICTs) have great potential to benefit women worldwide. As a vast source of information, ICTs constitute a powerful learning tool; they provide access to training and market information that can help women's businesses succeed...[9]

UNIFEM has been supporting technology-related programs and projects for the past twenty years, starting with labor-saving technologies in Africa. These efforts were to develop appropriate technologies to reduce the drudgery of domestic work and for income generation in villages and rural areas. Although they were critical to addressing women's economic empowerment, UNIFEM's strategy changed over the years from small-scale village-based activities to regulatory and policy frameworks that determined the relevance of technology to poverty eradication efforts.[10] Closely linked with the focus on economic empowerment is the Results-Based Management style used by UNIFEM to address gender issues.

Results-based Management Approach

The Results-based Management (RBM) approach focuses on results and requires monitoring and self-assessment of progress towards results and reporting on performance.[11] The RBM approach has been used by many UN agencies as a way

---

    8   Speech given by Noeleen Heyzer, Executive Director of UNIFEM at the WSIS Gender Caucus high level panel "Towards an Action Plan for an Equitable Information Society" December, 2003.

    9   Fact Sheet on "Women and Information Communication Technologies."

    10   "Technology and the Dynamics of Gender: Insights from UNIFEM's experience" by Joanne Sandler, UNIFEM at the World Bank Infrastructure Forum, May 2001. Available at: <http://www.unifem.org/news_events/story_detail.php?StoryID=199> accessed 5 April 2007.

    11   Frequently asked questions on a human rights-based approach to development cooperation report by the UNHCR, New York and Geneva, 2006. Available at: <http://www.ohchr.org/english/about/publications/docs/FAQ_en.pdf> accessed May 2006.

to demonstrate or account for their performance and use of funds. According to Isserles (2002), UNIFEM shifted to a Results-based Management Approach in 1998 to attract donors. The attractiveness of foreign donors might explain the rationale for its use especially in majority of ICT projects where UNIFEM has partnerships with private corporations. This approach has an underlying economic model and measures outcomes of projects and programs in quantitative and economic terms by focusing on data and indicators. In terms of ICTs therefore, UNIFEM is focused on improving entrepreneurial skills of women's participation in economic activities. Quantitative measures of ICTs concentrate on the number of women with access to ICTs without indicating which group of women are targeted and who is marginalized. For example the Millennium Development Goals (MDGs) measure ICT progress in countries by the number of who have access to telephones, Internet and cell phones without addressing how meaningful these technologies are in the lives of the people using it. With RBM, the expected results are identified from the outset. The target oriented agendas (found in the results-based approach) tends to privilege the institutions' goals over participants' experiences and goals (Riano 1994). However, the participatory approach may lead to changes in planned results during the programming process. If a development program is truly participatory and locally owned, this will likely necessitate changes in planned results during the programming process. The Results-based Management Approach in the ICT discourse therefore makes it difficult for local and grassroots organizations and women to develop a strategy of using ICTs to creatively design programs.

UNIFEM's activities on ICTs have in large part been influenced by the Millennium Development Goals (MDGs), which serves as the blue print of the development activities of the United Nations. The MDGs which also set targets and quantitative measures is a further reflection of evaluating progress by numbers. It created the link between ICTs and the achievements of all the targets in the MDGs. The influence of MDGs on the work of UNIFEM is somewhat problematic because of the focus on quantitative measures. The World Summit on the Information Society (WSIS) and the MDGs both highlighted the importance of aligning ICT policies with national poverty reduction strategies. Although the Platform for Action did not specifically define what empowerment meant, sections on "Women and Poverty" and "Women and Economy" linked information technologies to economic empowerment of women. The strategic objective (F.4) stated that information communication technologies could be used to strengthen women's economic capacity and commercial networks.

The ICT activities of UNIFEM are also influenced by the Multi-Year Funding Framework (MYFF) which provides strategic policy and management direction for the organization. At an Executive Board Meeting of UNDP and UNFPA in January 2004, the Executive Director of UNIFEM, Noeleen Heyzer, noted that in the MYFF for 2004-2007 UNIFEM has strengthened its capacity to program from a results-based perspective and had developed straightforward ways of tracking outputs, outcomes and processes. The Strategy and Business Plan, which is part of the MYFF has also influenced the focus and substance of UNIFEM programming on economic empowerment.[12] The 2000-2003 Strategy Plan included the following: increasing options and opportunities for women especially those living in poverty; strengthening the United Nations system capacity to support women's empowerment; strengthening UNIFEM effectiveness through strategic partnerships; lastly, ensuring that UNIFEM personnel, financial and program management systems support the goals and programs of the organization.[13] The plan was formulated as governments worldwide were preparing for the five-year review of the Beijing Platform for Action. The Strategy and Business Plan for 2000-2003 also argued for the importance of ICTs to increase options and opportunities for women's economic and political empowerment. Other materials showing the link between economic empowerment and ICTs are reflected in annual reports, biennial reports and speeches of representatives of the organization.

UNIFEM's annual reports give a snapshot of the organization's activities throughout the year as well as their initiatives and interventions.[14] In the 2002-2003 Annual Report the theme was "Working for women's empowerment and gender equality." The Fund devoted about 2.3 million dollars to economic and security rights initiatives in Africa. There were three projects under economic and security rights. First, throughout Africa, there was a project on "African Women's Economic Security Rights" aimed at promoting women's access to technology, finance and markets through training, setting up networking structures and advocating to shape macro-level policies and globalization instruments. Another project in Ghana and Nigeria called "Energy for sustainable women's livelihoods" aimed at increasing women farmers' income-generating opportunities through the introduction of better technologies and by linking women producers to external markets. The third project in Somalia, "Integrated approach to actualize women's human rights and economic security," targeted at strengthening the capacity of women and their organizations by establishing multi-purpose empowerment centers to increase access of poor women producers to information and appropriate technology.

In the 2003-2004 Annual report, UNIFEM devoted about $894, 294 on an ICT initiative titled "Bridging the gender digital divide in Africa through strategic partnerships." The project aimed at linking with the private sector to enhance women's ability to access and influence ICT policies. There were two components linked to the program. The first was a pilot initiative to build the capacity of women's organizations in the use of ICT and to influence ICT policy formulation in Rwanda. The second component was a multi-stakeholder network, to integrate

---

12   "Progress, gaps and lessons learned from the Strategy and Business Plan, 200-2003," January 2004 (DP/2004/CRP.3).

13   The Strategy and Business Plan identified UNIFEM core partners as governments, civil society organizations (especially women's organizations and networks), and United Nations system organizations.

14   It provides details on new UNIFEM initiatives approved in a particular year, and does not represent the entire portfolio of ongoing programs.

gender equality perspectives into the process of the WSIS. The 2004-2005 Annual report was divided into regions. For Africa, the focus was on opening political spaces in Sudan and fighting HIV/AIDS. All the four new initiatives that year were geared toward HIV/AIDS and human rights. UNIFEM developed four new web portals on AIDS and human rights in collaboration with its partners. The portals provided a resource base on areas of priority concern for women.

UNIFEM's biennial report published in 2005,[15] also illustrates further UNIFEM's focus on economic empowerment of women, especially in Africa. The report illustrated the organization's support for linking women producers to local marketplaces and international trade fairs for product promotion and marketing and macroeconomic policies. It also reported on UNIFEM's support for the inclusion of women in policy making nationally and globally through e-working group sessions with NGOs and activists. In the case of economic and security rights, the three sub-goals guiding UNIFEM's work were building understanding of the impact of economic globalization on women; incorporating gender perspectives in economic policy-making; and linking low-income women entrepreneurs, producers and informal sector workers to markets.

Speeches and Statements

The Executive Director of UNIFEM,[16] argues that the organization's overall approach to gender and ICTs is guided by the four Cs. They are: Content, Connection, Capability and Control. Content deals not only with access to language but with the substance of language, and identifies the lack of indigenous content that is relevant to rural women. Connection has to do with the physical access to ICTs. Capability is about the design of computer software and the need to educate women to design ICTs and to integrate gender dimensions into its design. Lastly, Control is the ability to have a voice in ICT development, deployment and regulation. This issue is addressed primarily by organizing electronic workshops and discussions with gender advocates and NGOs particularly in developing countries to influence ICT policies nationally, regionally and also globally. The four Cs that highlight the use of ICTs for the economic, social and political empowerment of women are reiterated by UNIFEM personnel in speeches, reports and workshops on gender and ICTs.

---

15   Chen et al. (eds) (2005), "Women, Work and Poverty" in *Progress of the World's Women*, New York: UNIFEM. Also available at: <http://www.unifem.org/resources/item_detail.php?ProductID=48> accessed August 2006.

16   Noeleen Heyzer, Executive Director of UNIFEM's speech at the special session of the General Assembly, "WomenAction 2000: Equality, Peace and Development for the 21st Century." Available at: <http://www.unifem.org/news_events/story_detail.php?StoryID=186> accessed August 2006.

The Deputy Director of Programs at UNIFEM identified further, two overarching principles that shape UNIFEM's work on addressing feminized poverty using ICTs as follows:

> Principle #1: Technology can play an important role in increasing women's income-earning potential, but other factors-such as land rights, market linkages, and collective approaches to negotiating for better terms-have a far greater strategic influence on creating and sustaining options and opportunities for women. Principle #2: Women and gender considerations must shape the regulatory environments that surround the design, introduction and deployment of technologies.[17]

Nevertheless, in Africa, the focus seems to be on economic empowerment rather than on innovative ways of utilizing ICTs for community participation or on making women active decision-makers in utilizing ICTs for development. The issue of access to economic empowerment, however, features highly not only in the speeches and reports of the organization, but also in the individual ICT projects in Africa.

Snyder (1995) in an assessment and history of UNIFEM notes that the organization's mandate is to give special attention to rural and poor urban women, and to bring about "grassroots economic empowerment." Nevertheless, in terms of ICTs, the attention has shifted from rural women to women in urban areas. This shift might have to do with the fact that UNIFEM is focused on access to ICTs as the major ICT challenge facing women. Rural women are defined as obstacles to ICT access because of illiteracy and poverty. Nevertheless rural and illiterate women have a long history of their role in traditional communication techniques such as drama, songs and dance. Also rural women's active engagement with old technologies such as radio and television are ignored in this discourse. They are treated as a blank slate with no knowledge of the importance of communication for development. Therefore there are no creative projects to ensure that rural women do not only participate in utilizing ICTs, but also gain control over them (this is discussed further in the next chapter). Although speeches, statements and reports of UNIFEM have outlined the need to address not only access to ICTs but also issues such as indigenous content and the decision-making role of rural women in ICTs, UNIFEM projects on the ground in Africa do not match this discourse. They rather focus on utilizing ICTs for economic empowerment, and target women and NGOs in urban areas. Some of the projects reflecting an economic bias as well as a focus on urban literate women include the DDI, and WINNER projects.

---

17 "Technology and the Dynamics of Gender: Insights from UNIFEM's Experience" lecture by Joanne Sandler, UNIFEM at the World Bank Infrastructure Forum, May 2001. Available at: <http://www.unifem.org/news_events/story_detail.php?StoryID=199> accessed July 2006.

The Digital Diaspora Initiative (DDI)

One of the major projects undertaken by UNIFEM in Africa is the Digital Diaspora Initiative (DDI). According to the Executive Director of UNIFEM, the Digital Diaspora initiative "offers not only e-mail, e-commerce, and e-jobs, but E-quality."[18] The initiative seeks to undertake projects to empower women economically through capacity building in the use of ICTs, identifying business opportunities, creating business partnerships and providing access to finance for poverty alleviation. The main objective is to build the capacity of selected African women's organizations and business associations to provide ICT access and training to enhance their economic activities. This will occur largely through technology transfer program utilizing African Diaspora experts in the area of information technology and business management.

In January 2002 in New York, UNIFEM launched the DDI to build strategic partnerships between African information technology entrepreneurs in the Diaspora and women's organizations and business associations in Africa. The DDI was re-launched in Africa in May 2003, during a Regional meeting hosted by the Government of Uganda and organized by UNIFEM with UNDP, and UN ICT Task Force. UNIFEM devoted about $894,294 to the DDI initiative (Annual Report, 2003-2004). The underlying message of this project is that ICTs can become powerful tools for economic empowerment, for women in Africa. The three main objectives are as follows: first, establishment of business linkages between African entrepreneurs in the Diaspora and women entrepreneurs based in Africa through networking activities, pilot projects and partnerships with the private sector and private foundations; second, cooperation in capacity-building initiatives at the country level through technology transfer programs, information technology management training and job-placement activities; third, the creation of an enabling ICT environment for African women that addresses policy and regulatory mechanisms as well as infrastructure issues. The overall objective of the DDI was to facilitate the creation of a significant number of jobs for poor women through exploiting business opportunities presented by ICTs. This will ensure according to the interviews "that women are active participants in the information technology revolution, as opposed to being passive victims."[19]

In June 2003, the implementation of the first pilot project of the DDI started in Rwanda. The project linked Rwandan women entrepreneurs with ICT trainers and ICT entrepreneurs from the African Diaspora, and built a national advocacy group on gender and ICT issues. As of January 2005, UNIFEM undertook research to explore the possibility of establishing a Venture Capital Fund to support entrepreneurship activities of Rwandan women. The next steps include the expansion of the pilot to eight countries, capacity building at local levels, and the

---

18   UNIFEM website: <http://www.unifem.org>.
19   Interview with UNIFEM program specialist. June 2004.

continuation of information technology transfer and linkages with multipurpose community telecenters.

Although the DDI does not state categorically the group of women entrepreneurs targeted, the nature of the project implies that literate women from urban areas are those that benefit from this program. Although the aim of the DDI is to assist poor women to exploit business opportunities, the process itself of linking women entrepreneurs to those in the Diaspora mainly through the Internet exclude women in rural areas who by default do not have access to these technologies.

The WINNER Program

With UNIFEM support, the Development Network Association International (DEVNET)[20] established the Women into the New Network for Entrepreneurial Reinforcement (WINNER), a global program that seeks to strengthen the practical and technical skills of women entrepreneurs through basic training on the Internet, e-commerce, international trade, business management and gender issues. Over 1,500 women have already received WINNER training in countries like Ecuador, Albania, Romania, Nepal, Philippines, China, Bangladesh and Zimbabwe. The underlying rationale for UNIFEM's activities in this project is to link women producers and traders directly to markets at national, regional and global levels, allowing them to restructure their economic activities and bypass middlemen and male-dominated and exploitative market structures.

It is estimated that between one quarter and one third of the world's businesses are owned and operated by women (Zabludovsky 1998). However, despite the growing number of women entrepreneurs worldwide, women in developing countries, particularly small business owners, continue to face countless difficulties when creating, consolidating and expanding their businesses. One such challenge is limited access to ICTs in developing regions. While North America and Europe accounted for almost eighty percent of Internet users in 1999, Africa, with thirteen percent of the world's population, had less than one percent of total Internet users worldwide. Recognizing the importance of ICTs for business development and their potential to empower women by building the capacity of women entrepreneurs, the WINNER project was launched by DEVNET and UNIFEM.

The second phase of the program was expanded to women in Africa including Zimbabwe. It focused on providing training to participants in the application of ICT instruments to promote better business operation and access to local, regional and international markets. Participants received training in e-commerce, international trade and entrepreneurial management and were provided an opportunity to gain a global presence through showcasing their products on an Electronic Market Space

---

20   DEVNET is an international NGO that provides business information and management assistance services to enhance the competitiveness of micro size enterprises worldwide.

(EMS), thus gaining access to a global market. The beneficiaries of this program were women entrepreneurs with micro and small enterprises, and intermediary women's organizations in developing countries that support women entrepreneurs. The second phase intended to build women's capacity in the area of ICTs and business management in the micro enterprise sector, particularly in terms of e-commerce capabilities with a view to improve their business operations and expand their opportunities in the context of globalization. This objective falls in line with UNIFEM's Strategy and Business Plan 2000-2003, by aiming to strengthen women's economic capacity, rights and sustainable livelihoods as entrepreneurs, producers and home-based workers (WINNER Fact Sheet 2005). Again, like the DDI project the WINNER project does not address the participation of rural and illiterate women.

UNIFEM and Private Partnerships

> UNIFEM recognizes the importance of guaranteeing women's active and equal participation in the rapid march towards the development of knowledge societies. The Fund is partnering with governments, NGOs, UN organizations and the private sector to facilitate women's participation in developing programs which demonstrate women's visions of the use of ICTs, encourage women's employment in ICT fields and facilitate the access of women to new technologies.[21]

The above statement shows the linkage UNIFEM has with private corporations in ICT projects. The linkage between ICTs and private partnerships in the Millennium Development Goals (MDGs) has provided a context for analyzing UNIFEM's partnerships with private corporations in ICT projects. According to Robbins (2002) ICT projects with private corporations coincided with the privatization of telecommunications in Africa. For example, Mohammadi (1997) notes how USAID development projects were created within a context of foreign policies that have supported privatization and commercialization since the early 1980s.

One ICT initiative by UNIFEM where partnership with private corporations features highly is the Digital Diaspora Network-Africa (DDN-A) launched six months after the Digital Diaspora Initiative (DDI). The report titled "Digital Bridge to Africa" aimed to bridge the gap between the African Diaspora and partners in Africa. Over one hundred and thirty leaders attended this all-day meeting to explore ways in which the combined knowledge, experiences and resources of the public and private sectors could be harnessed to effect positive and sustainable change in Africa. The DDI is a collaborative effort between the UN ICT Task Force, the United Nations Fund for International Partnerships (UNFIP), UNIFEM,

---

21 "Women and Information Communication Technologies" Fact Sheet by UNIFEM. Available at <http://www.unifem.org>.

Digital Partners and Gruppo Cerfe. The primary objective of this network is to engage individual ICT and business leaders, with a particular focus on women, youth, and support of aspiring entrepreneurs. DDN-A has developed a Social Entrepreneurship Fund to provide financial support for people in African countries hoping to undertake entrepreneurial activities. The report also recommended new organizations to solicit more financial support from multinational corporations. Another recommendation was to match corporations with appropriate projects by tapping into corporations' desire to be socially responsible, and make it easy for multinationals to find projects that match interests.

The UNIFEM Chief in Africa describes the link between this initiative and partnership with private corporations as follows:

> This initiative…is in line with UNIFEM's 2000-2003 strategy and business plan
> that recognizes the importance of ICT and innovative uses of new technologies
> to tackle the feminization of poverty. Within this context, UNIFEM is fostering
> E-quality in Africa through strategic partnerships with the private sector…[22]

Another major ICT initiative by UNIFEM is the Gender Initiative, which is part of the Least Developed Countries Initiative (LDC). This program, was introduced in July 2000 to provide opportunities for Information technology training in an effort to bridge the digital divide in the least developed countries of the world. Following the G-8 Summit, Cisco Systems (a private information technology corporation), the United Nations Development Fund (UNDP), UNIFEM, and UN volunteers announced the formation of this strategic partnership to help train students in Least Developed Countries (LDCs) for jobs in the Internet economy. The gender initiative became part of the LDC initiative, in order to address the gender digital divide globally. This initiative seeks to increase women's access to IT training and career opportunities beginning with the Cisco networking academy program, to narrow the gender gap and increase female participation in the Internet economy. According to Cisco Corporation, all female classes create a comfortable learning environment for women and help foster a network of women involved in information technology. Female academies established in Africa are in Ethiopia and the Democratic Republic of Congo. The project is a leading example of the collaboration between the UN and the private sector to meet the so-called needs of least developed countries.[23]

It is clear from UNIFEM's major projects and activities in Africa that there is a focus on economic empowerment which is defined as a mechanism to bridge the digital divide. This repeats the WID rhetoric that once this divide is bridged, women would benefit from ICTs. Also women are defined as a coherent group in

---

22   Statement made by Ms Dirasse, UNIFEM Chief in Africa at the Launch of the Digital Diaspora Network Africa in 2002 in New York.

23   "Networking with Cisco Systems" UN Chronicle online. Available at: <http://www.un.org/Pubs/chronicle/2001/issue4/0104p61.html> accessed March 2006.

the discourse of the gender digital divide, which also assumes that access to ICTs is defined mainly by gender and not its intersection with class or social position. Nevertheless, other development agencies, notably the International Development Research Centre's (IDRC) *Acacia Initiative* has integrated rural women and other marginalized communities into its ICT activities (Primo 2003).

Concluding Thoughts

Michiels and Crowder (2001) maintain that there is an economic bias in ICT projects. However, the degree to which these efforts contribute to wealth generation, especially among poorer participants, remains to be seen. In addition, partnerships with private corporations raise questions about whose agenda is being advanced in this discourse on ICTs. I argue that the ICT discourse of UNIFEM which privileges expert knowledge "robs" the opportunity for grassroots women to determine their own information needs and create innovative projects to utilize ICTs effectively for development. The content of information should reflect the viewpoints, knowledge and interests of grassroots women. Women, including grassroots women's exclusion from information production mean the diversity of their viewpoints, experiences and concerns are not represented. If women participate actively in their information needs, ICTs could be utilized in varied ways, for economic, social and political goals. An InfoDev report published in 2003[24] suggests that despite the vast amounts of resources that have been invested in efforts to increase access to ICT in developing countries and among the poor, these technologies have not proven as transformative as expected.

UNIFEM, employs a neoliberal ideology of equating development with economic progress. Thus, the discourse of ICTs in terms of speeches, reports, projects and initiatives are couched in economic terms. Empowerment is defined as economic empowerment, and women entrepreneurs are targeted in ICT projects. Partnerships with private corporations and the results-based approach used to evaluate projects mirrors the neoliberal agenda inherent in ICT programs. The economic bias underlying ICT projects should be addressed. As shown by UNIFEM, private partnerships play a huge role in ICT projects. It has been documented (Iserles 2002) that the role of private corporations in UNIFEM's project played a role in the organization adopting a results-based agenda as a way to demonstrate or account for their performance and use of funds to donors. This approach has an underlying economic model and measures outcomes of projects and programs in quantitative and economic terms by focusing on data and indicators. Quantitative measures of ICTs by UNIFEM concentrate on the

---

24   McNamara, K. (2003), "Information and Communication Technologies, Poverty and Development: Learning from Experience" Background Paper for the InfoDev Annual Symposium. 9-10 December, 200, Geneva, Switzerland (Washington,D.C: The World Bank).

number of women with access to ICTs without indicating which group of women are targeted and who is marginalized. The implication of this approach is that it makes it difficult for local and grassroots organizations and women to develop a strategy of using ICTs to creatively design programs.

In order to effectively use ICTs to address development issues, there needs to be an integrated approach, with a strong focus and involvement of rural communities. This integrated approach does not focus only on economic empowerment, but social and political empowerment of women as well. According to Michiels and Crowder (2001), local appropriation of ICTs takes place when communities define their own information and communication needs and preferences, and adapting technologies to suit their own needs. This reduces the role of the expert, which imposes its agenda on the needs of the population in question. Local appropriation of ICTs is important because it does the following (Bachelor and O'Farrell 2003):

- It contributes to reducing the digital divide;
- It gives a voice to the voiceless; fosters and facilitates community decision-making and action and empower people to take control of local development processes;
- It advances community ownership of ICTs for development;
- It ensures that ICTs serve the purposes of local communities.

Through appropriation, communities select and transform technologies and content to fit their needs, rather than reflect the interests of external groups. There are limited numbers of cases of community-driven, locally appropriated ICT initiatives or projects. However, the few that do, receive scant attention in part because they are not donor-driven (Michiels and Crowder, 2001). Also most of the community-driven projects are relatively new and therefore it is difficult to measure the impact or sustainability of these projects.

One development organization such as the International Development Research Centre (IDRC) has been a leader in exploring linkages between new ICTs and community development.[25] The IDRC established the Acacia Initiative in 1997 to develop the potential of information and communications technologies for the empowerment of poor African communities. This initiative is an international program to empower sub-Saharan communities with the ability to apply ICTs to their own social and economic development. It aims at enabling rural communities to address development challenges in ways that build firmly on local goals, cultures, strengths and processes, as well as promoting the affordable and effective use of ICTs by marginalized communities such as women. The reason why the Acacia Initiative is different from others is its strong focus and involvement of rural communities as well as the integrated

---

25 Executive Summary of Acacia Activities. Available at <http://www.idrc.ca> accessed March 2007.

approach to utilizing ICTs for development. This integrated approach does not only focus on economic empowerment, but social and political empowerment of women as well. The involvement of rural communities ensures that community voices shape the innovative solutions to development problems and shifts some of the development decision-making away from the metropolitan centers and international development organizations and towards rural communities. The Initiative is therefore grounded in participatory community-level research and experimentation.

Engaging local women in identifying their communication needs is significant in turning grassroots women, not just as recipients and consumers of ICTs but producers of them. Michiels and Crowder (2001) contend that access without local capacity and skills for purposeful and meaningful use of ICTs, and decisive control by local groups and communities over ICT resources and applications, will most likely have little impact. This is reiterated by the Gender and Information Working Group of the International Development Research Centre (McConnell 1995), which maintains that due to the lack of appropriate content available through ICTs, not many women are convinced that it is worth taking the time and making an effort to use ICTs for improving their conditions. The challenge for organizations including UNIFEM is to encourage and support community initiatives without denying or stifling the autonomous control of local communities and groups to be involved in the ICT discourse. In order to make ICTs meaningful to majority of women in Africa who are non-literate, poor and in rural areas, there should be a move away from expert knowledge to a more democratic one that recognizes the multiple and diverse voices of women and "others" who are seldom heard in the development discourse.

I conclude that ICTs are not the panacea for addressing development problems faced by developing countries, especially those in sub-Saharan Africa. For ICTs to be used as a tool to empower women and to effect economic, social and political change in society it is imperative for women to be active and not passive users. It requires the active use of these technologies by women themselves to set their own agenda and find ways of using it to address any development issues that they face. Furthermore, the top-down approach to development, where experts from the north, western and developed countries, define development needs of those in the south (developing countries), should be changed to a bottom-up approach where poor, non-literate and rural women act as their own experts by actively using these new technologies in combination with the old (such as radios and videos) to address their own needs. For the rhetoric of the significance of ICTs for development as put forth by international organizations such as UNIFEM to become reality, there should be a focus on the participatory use of ICTs by majority of women to not only bridge the digital divides but also to ensure the active role of women marginalized in the development process.

References

Acosta-Belen, E. and Bose, C. (1990), "From Structural Subordination to Empowerment: Women and Development in Third World Contexts," *Gender and Society* 4:3, 299-320.

Afshar, H. (ed.) (1998), *Women and Empowerment: Illustrations from the Third World* (New York: St. Martin's Press).

Anderson, M. (1985), "Technology Transfer: Implications for Women," in C. Overholt, et al. (eds), *Gender Roles in Development Projects: A Case Book* (West Hartford, Connecticut: Kumarian Press).

Atack, I. (1999), "Four Criteria of Development NGO Legitimacy," *World Development* 27:5, 855-864.

Bachelor, S. and O'Farrell, C. (2003), "Guiding Principles for ICT Interventions," in *Revisiting the "Magic Box": Case Studies in Local Appropriation of Information Communication Technologies* (Rome: FAO), 1-27.

Batchelor, S. (2002), *Using ICTs to Generate Development Content* (The Hague: International Institute for Communication and Development).

Batliwala, S. (1994), "The Meaning of Women's Empowerment: New Conceptsfrom Action," in Sen, G. et al. (eds), *Population Policies Reconsidered: Health, Empowerment and Rights* (Cambridge, MA: Harvard School of Public Health).

Belbase, S. (1988), "Video Survey: Do Rural People Learn from Video?," *Media Asia* 15:2, 108-112.

Beneria, L. and Sen, G. (1981), "Accumulation, Reproduction and Women's Role in Economic Development: Boserup Revisited," *Signs* 7:2, 279-98.

Bisnath, S. and Elson, D. (1999), "Women's Empowerment Revisited" Background Paper Commissioned by UNIFEM for *Progress of the World's Women 2000* (New York: UNIFEM).

Blumberg, R. (1989), "Toward a feminist theory of development," in R. Wallace (ed.), *Feminism and Sociological Theory* (Beverly Hills: Sage).

Boserup, E. (1970), *Women's Role in Economic Development* (New York: St. Martin's Press).

Buvinic, M. (1986), "Projects for Women in the Third World: Explaining their Misbehavior," in Lycette, M. and McGreevey, W.P. (eds), *Women and Poverty in the Third World* (Baltimore: Johns Hopkins University Press), 14-33.

Castells, M. (2000), *The Information Age: Economy, Society and Culture. Volume I: The Rise of the Network Society*, 2nd Edition, 3 Volumes (MA: Blackwell Publishers).

Contreras, M. (2003), "Integrating Community Radio and ICTs for Development in Rural Mexico," in *Revisiting the "Magic Box": Case Studies in Local Appropriation of Information Communication Technologies* (Rome: FAO), 71-100.

Crush, J. (1995), *Power of Development* (London and New York: Routledge).

Elson, D. (2002), "Gender Justice, Human Rights, and Neo-liberal Economic Policies," in M. Molyneux and S. Razavi (eds), *Gender Justice, Development, and Rights* (New York : Oxford University Press).

Escobar, A. (1995a), *Encountering Development: The Making and Unmaking of the Third World* (Princeton, NJ: Princeton University Press).

—— (1995b), "Imagining a Post-development," in J. Crush (ed.), *Power of Development* (New York: Routledge), 211-227.

—— (1984), "Discourse and Power in Development: Michel Foucault and The Relevance of his Work to the Third World," *Alternatives* 10:3, 377-400.

Everts, S. (1998), *Gender and Technology: Empowering Women, Engendering Development* (London: Zed Books).

Hafkin, N. and Taggart, N. (eds) (2001), *Gender, Information Technology, and Developing Countries: An Analytic Study* (Office of Women in Development, USAID).

Hall, M.C. (1992), *Women and Empowerment: Strategies for Increasing Autonomy* (Washington: Hemisphere).

Hamelink, C. (1996), *World Communication: Disempowerment and Self-empowerment* (London: Zed Books).

Harcourt, W. (ed.) (1999), *Women @ Internet: Creating New Cultures in Cyberspace* (London: Zed Books).

Hartmann, H. (1981), "The Unhappy Marriage of Marxism and Feminism," in L. Sargent (ed.), *Women and Revolution* (Boston: South End Press), 1-41.

Heyzer, N. (ed.) (1995), "A Women's Development Agenda for the 21st century," in *Perspectives on Development for Beijing and Beyond* (New York: UNIFEM).

Hirshman, M. (1995), "Women and Development: a Critique," in M. Marchand, and J. Parpart (eds), *Feminism, Postmodernism, Development* (New York: Routledge), 42- 55.

Huyer, S. and T. Siskosa (2003), "Overcoming the Gender Digital Divide: Understanding ICTs and their Potential for Empowerment of Women," *Instraw Research Paper Series* no. 1, April 2003.

Iserles, R. (2002), "Ideology, Rhetoric and the Politics of Bureaucracy: Exploring Women and Development," Unpublished PhD Dissertation, The City University of New York.

Kenny, C. (2002), "Information and Communication Technologies for Direct poverty Alleviation: Costs and Benefits," *Development Policy Review* 20:2.

Marcelle, G. (2000), "Getting Information into African ICT Policy: A Strategic View," in E. Rathgeber and E. Ofwona (eds), *Gender and Information Revolution in Africa* (Ottawa, ON: International Development Research Center), 35-83.

—— (1999), "Creating an African Women's Cyberspace," in Mitter et al. (ed.).

—— (1995), *Using Information Technology to Strengthen African Women's Organizations* (Abantu for Development, London UK).

McMichael, P. (2000), *Development and Social Change: A Global Perspective*, 2nd Edition (Thousand Oaks, CA: Pine Forge Press).

McNamara, K. (2003), "Information and Communication Technologies, Poverty and Development: Learning from Experience," Background Paper for the InfoDev Annual Symposium. 9-10 December, 200, Geneva, Switzerland (Washington, D.C: The World Bank).

Michiels, S. and Van Crowder, L. (2001), *Discovering the "Magic Box": Local Appropriation of Information Communication Technologies (ICTs)* (Rome: FAO). Also available at: <http://www.fao.org/sd/2001/KN0602a_en.htm> accessed 11 May, 2008.

Mies, M. (1982), *The Lace Makers of Narsapur: Indian Housewives Produce for the World Market* (London: Zed Books).

Mitter, S. and Ng, C. (eds) (2005), *Gender and the Digital Economy: Perspectives from the Developing World* (New Delhi, Thousand Oaks, CA: Sage Publications).

Mitter, S. (2004), "Globalization, ICTs, and Economic Empowerment," *Gender, Technology, and Development* 8:1, 5-29.

Mohammadi, A. (ed.) (1997), *International Communication and Globalization: A Critical Introduction* (London: Sage Publications).

Nath, V. (2001), "Empowerment and Governance through Information and Communication Technologies: Women's Perspective," *International Information and Library Review* 33:4, 317-339.

Ngwaimbi, E.K. (1999), *Exporting Communication Technology to Developing Countries: Socio-cultural, Economic and Educational Factors* (Lanham, MD: University Press of America).

Parpart J. (1995). "Deconstructing the Development 'Expert', Gender, Development and the 'Vulnerable Groups,'" in Marchand, M. and Parpart, J. (eds), *Feminism, Postmodernism and Development* (New York: Routledge) 221-243.

Parpart, J. (1995b), "Post-modernism, Gender and Development," in Crush (ed.).

—— (1993), "Who is the 'Other'?: A Postmodern Feminist Critique of women and Development Theory and Practice," *Development and Change* 24:3, 439-64.

—— (1989), *Women and Development in Africa: Comparative Perspectives* (Lanham, MD: University Press of America, Inc).

Patil, P. (ed.) (1999), *Gender Perspective: Participation, Empowerment and Development* (New Delhi: Radha Publications).

Riano, P. (ed.) (1994), *Women in Grassroots Communication: Furthering Social Change* (London and New Delhi: Sage).

Robbins, M.B. (2002), "Are African Women Online just ICT Consumers?" *Gazette* 64, 235-249.

Sen, A. (1999), *Development as Freedom* (New York: Knopf).

Senker, P. (2000), "A Dynamic Perspective on Technology, Economic Inequality and Development," in S. Wyatt et al. (eds), *Technology and In/Equality: Questioning the Information Society* (London: Routledge), 197-217.

Snyder, M. (1995), *Transforming Development: Women, Poverty and Politics* (London: Intermediate Technology Publications).

Stamp, P. (1990), *Technology, Gender and Power in Africa* (Ottawa, Ont: IDRC).

Sweetman, C. (ed.) (1998), *Gender and Technology* (Oxford: Oxfam).

Tandon, N. (1999), "Global Business, National Politics, Community Planning: Are Women Building the Linkages," in Harcourt. (ed.).

Tesner, S. (2000), *The United Nations and Business: A Partnership Recovered* (New York: St. Martin's Press).

UNIFEM. (2005), *Women 2000 and Beyond: Gender Equality and Empowerment of Women Through ICT* (New York: UNIFEM and DAW).

Wambui, M. (2005), "Development through Radio: A Case Study from Sierra Leone," in S. Cummings et al. (eds), *Gender, and ICTs for Development: A Global Sourcebook* (The Netherlands: Oxfam and KIT, Royal Tropical Institute).

Wilkins, K. (1999), "Development Discourse on Gender and Communication Strategies for Social Change," *Journal of Communication* 49:1, 46-68.

Zammit, A. (2004), *Development at Risk: Rethinking UN-Business Partnerships* (Geneva: UNRISD).

Zabludovsky, G. (1998), *Women Business Owners in Mexico: An Emerging Economic Force* (Mexico: Autonomous National University of Mexico UNAM).

Chapter 10

Globalization and Women's Empowerment in Africa

Robert Dibie

Introduction

This chapter examines the impact of globalization in the social, economic and multi-dimensional aspects of women's lives in Africa and the process of their empowerment. It argues that globalization has an uneven impact on women's rights. It contends that globalization has led to increasing violations of women's economic, political, and cultural rights in a large measure due to structural adjustment programs that were adopted by several African countries. The chapter also explores the social and economic factors that militate against the integration of women into political leadership positions in the continent. However, amidst these obstacles, women in Africa seek increasing opportunities to work in solidarity at national, regional, and international levels to demand their rights.

This chapter also advances the notion that a society that promotes gender equality is likely to achieve stable, continuous development. No development process will be totally beneficial to a nation if it does not involve women. Given a patriarchal culture in Africa, is the present involvement of women in the society the best possible one for the continent? The concluding section calls for an equal opportunity and sexual harassment policies that would effectively reduce discrimination against women in the African society as well as stimulate and integrate women's interest in the social, economic, leadership, and political development in Africa.

Women and Ethnographic Paradigms

Feminists and the United Nations declaration for women have promoted the people-centered development paradigm in achieving sustainable development (Disch 2006; Kerbo 2006). This paradigm postulates that women should be placed at the center of the national development process. From the African continent perspective, women's unequal and subordinate positions have been said to hamper sustainable development efforts. The paradigm advocates that the coexistence of women's multiple roles as reproducer, producer of goods and services, and traditional manager of resources is paramount to development. Further, the women's discriminatory cultural beliefs that infiltrate institutions at various levels of society in Africa may not be appropriate for the implementation of sustainable development goals (Dibie 2008).

The liberal feminist theory, the radical feminist theory and the Marxist feminist theory have been propounded to explain gender inequality and women's underdevelopment in the world. Herold Kerbo (2006) contends that liberal feminists locate gender inequality in gender role differentiation, socialization, and sexism. The limits on women's individual rights and freedoms as compared to men have aided to promote a culture whereby women are confined to the private sphere. These imposed constraints have limited women's access to equal opportunities in education, work outside the home, and in political participation. Since sustainable development and political power resides in activities in the public sphere, gender equality must be enforced (Gagne and Tewksbury 2003). Some critics of the liberal feminist theory have argued that if all women and men are well educated and work long hours in order to be successful in modern industrial Africa, how will all the care work and domestic work be done? (Kerbo 2006).

The radical feminist theory presents the argument that women's subordination in a patriarchal system encourages male domination and control of all institutions in public and private life (Brettell and Sargent 1997; Kerbo 2006; Disch 2006). Male domination of women according to the radical feminists, covers economic power and privilege as well as control over female sexuality and reproduction. The bone of contention of the radical feminist theory is that gender equality requires institutional and structural transformations. Such transformations should help to galvanize the consciousness of women's importance in any society. This consciousness would also help to reconstruct male and female relationships in a more egalitarian and flexible way. Most men in several African nations reject any equitable power sharing or relationship with women in their society.

The Marxist feminist theory argues that gender inequality is rooted in class oppression under capitalism. Capitalism is used in this chapter to refer to a political economy system based on private ownership of the means of production. Marxist feminists also stress that an effective control over property leads to monogamous patrilineal and patriarchal nuclear family structure. The mechanism of control is rooted in the fact that husbands control the means of production and thus subordinate their wives and children. This practice is common in several African nations because husbands and fathers are the owners of property rights (Kerbo 2006; Akinboye 2004). Figure 10.1 shows the relationship between the three theories to women's liberation and sustainable development.

Global transformation mechanisms in the form of neo-liberal policies – for example the structural adjustment program (SAP) that was prescribed by the World Bank and IMF – have increased the level of inequality and poverty among men and women in several African countries. The neo-liberal policies postulated that several countries that seek financial aid from the World Bank and IMF should adopt privatization, monetary liberalization, fiscal discipline, flexible labor market, removal of subsidies, budget cutbacks, tax cuts and trade liberalization polices (Olukoshi et al. 1994). One of the consequences of these neo-liberal economic

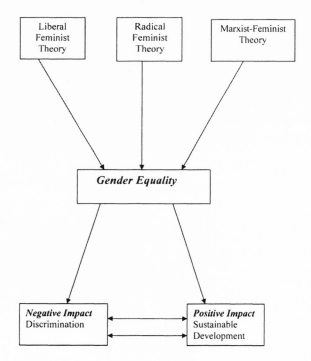

Figure 10.1   Relationship between development and women's liberation

policies is the deregulation of work that increased unemployment forcing affected families to seek alternative ways of livelihood. Thus, the neo-liberal policies that were adopted by several African nations have affected women traders in many ways depending on the form of business that they are engaged in (Pam Sha 2007; Okpeh and Angya 2007). It is interesting to note that the impact of the neo-liberal policies, the structure of the informal sector and the role of the national and regional governments in several African countries have influenced to a large extent, the ability of women to organize effectively.

The ethnographic literature describes how women in pastoral and sedentary societies in Africa adapt to dual and separate worlds (Nelson 1997; Disch 2006; Kerbo). The cultural practices of most African countries is such that fewer women than men are in the administrative, political, social and legal institutions of their society. Cynthia Nelson (1997) and December Green (1999) contend that the African women's world has two major spheres. These are the home and the private communication patterns between women of several homes. Thus, the African women's world in most cases is narrowly circumscribed like most civilizations. In the rural areas these cultural and Islamic religious restrictions on women also provided a complicated system of devices for cushioning or limiting access to the men's world. However, Veronica Adeleke (2002) argue that despite the dual world that several women live in Africa, the combine wealth of wife and husband often provides for the maintenance of their children.

Women and Negative Consequences of Globalization

The negative consequences of globalization are enormous in the African continent. The consequences include exploitation, exclusion, deliberate deprivation and human rights violation. The extent to which globalization has affected the institutionalization of gender inequality in both the public and private sphere in several African nations can be explained by six perspectives: (1) the traditional perspective, where the African woman was an appendage to her husband or father, family, village or ethnic group; (2) the rural settings or spatial dimension, where marriage was between two families rather than the joining together of man and woman; (3) the woman through her childbearing contributes to the manpower required by the husband for farming; (4) women are expected to market and distribute the farm products, thus acting as economic partners which makes their social relationship stronger; (5) in some rural areas in Africa the versatility of women has been widely acclaimed; and (6) due to the weakening of families as a result of more urban living, several African women's associations established by both domestic and foreign NGOs are beginning to protest against the discrimination of women.

The debate on why African nations should hold on to their tradition and culture of unequal treatment of men and women is still framed within cultural relativism versus universal human rights (Beneria 2003; Dahlerup 2005; Pan Sha 2007; Ibe 1994). In several African families a husband uses these same cultural beliefs as a reason to physically abuse or discipline his wife. This practice is acceptable among several African ethnic and religious groups.

As stated earlier, several African nations have a strong patriarchal structure that maintained the sexual division of labor in the household and families. This same structure directly restricts women's availability for paid work and indirectly affects the terms of employment for those women who enter the public and private sectors. There is a clear gender differentiation, in terms of occupational status and work conditions in several African nations. Specifically, women in the public service and private sector are characterized by limited and insecure employment opportunities and marked substandard wages, poor working conditions, unstable hours and disadvantageous employment contracts (Ifedi 1994; Karanja 1987; Mba 1982). Women are predominantly employed in low wage jobs or in small-scale ventures, which shunt them into segregated occupation and repetitious manual production.

Despite the fact that the majority of the women who work in public services and the private sector in several African nations occupy junior positions, there are few women who hold positions of power in the government. In the private sector, there are few women who are entrepreneurs and directors. Few women who are handicapped lack affordable childcare, experience spousal abandonment, increasingly high cost of living and gender stereotyping. These conditions deny women in the public and private sectors the requisite skills, training, and capital to secure more lucrative and secured employment (Nweke 1985, Ifedi 1994; Obadina 1985). Moreover, because most African women tend to be concentrated in transitory, low-paid, and low status jobs they typically replicate their household tasks, and their activities as survival victims.

In most African public and private sectors, the marginalization of women in the continent has two contrasting gender ideologies, which ironically produce the same outcome. The first is related to the aforementioned state-promoted gender identity. The state rhetoric and action imply that women in most African nations do not need to engage in income-generating activities and that those who do engage in such activities do so for reasons other than economic necessity. The second gender ideology undergirding the marginalization of women micro-entrepreneurs is related to gender bias embedded in development practice that perceive women as vulnerable and isolated groups and their activities as a collection of inconsequential endeavors (Aderibege 2004; Waylen 1996; Dahlerup 2005; Reimann 2006). Gender specific ideologies, such as these, which underpin the marginalization of women within the public and private sectors in Africa, are often nuanced by cultural, ethnic and religious undertones.

In several African nations, the rigid and hegemonic nature of prevailing notions of work not only denigrates the work of women but dis-empowers women producers themselves. Interviews conducted in several African nations in the summers of 2006, 2007 and 2008 reveal that, although women consider themselves to be producers of goods and providers of services for a large segment of the society, most African women have a low estimate of the value of their own labor. Hence, it would seem that the particular constructions of gender to which some African working women are subjected and which inform their notions of self not only deny them the value of their daily activities but also undermine the potential of their private sector or public agencies, as well as discourage them from developing the concept of self worth.

The traditional practice of early marriage is still very common in several African countries. This practice often encourages parents to give their young girl to potential suitors at an age between 9 and 16 years old. Since such girls were generally younger than their husbands, it was easy for their spouse to dominate them and limiting their opportunity for self-actualization. Husband domination often leads to abuse (Green 1999; Akinboye 2004). Motherhood and demands of esteem also made women more home-centered and limited in their social, political, and economic engagement. Eno Ikpe (2004) contends that the attitude of women in several African countries has also contributed to the legacy of inequality between genders. She argued that some women seem to have developed an attitude which does not stimulate other women to seek leadership and political positions. Many women through social conditioning do not seem to see themselves as capable of participating meaningfully in polities and functioning leadership position. As a result such women would develop negative attitudes toward political participation and leadership positions. In most cases, women seem to have a high level of distrust for fellow women who seek political positions. This lack of support for their own fellow women has immensely contributed to subordination of women in several African nations.

The exclusion of women from senior public management and political positions at the national and regional government levels as well as private sectors reinforce the argument that women do not have economic and political power in several African nations. After almost six decades of independence how can women in most African nations be empowered to participate in economic, social and political aspects of their society and nation? The implementation of appropriate strategies to enhance female empowerment in Africa is one of the major steps for the continent to achieve sustainable development.

It is important to note that gender and equality issues are central to the social and economic life of every nation in Africa. Therefore, creating a new value system in society in which equality is a core value not only between men and women but also for children is very important. This is the sustainable human development aspect of gender mainstreaming that involves elevating the potential of all people regardless of gender, race, class and ethnicity to attain better development goals (Dauda 2004).

Scholars such as Thomas-Sayter and Rocheleau (1995), Adepoju (1994), Kalu (1993), and Hyden (2006) have argued that masculine-oriented culture that is practiced in several parts of the African continent has helped to shape the opportunities and constraints women and men face in securing employment in the government, the nonprofit and private sectors. They contend that the systematically inferior position of women inside and outside the public service and household in the continent points to the necessity of treating gender as a force of its own in the sustainable development processes in Africa. Although the relative deprivation of women when compared with men varies among the 54 African nations, it is very important to note that giving qualified women more senior public management positions in government organizations will galvanize the continent's role in sustainable development (Dibie, 2008). Sustainable development as used in this chapter refers to consideration of the strong inter-linkage between economy, ecology, social development, and inclusive society as well as respect for human rights (including women's rights).

The lack of any sustained women's empowerment policies and the dynamics as well as the contradictions of household politics and gender relations has made most African governments vulnerable to international nongovernmental organizations (INGOs). Thus African women with the help of several NGOs have been struggling to achieve equality with men in leadership and decision-making. The drafting of the communiqué for the Eradication of all Discrimination Against Women (CEDAW) in 1979 by the United Nations, has also galvanized gender-oriented foreign NGOs in several nations in Africa to call for more equitable treatment of women (Kuye 2003; Antrobus 2004).

During the past three decades most African governments are beginning to accept women's equity rights. Despite these new development poverty reduction policies several African nations no longer talk of women, but, stress human capital development, down-sizing, devaluation, privatization of public corporations, and out-sourcing (Okpeh and Angya 2007). The most troubling aftermath across the African continent includes disturbing indicators of the overall status of women. The spread of poverty from Sudan to the Democratic Republic of Congo, Rwanda, Ethiopia, Chad, Niger and several other African nations have also increased the practice of women trafficking, the high incidence of material morality and female illiteracy (World Bank Report 2005; Meekers and Richter, 2005).

The impact of women's poverty has spilled over to child malnutrition in several African nations. Most women and their children have become losers in the structural adjustment program (SAP) that was prescribed by the World Bank and IMF and adopted by several African nations. Rather than promoting production, trade liberalization and the structural adjustment policies have enhanced poverty. As a result of lay off of their husbands' withdrawal of social support by the government, women's domestic and economic responsibilities have increased in several nations in the African continent. In general, women have become the victims of society while men play the role of political control and major decision makers of the state and family (Opeh and Angya 2007).

There is a widespread acceptance of the critical role played by women and public institutions in the development process (Disch 2006; Kerbo 2006; Okpeh and Angya 2007; World Bank 1997). Women have a major part in the transformation process, whether in terms of their direct involvement in the economy or their more tempered role as catalyst, facilitator and regulator of economic activity (World Bank 2005). At the same time, there has been a growing concern with the representation of women and the management of diversity within Africa's public sector (Akinboye 2004; Kuye 2003). The concern of unequal representation of women in leadership positions in the nonprofit, private and public sectors has affected reform efforts that stresses human resources management issues such as capacity-building, participatory management styles, cross gender mentor–protégé relationship, constant innovation, entrepreneurial initiative, teamwork, strategic thinking and planning as crucial.

A World Bank (1997 and 2005) report pointed out that when women are not offered equal opportunities in the public sector there is the danger that some skills and talents in a nation could be wasted. The idea that recruitment and promotion are based on gender rather than merit can contribute significantly to a decrease of morale and performance among talented and innovative women.

As Dahlerup (2005) and Disch (2006) have pointed out, ethnic politics largely ignores public administration or socioeconomic development, in much the same way that the literature on economic development overlooks ethnic cleavages. Yet in many societies across the African continent, ethnicity and gender stereotype plays such a pervasive role in the development process. This is why Adepoju (1994) and Matland (2006) describe gender and ethnic politics as "an important dimension in public affairs, pervading the environment in which public administration functions in sub-Saharan Africa."

Jerald Greenberg (2008) and Modupe Kolawole (1998) presented three reasons why men have more access to mentor than women. First, there are simply fewer female executives available to serve as mentors for young female employees. Second, women are less willing to enter into mentoring relationships because they anticipate greater risk than men in doing so. Recent surveys in some African nations found that women expressed more concern than men did about the vulnerability to sexual harassment that might come from the increased visibility they assume because of their protégé status. This is specifically very important because most African nations do not have sexual harassment laws. Third, barriers to mentoring exist not only between men and women, but also between members of different religious and ethnic groups. Insofar as mentor and protégé often get together because they have similar backgrounds and share similar attitudes, it is not surprising to find that people from different ethnic and religious groups face difficulties in their mentor-protégé relationships – if they form one at all.

Pam Sha (2007) and Okpeh and Angya (2007) describes the current wave of policy reforms in Africa in an attempt to expand the role of women in both public and private sectors. Although these reforms also make it difficult for African governments to introduce programs that would discourage discrimination against women, prejudice against women continues to exist in the public and private sectors. A glass ceiling that limits all women from enjoying true equal opportunities and a working environment free from sexual harassment in the nation are also very evident in several African nations. Some indicators of women's underdevelopment includes high unemployment among educated women, low level of literacy, lower income compared to men, high fertility rate, lower usage of contraception, lower capitalization and lower savings. It becomes obvious that, gender balance will not come about by itself unless government and NGOs take some crucial actions (Dahlerup 2005). Therefore, the responsibility for dealing with the under-representation of women rests with the government, the private sector, and NGOs. It is therefore paramount that public policy should address women's under representation, such as setting up electoral gender quotas for the recruitment and election of female candidates. Progress for women will be likely to come in the twenty-first century inevitably in several African nations with the support of foreign NGOs and reform in public policy.

Policies Toward Women's Empowerment

How can the negative consequences discussed previously be prevented by giving women a greater and appropriate place in the African society, the economy and government? What would be the appropriate approach to resisting neoliberal globalization that reinforces or increases gender inequality? Given the cultural, political, and economic environment in which the African society finds itself, what can be done to liberate women? To what extent has the kinship system, the traditions, and religious ideologies reinforce the level of gender inequality in the society?

In the past three decades some African and international laws on human rights have given women in the continent the legal instrument to fight for their rights (Akinboye, 2004). No doubt women are the pillars of the African family. Generally men acknowledge that the physical, psychological and mental health of each member of their family depends on the woman in the family. This assumption leads us to argue that the promotion of a woman's well-being is control to solving to the ills of patriarchal values in the African continent.

It has also been argued that the continuing exclusion, exploitation, poverty, humiliation, oppression, and marginalization that are mechanisms of neo-liberal globalization, are the reasons for women's call for social justice and equality in the 21st century. Josephine Dibie and Robert Dibie (2007) contend that history and culture are not static values, they could be modified incrementally.

An effective tool for women's resistance to neo-liberal globalization can only come in the context of a woman's movement oriented toward the basic social problems affecting women. The bone of contention is the economic dependency trap, educational disadvantages, and other obstacles to empowerment such as the birth of a child and lack of day care facilities for urban workers. To improve women's social and economic security, marital customs must be challenged, and new civil laws must be implemented to offer additional protection to married and divorced women concerning child custody, rights in marital property, and financial support – going beyond the present provisions of common law, Islamic and customary laws in several African nations (Gruenbuum 1997).

Therefore, the empowerment of women in the African continent through education, technical skills, enhanced self-worth, and economic independence will lead toward equality and a more inclusive society and way of life. Training in personal and family hygiene, knowledge about healthy food production and preparation would help to alleviate the living standards of women in several African nations. Policies that could promote women's freedom from harmful activities as well as give ladies choice in sexual and reproductive matters, including the right to have safe sex will help to empower African women to be the custodian of their bodies and health.

There are different approaches to dealing with institutional gender discrimination in Africa. One approach emphasizes demographic representation of women in the public and private sectors of Africa. Another approach recognizes the cultural, religious and political determinants of discrimination against women (Waylen 1996; Dahlerup 2005; Reiman 2006). From these perspectives arise policies such as equal opportunity and other ethnic-conscious instruments designed to benefit the marginalized groups. Equality of opportunity is predicated on the idea of fair competition on the basis of merit, and the role of public policy is to ensure that all qualified individuals (men and women) can enter the competition and be judged according to the same criteria. Thus the state must act to (1) ensure that the

Table 10.1   Policies for women's empowerment

Policy Variable	Description
Equal Employment Opportunities	Equal opportunities and other ethnicity-conscious instruments designed to benefit the marginalized girls and middle age women.
Gender Discrimination	Takes action to stop gender discrimination in the hiring and promotion process.
Child Day Care Assistance	Public and private institutions should be encouraged to provide child day care facilities around their location.
Women Participation in Politics	Creates an environment that will encourage women to participate in politics and occupy key positions in political parties.
Diversity in Women's Education	(a) Girls and middle age women should be encouraged to complete at least high school diploma. (b) Women should be encouraged to be Scientists, Engineers, Pilots, Computer Experts and Doctors.
Law Abuse of Women	Takes action to prosecute men who abuse their wives.
National Sexual Harassment Policy in the workplace	Prosecutes men especially senior administrators who use their position to intimidate junior female employees or demand sex as a condition for continuous employment or promotion.
Women Co-operative Societies and NGOs	Encourages the consolidation of women economic power through co-operative societies and NGOs around the nation.
Public Education Campaign to change traditional, social, cultural, and religions stereotypes on women	Introduces civil society campaign to educate both rural and urban communities that the time is right for the nation to change some of its outdated values about girls and women.

competition is equal, and (2) equalize starting points where necessary (Lovenduski 1989: 8; Steinman 1991; Weisner 1997). Table 10.1 shows a framework of how women's empowerment can be achieved in Africa.

Several African nations are beginning to enact policies to stimulate economic, political and social participation of women in both the public and private sectors. Some of the policies include:

- Married women that were transferred from the city where their husbands worked are now entitled to government residents.
- There are gender equality in respect to annual vacation, transportation allowances and bonus pay.

- Children's allowance for female officers working abroad.
- Free medical treatment.
- Equal pay for equal qualification and work.

Political Leadership

There is the need for all African governments and NGOs regardless of culture, religion, political system, history and custom, to protect the universally recognized human rights all nations have agreed to as well as the Beijing declaration to protect women's right. African governments need to prosecute those who violate the human rights laws. African governments must enforce laws against rape, gender-based violence, murder and torture. No African nation should condone discrimination against women or any form of sexual abuse.

It is also important that the government, the private sector and NGOs operating in the African continent elevate the priority for women in development. In the 21st century development should not only focus on power plants, good roads, health care, technology, dams, and defense, rather governments need to put people and families first. They can do this by investing in women, young girls, welfare and education, women's needs, in creating women's opportunities, and in promoting women's rights. It is therefore paramount for NGOs, the public and private sectors to ensure that women are their top priority in achieving sustainable development in Africa.

Protection of Women from Disease

The problem of the spread of HIV/AIDS in Africa is alarming. It is therefore essential that governments, NGOs and the private sector unite to form a sexual and reproductive health movement in seeking solutions to address the HIV/AIDS disease in the continent. NGOs should collaborate with local health departments and family planning agencies and clinics on the front lines in preventing the spread of sexually transmitted infections. It is not enough to condemn illiterate African women who are affected because of indifference to science and by failure to provide tools for their own protection. Doing so will insinuate blaming the victim and condone crimes against humanity. African governments and NGOs must collaborate to fight back and mobilize a comprehensive prevention program that experts estimate could prevent the HIV/AIDS epidemic from further spreading in the African continent. There is also the need for the manufacturing of female condoms. These condoms should be made more affordable and acceptable. These strategies can simultaneously prevent unwanted pregnancy, sexually transmitted infections and limit the spread of the AIDS virus itself. It is crucial that NGOs, CBOs, the private sector, and all relevant stakeholders collaborate in the design and implementation of health sector reform with the cooperation of the government.

Access of health services to vulnerable groups especially women in the rural areas must be ensured.

Culture, Tradition and Religion

There are over 1,000 ethnic groups and languages in Africa. Nigeria for example, has nearly 250 different languages and ethnic groups, while Tanzania has more than 100. Kenya alone has more than 40 ethnic groups and languages (Khapoya 1998). The interesting thing about the different ethnic groups is that they all have distinct or specific cultures and traditions. In several parts of Africa the values of culture and tradition are both dynamic and affected by changing legal, economic and political forces (Khapoya 1998). In some cases these cultured elements impedes human rights and development in contemporary Africa. Therefore it is paramount for African governments and NGOs to work together in eliminating those culture and religious values that infringe upon women's rights. They should also strengthen the exiting positive cultural values that promote gender equality and human dignity. The strengthening of positive cultural practices could be done through reinforcement of human rights education and law reform. Traditional methods of dealing with sexual and life-skills education need to be reevaluated. There is also the need for partnership or collaboration with religious, customary laws and traditional stakeholders to realize the rights of vulnerable groups especially women and young girls who are affected by parochial traditional practices such as female mutilation, child marriages and obnoxious initiation and widowhood rites. National governments should introduce reforms in customary laws, constitutional and judicial laws pertaining to marriage, land inheritance rights and family life.

Equity and Women's Citizenship

In any nation men and women contribute to the development process. African nations must recognize that equity, equality and the empowerment of women as the necessary pre-requisites for women's ability to enjoy the right to the highest attainable standard of sexual and reproductive health. Women must be encouraged to be equal partners to men, in order to transform gender relations and achieve sustained equity and social justice. Therefore African nations should introduce ground-breaking public policy that would encourage progressive measures that will ensure the fulfillment of women's rights. NGOs and government institutions should promote popular education campaign on gender rights, gender-sensitive issues and the socialization of children. In addition, African governments and NGOs should promote women's sexual rights, including their rights to bodily integrity, their freedom to determine their sexual lives and their freedom from sexual violence, coercion, discrimination and ostracism. The current entrenched structural gendered inequities manifested in economic powerlessness, and in inadequate legal protection from violations such as gender based violence. Several African nations have resulted in women and girls not being accorded their equal rights and citizenship. Passing public policy that allocates seats for women and engaging in electoral politics are some initial means for reaching the goals of achieving and expanding women's citizenship across the African continent.

Diversity and Equal Opportunies

There has been much debate and political controversy surrounding equal opportunity policies and quota system in several African nations. At the heart of the debate is the question of whether preferential treatment is justified and, if so, on what grounds. While accepting that there may be reason to challenge the arbitrary criteria on which preferences are to be allocated, there is no alternative but to support Edwards' (1995) position that, in principle at least, they (i.e. preferences to one or other group) are acceptable once they are designed to remove inequality and do not create greater injustices than those they seek to overcome.

Diversity ought to be an end in itself and not a means to achieving some less noble, politically motivated objective (Harvey and Allard 2002). Second, if equal opportunities are intended to serve as compensation for past injustices, then they are flawed as a form of redress since there is seldom anything that links past victims and present beneficiaries. What they do, in effect, is to seriously devalue (or certainly undervalue) the qualifications of those whose forebears stand accused of discriminating against previous generations of the new "in-group." This is surely tantamount to replacing one system of injustice with another.

African governments and NGOs not only must understand the dynamics of family abuse, but also be prepared to offer support and guidance to victims as they move through the difficult period in their lives. Repairing the body and spirit is only half the battle; society must be able to make the victims of family abuse completely whole. This has to include financial reimbursement from the offender. The people of Africa are beginning to accept the fact that victims of crimes in general and victims of family abuse in particular, have rights and need to be active participants in the criminal justice system. This includes giving their input during sentencing of offenders. The use of victim impact statements is a giant step forward for victims of family violence.

The various policy instruments for ensuring women's development are not exclusive to the government's official policies. Legal aid and legal literacy are the most popular components of government's effort to reduce family abuse. To rectify this situation in several African nations, the Family Law Center offers free legal advice on all family legal problems to low-income people. The center's founders were careful not to restrict its services to women because of fear that it would be stigmatized as another "women's liberation project." Such a label might have jeopardized the center's existence for a number of reasons. To be more inclusive the center publishes booklets in four of the main languages in some African nations. These publications are free and target school-age children in the hope that they will read it to their mothers while also learning on their own (Akande and Kuye 1986; Kuye 2003).

In recent years, some NGOs have become increasingly proactive in their attempt to eliminate prejudice. Their approach is not just to hire a broader group of people than usual, but to create an atmosphere in which diverse groups can flourish. The NGOs above are not merely trying to obey the law or attempting to be socially responsible, they also recognize that diversity is a public issue that needs to be addressed. The government should therefore make sure that all its agencies introduce appropriate diversity management programs that will give women access to senior management positions. As Otobo (1999) pointed out, the increasing success of the government depends on its managers' ability to naturally tap the full potentials of a diverse workforce that includes women, men, young adults.

The introduction of diversity management programs in African nations' public service would constitute an effort to celebrate diversity by creating supportive work environments for women and minority ethnic groups in the continent. The national and regional governments should adopt the underlying philosophy of diversity management programs so that they may crack the glass ceiling preventing women and minority groups in the continent from excelling and contributing effectively to the nation's sustainable development process.

There are some non-official organizations or associations that are committed to women's development. These NGOs include: Association of Working House Wives, Association of Media Women, Army Officers Wives Association, and National Council of Women Society of Nigeria. The interests of these groups are basically confined to the welfare of their members. In the future the government should encourage women's groups to consolidate their economic power by establishing co-operative that will enhance their quest for liberation. The current activities of the National Council of Women for example, include the operation of child welfare services scheme, and market nurseries to cater for the children of market traders. The council runs adult education programs aimed at increasing political awareness and participation of women in development with particular references to women franchise – the right to vote and be voted for. It also runs hostel accommodation for women in various towns and cities in Africa in order to alleviate accommodation problems for women in urban centers. These activities are not enough. New women co-operative societies should be formed around the African continent to further promote these causes.

Community Home Economics Program

The formal instrument for women development in several African nations is the Ministry or Department of Social Development, Youth and Sports and the Ministry of Women Affairs. Broad policies and guidelines on women development emanate from these ministries. Prominent among such development programs is the Community Home Economics that include day care center management. This is designed to enlighten women in rural areas on modern methods of home keeping and childcare. Another women development program is the Community Development Training Center. The center undertakes the training of rural women, teachers, and front line women leaders to enable them to motivate the citizens toward undertaking self-help projects and manage the various day care centers (Buchanan 1993: Kuye 2003). Although women dominate the teaching and nursing professions in several African nations, the Ministry of Women's Affairs should do a better job in performing their roles in the women empowerment process to both women and men.

Adult Education Program

The Adult Education program of the Ministry or Department of Education, though not exclusively related to women's affairs, has also presented a policy instrument for enhancing women's development. Women are largely illiterate in comparison with their male counterparts and would therefore benefit more from adult education programs of the national and various regional governments. It is pertinent to note that most African nations have set up a National Education Agency and, subsequently several regional governments have been directed to set aside some of their capital budget on education for the agency (Ibe 1994).

Some African governments have started operating a scholarship scheme for interested female candidates who do exceptionally well in science, technology, mathematics and other science-related subjects. Some technical colleges have been devoted to the enhancement of women's development in a number of African countries (Buchanan 1993). Also indicative of government policy, is the use of mass media to propagate education for women. In this vein, both the national education ministry and state governments seek to encourage parents to send their female children to school. In most rural regions, the official position is to prosecute parents who either withdraw their daughters from school for marriage, encourage their daughters to trade on the streets or farm. Several African governments have also established the Commission for Women's Affairs to enhance the status of women socially and economically. In addition, NGOs and several African governments have issued decrees abolishing abuses against women, improving their health status, and discouraging such practices as early marriage and female circumcision. The President of Nigeria, Olusegun Obasanjo announced the establishment of a new Ministry for Women Affairs in his 2000 budget speech. This is a continuation of General Sani Abacha's legacy of 1995. The rationale for the establishment of a women's ministry is that it will encourage women to enter the labor force and supply a wide range of talents and services that is required for the sustainable development of Nigeria. This in turn will improve productivity and economic growth of the continent. In the management of businesses and industries, however, women are conspicuously absent. The government and NGOs in Africa should establish an atmosphere where women will be seen as transformational managers and innovative entrepreneurs. It is not the technical, but the social and cultural aspects of industrial and business management that militates against success for women in the professional occupations.

Pressure from Civil Society Groups

Further political pressure from NGOs, and civil society groups, by both men and women dedicated to gender equality will be vital to promoting women's interests are not neglected. These groups range from rural co-operative societies to professional occupational associations, to urban business enterprises, to social welfare, church, and entertainment groups. Although they may not have originated as such, many of these groups have developed an expressly political focus. Through the use of these NGOs or civil society groups, women's protests have assumed widely divergent forms. Some civil society organizations are seeking to politicize the private domain in certain contexts. Nonsexist education and training for women and men as well as equal access to jobs, property, and leadership positions must be provided. African nations will not achieve their development goals if women's full humanity and citizenship is not acknowledge and vigorously protected.

Even if legal reforms make the economic situation of wives more secure, African men must be educated on other ways to improve their self-image, redirect their anger and curb their chauvinism. Beating wives should not be tolerated. The media should be used to educate the people of Africa, to raise their awareness of cultural values that encourage family abuse.

African women should realize that the degree of success that they will experience in curtailing any opposition from men and in averting gender stereotype in their nation is dependent on their ability to enlist men as allies. The extent to which this would be possible in Africa hinges on women's ability to convince men that their new social space and new gender identities are non-threatening, mutually benefiting, and greater than a zero-sum game. In the 21st century African nations should change the notion of women as specialized homemakers and men as providers. There should be a mutual understanding that both women and men have the obligation to participate in the labor market regardless of gender and domestic responsibilities.

The lack of cooperation between various government services – such as police, courts, social welfare, and health – only exacerbates women's problems. Abused women need various services that cannot be provided by only one agency. The lack of collaboration between agencies results in increased inaccessibility. Although some African nations are beginning to address this problem by fostering the collaboration between nongovernmental organizations (NGOs), the private sector, and governmental agencies for abuse women. More efforts and resources need to be deployed in most African nations to help women faced with this dilemma.

Finally, African nations would be able to strive toward achieving sustainable development if they could anchor the effective mobilization of women in politics and governance. Placing women in political position and leadership in governance constitutes an important piece of what is representative democracy. Politics and governance are not just about governments, states and elections. Politics encompass the broader questions of voices, identities, parity, justice and social change that women can benefit from across Africa.

Conclusion

This chapter has examined the impact of globalization on women in Africa. It calls for the effective implementation of empowerment policies that would give women equal rights in all countries in the African continent. It argues that gender balance will not come about by itself. Therefore the United Nations, governments in the African continent, the private sector and NGOs must assume the responsibility for dealing with the under-representation of women in the continent. It calls for African governments to introduce gender-sensitive policies that would raise national awareness of women's rights as well as remove cultural and religious constraints against women's attainment of social justice and equity in the society. These policies should be adopted by the national and regional governments as a means for empowering women in economic, social and political aspects of life. It also suggests that if class oppression is overcome in several African nations, then gender oppression and inequality would not be necessary.

The liberal feminist, radical feminist and Marxist feminist theories help to explain the situation of African women beyond patriarchy to include the global exploitation of men and women with the modern capitalist system. It should be noted that globalization has caused most African women to be constrained by factors from other parts of the world. The African woman's faith has been shaped by culture and the system of values as much as by the global economy and politics. Women in the African continent can no longer wait to achieve equity and equal rights in contributing to the processes of sustainable development in the continent? If the problem of under-representation is not rooted in women's lack of resources, but in their lack of knowledge of these resources and experiences that women actually bring into the political life and sustainable development processes, then there is no need to wait for women to be more educated or experienced. There is therefore the need for governments and NGOs in Africa to promote an effective popular education on gender and rights and gender-sensitive socialization programs for children. Because both men and women can contribute to Africa's development, governments, NGOs and other stakeholders should encourage initiatives with men as partners to transform gender relations and achieve gender equity and social justice.

This chapter also argued that in offering women the opportunity to access economic resources and to disentangle their identities from those of their families, diversity management programs will provide the space for women in Africa to clearly define their roles as equal partners in the sustainable development process of the continent. The chapter suggested ways in which subjective perceptions of discrimination can be minimized in Africa. Transparency in the affairs of treating women as equal members of the African society is critical. Public disclosure of entrance requirements and examination results, and even of the rationale for confidentiality where this is felt unavoidable, can ensure that injustice and unfairness are met with public censure. The composition of interview panels must be sensitive to issues of ethnicity as well as gender.

The precise nature of the jobs assigned to men and women is not important in itself. What is important is that jobs should be given to the people with the right qualifications or skills. Gender typing will not help the African continent to attain its industrialization goals. Given Africa's critical economic and political problems, it appears increasingly obvious that suppressing the talents and skills of women in order to protect men's privileges is an enormous waste of human resources that the country can no longer afford. The present situation does not meet the criterion of "the best person for the job." It therefore implies a kind of prodigality that those concerned with public interest can hardly be viewed with equanimity.

Although some bureaucratic structures are in place to provide for equal wages and equality of opportunity, women's economic position relative to men's has eroded. Enforcement of these myopic policies on gender equality clearly becomes difficult when left to men in top management positions. Culturally and religiously (in case of Islam and African traditional religion) prescribed gender roles limit women from asserting themselves as much as they are capable. It also prevents men from allowing women to function as equal partners. Gender balanced policies and women in senior policy-making positions should serve as role models for changing cultural stereotypes. If women's program units were allowed to control significant resources, build useful alliance, and create appropriate incentives, other parts of the public and private sectors would be more likely to respond to policy mandates on gender equality. A look at the past shows clearly that positive strides will not be made without sustained and conscientious efforts by the government.

The various governments, NGOs, private sectors and other civil society groups in Africa must ensure that women are given equal opportunity to contribute in the national development process. With such concrete resolution of the constraints militating against women's participation in development, the African continent will move faster in empowering women in Africa.

References

Abdullah, H. (1995), "Wifeism and Activism: The Nigerian Women's Movement," in Amerita Basu (ed.) *The Challenge of Local Feminisms: Women's Movements in Global Perspective* (Boulder, CO: Westview).

Adamolekun O. (ed.) (1999), *Public Administration in Africa* (Boulder, Colorado: Westview).

Adeleke, V. (2002), *Concept of Gender Equality as a Paradox in Nigeria's Democratic Experience* (Ikeja: Babcock University Nigeria).

Adepuju, A. (1994), "The Demographic Profile: Sustained High Morality and Fertility and Migration for Employment," in *Gender, Work and Population in Sub-Saharan Africa* (ed.), A. Adepoju and C. Oppong (London: J. Currey).

Aderibegbe, Y. (2004), "Women and the War Against Gender Violence," *The Guardian* (15), 21 October 2004.

Akande, J. and Kuye, P. (1986), "Nigeria: Family Law Project," in *Empowerment and the Law: Strategies of Third World Women* (ed.) M. Schuler (Washington, DC: OEF International), 335-345.

Akinboye, S. (2004), *Paradox of Gender Equality in Nigerian Politics* (Lagos, Nigeria: Concept Publication).

Alvarez, S. (1989), "Contradictions of a Women's Space in a Male-Dominated State: The Political Role of the Commissions on the Status of Women in Post -Authoritarian Brazil," in *Women, International Development and Politics* (ed.), K. Staudt (Philadelphia, PA, Temple University Press).

Angya, C. (2005), *Perspectives on Violence Against Women in Nigeria* (Abuja, Nigeria: Aboki Publishers).

Antrobus, P. (2004), *The Global Women's Movements: Origins, Issues and Strategies* (London: Zed Books).

Badejo, D.L. (1985), *Women in Nigeria Today* (London: Zed Books).

Bank, L. (1994), "Angry Men and Working Women: Gender, Violence and Economic Change in Qwaqwq in the 1980s," *African Studies*, Vol. 53, no.1: 89-114.

Beneria, L. (2003), *Gender, Development, and Globalization Economics As If All People Mattered* (London: Routledge).

Brettell, C. and Sargent, C. (1997), *Gender in Cross-Cultural Perspective* (Upper Saddle, NJ: Prentice Hall).

Buchanan, E. (1993), "Women: Struggle for Change," *West Africa*, November 1-7: 21-23.

Callaway, B. and Creevey, L. (1989), "Women and the State in Islamic West Africa," in *Women, the State and Development* (ed.) S. Ellen M. Charton, J. Everett, and K. Staudt (Albany, New York: SUNY Press), 86-113.

Callaway, B. (1987), *Muslim Hausa Women in Nigeria: Tradition and Change* (New York: Syracuse University Press).

Conway, M., Steuernagel, G. and Ahern, D. (2005), *Women and Political Participation* (Washington D. C.: Congressional Quarterly Press).

Dahlerup, D. (2005), *Women, Quotas and Politics* (London: Routledge).

Dahlerup, D. and Francisco, J. (2005), "Gender, Governance and Democracy," *Isis Monograph Series*, vol. 1, no. 1: 12-19.

Dauda, R. (2004), "The Economic Context of Gender Equality in Nigeria," in *Paradox of Gender Equality in Nigerian Politics* (ed.) A. Solomon (Lagos, Nigeria: Cocept Publication).

Dennis, C. (1987), "Women and the State in Nigeria: The Case of the Federal Military Government," in *Women, State and Ideology: Studies from Africa and Asia* (ed.) H. Afshar. (Albany, New York: SUNY Press), 13-27.

Dibie, J. and Dibie, R. (2007), "Current and Future Roles of NGOs in the Empowerment of Women in Africa," in *NGOs and Sustainable Development in Sub-Saharan Africa* (ed.) R. Dibie (Lanham, MD: Lexington Books).

Disch, E. (2006), *Reconstructing Gender* (Boston, MA: McGraw-Hill).

Dolphyne, F. (1991), *The Emancipation of Women: An African Perspective* (Accra: Ghana University Press).

Ebosele, M. (1993), "Political Emancipation of Women," *The Nigerian Observer*, October 5: 5.

Edwards, J. (1995), *When Race Counts: The Morality of Racial Preference in Britain and America* (London: Routledge).

Egonmwan, J. (1991), *Public Policy Analysis: Concepts and Applications* (Benin City, Nigeria: Aka and Brothers Press).

Esman, M. (1997), "Public Administration, Ethnic Conflict, and Economic Development" *Public Administration* Review, vol. 57, no.6, (1997): 527-33.

Gagne, P. and Tewksbury, R. (1999), *The Dynamics of Inequality* (Upper Saddle, NJ: Prentice Hall).

Green, D. (1999), *Gender Violence in Africa* (New York: St. Martin's Press).

Greenberg, J. (2003), *Managing Organizational Behavior* (Upper Saddle River, New Jersey: Prentice Hall).

Gentile, M. (1996), *Managerial Excellence through Diversity* (Prospect Heights, Illinois: Waveland Press).

Gruenbaum, E. (1997), "The Movement Against Clitoridectomy and Infibulation in Sudan: Public Health Policy and the Women's Movement," in *Gender in Cross-Cultural Perspective*, (eds) C. Brettell, and C. Sargent (Upper Saddle River, NJ: Prentice Hall).

Harvey, C, and Allard, J. (2002), *Understanding and Managing Diversity* (Upper Saddle River, NJ: Prentice Hall).

Hyden, G. (2006) *African Politics in Comparative Perspective* (New York, NY: Cambridge University Press).

Ibe, I. (1994), "A Look at the Gender Conflict in Africa." *The Punch Newspaper*, March: 7.

Ifedi, C. (1994), "Women Workers in Multinational Enterprises in Developing Countries," *Business Concord Magazine*, vol. 29, no.2, (June 1994): 7.

Ikpe, E. (2004), "The Historical Legacy of Gender Inequality in Nigeria," in *Paradox of Gender Equality in Nigerian Politics* (ed.) A. Solomom (Lagos: Cocept Publication).

Isekhure, N. (1998), *201 Solutions to Vision 2010* (Benin City, Nigeria: Oduna Communications).

International Family Planning Perspective (IFPP) (2002), "In Zimbabwe, Sexual Relationships with Older Men Put Young Women at high Risk of HIV Infection," *IIFPP*, vol. 28, no. 4, (December, 2002).

Kalu, W. J. (1993), "Battered Spouse As a Social Concern in Work with Families in Two Semi-Rural Communities of Nigeria," *Journal of Family Violence*, vol. 8, no. 4: 361-373.

Karanja, W. (1987), "Outside Wives and Inside Wives in Nigeria: A Study of Changing Perceptions in Marriage," in *Transformations of African Marriage*, (ed.) D. Parkin and D. Nyamwaya (Manchester: Manchester University Press).

Kerbo, H. (2006), *Social Stratification and Inequality* (Boston, MA: McGraw-Hill).

Khapoya, V. (1998), *The African Experience* (Upper Saddle, New Jersey: Prentice Hall Press).

Kingsley, D. (1944), *Representative Bureaucracy* (Yellow Springs, Ohio: Antioch Press).

Kolawole, M. (ed.) (1998), *Gender Perceptions and Development in Africa* (Lagos: Arrabon Academic Publisher).

Konjo, K. (1976), "The Dual-Sex Political System in Operation: Igbo Women and Community Politics in Midwestern Nigeria," in *Women in Africa* (ed.) N. Hafkin and E. Bay, (Stanford CA: Stanford University Press).

—— (1991), "Nigerian Women's Participation in National Politics: Legitimacy and Stability in an Era of Transition," Michigan State University Working Paper (July 1991): 221.

Krislov, S. (1997), *Representative Bureaucracy* (Englewood Cliff, NJ: Prentice Hall).

Kuye, P. (2003), "Economic and Political Empowerment of Women," *Nigeria Vanguard Newspaper* 6 January: 2-3.

Ljjphart, A. (1997), *Democracy in Plural Societies* (New Haven: Yale University Press).

Lovenduski, J. (1989), "Implementing Equal Opportunities in the 1980s: An Overview." *Public Administration*, vol. 67, (1989): 7-18.

Matland, R. (2006), "Electoral Quotas: Frequency and Effectiveness," in *Women, Quotas and Politics*, (ed.) D. Dahlerup (London: Routledge).

Mba, Nina, E. (1982), *Nigerian Woman Mobilized: Women's Political Activity in Southern Nigeria 1900-1965* (Berkeley: University of California).

Meekers, D. and Richter, K. (2005), "Factors Associated with use of the Female Condom in Zimbabwe," *International Family Planning Perspective (IFPP)*, vol. 31, no. 1 (March): 1-5.

Meier, K. (1993), "Representative Bureaucracy: A Theoretical and Empirical Exposition," in *Research in Public Administration* (ed.) J. Perry (Greenwich, Connecticut: JAI Press).

Mohanty, C., Russo, A. and Torres, L. (1991), *Third World Women and the Politics of Feminism* (Bloomington, Indiana: Indiana University Press).

Matland, R.(2006), "Electoral Quotas: Frequency and Effectiveness," in *Women, Quotas and Politics*, (ed.) D. Dahlerup (London: Routledge).

Nelson, C. (1997), "Public and Private Politics: Women in the Middle Eastern World," in *Gender in Cross-Cultural Perspective*, (ed.) C. Brettell and C. Sargent (Upper Saddle, NJ: Prentice Hall).

Nweke, T. (1985), "The Role of Women in Nigerian Society: The Media," in *Women in Nigeria Today*, (ed.) E. Obadina (London: Zed Books).

Obadina, E. (1985), "How Relevant Is the Western Women's Liberation Movement for Nigeria?" in *Women in Nigeria Today*, (ed.) E. Obadina (London: Zed Books).

Ofei-Aoagye, R. (1994), "Altering the Strands of the Fabric: A Preliminary Look at Domestic Violence in Ghana," *Signs*, vol. 19, no. 4: 924-940.

Okpeh, O. and Angya, C. (2007), *Women and Trade Unionism in Nigeria*. Benue State University Center for Gender Studies, Monograph Series no. 1, 2007.

Olowu, D. (1999), "Accountability and Transparency," in *Public Administration in Africa* (ed.) O. Adamolekun (Boulder, CO: Westview).

Olukoshi, A., Omotayo, O. and Aribisala, F. (1994), *Structural Adjustment in West Africa* (Lagos, Nigeria: Pumark Publishers Limited).

Otobo, E. (1999), "Nigeria," in *Public Administration in Africa* (ed.) O. Adamolekun. (Boulder, CO: Westview).

Pam Sha, D. (2007), *Globalization and Challeneges of organizing among Women in the Informal Sector in Nigeria*, Benue State University Center for Gender Studies, Monograph Series no. 2, 2007.

Reiman, K. (2006), "A View from the Top: International Politics, Norms and the Worldwide Growth of NGOs," *International Studies Quarter*, vol. 50: 45-67.

Robertson, C. and Berger, I. (1986), *Women and Class in Africa* (New York: Africana Publishing Company).

Scott, C. (1995), *Gender and Development* (Boulder, CO: Lynn Rienner Press).

Steinman M. (1991), *Women Battering: Policy Responses* (Highland Heights, KY: Academy of Criminal Justice).

Thomas-Sayter, B, and Rocheleau, D. (1995), *Gender, Environment and Development* (Boulder, CO: Lynne Rienner Press).

Turner, M. and Hulme, D. (1997), *Governance, Administration and Development: Making the State Work* (London: Macmillan Press).

Vargas, V. (2000), "Democratic Institutionality and Feminist Strategies during the Nineties," in *About Women's Powers and Vision*, (ed.) V. Vargas. (Montevideo: Dawn and Repem).

Wallace, H. (1999), *Family Violence: Legal, Medical, and Social Perspectives* (Boston, Massachusetts: Allyn and Bacon).

Waylen, G. (1996), *Gender in Third World Politic* (Boulder, Colorado: Lynne Rienner Press).

Weisner, T., Bradley, C. and Kilbride, C. (1997), *African Families and the Crisis of Social Change* (Westport, CT: Bergin and Garvey).

World Bank (1989), *Sub-Sahara Africa: From Crisis to Sustainable Growth: A Long Term Perspective Study* (Washington, DC: World Bank).

World Bank (1997), *World Development Report* (New York: Oxford University Press).

World Bank (1998-1999), *World Development Report* (New York: Oxford University Press).

World Bank (2005), *World Development Report* (New York: Oxford University Press).

Chapter 11

Globalization and the Sexual Commodification of Women

Sex Trafficking Migration in South Asia

Bandana Purkayastha and Shweta Majumdar

Introduction

In South Asia,[1] as in all other parts of the world, sex has long been a commodity for sale. We find, for instance, that the boundary between voluntary exchange of sex (for example by courtesans) and coerced sex—from "nautch girls" (dance girls), "comfort women" gathered in colonies to service British imperial troops, or "beshyas"/prostitutes—as well as the "plight" of sexually exploited women and children was a much debated topic throughout the nineteenth century on the Indian subcontinent.[2] Thus, sex trafficking is not a new phenomenon in this region. Contemporary globalization has intersected with local socio-economic-political processes and re-energized some of the "older" forms of trafficking by expanding the "catchment area" from where socio-economically women and girls are trafficked. It has also fuelled the rapid growth of a large market for the commodification and commercialized consumption of sex.

In this chapter, we provide a brief glimpse into sex trafficking in South Asia. We show how global, regional and local, i.e. glocal, trends intersect in this region and shape sex trafficking and responses to it. We describe trafficking in and

---

1   Though South Asia, as a geo-political entity consists of eight countries: India, Pakistan, Afghanistan, Nepal, Bangladesh, Sri Lanka, Maldives and Bhutan. In this chapter we focus only on India, Pakistan, Nepal and Bangladesh. We made this pragmatic selection because, relatively, there is more information available on trafficking for these four countries.

2   According to Kumar (1990), prostitution, organized in public "red light areas" grew rapidly as "comfort women" colonies were created by the British to serve imperial troops. But as venereal diseases spread, the British attempted to regulate prostitution through an Act that allowed them the power to medically examine all women suspected of prostitution. Women suspected of prostitution were penalized under laws that against "immoral acts;" male clients were not charged at all. The Indian opposition was varied: many reformers fought back against the British definition of "prostitute" which did not distinguish between courtesans, mistresses, and prostitutes. Other male and female Indian reformers tried to rehabilitate prostitutes.

between India, Pakistan, Nepal and Bangladesh to show how local hegemonies drive the process and organization of sex trafficking. We also document responses to sex trafficking by governments and non-governmental actors. We conclude by weaving academic debates in the West about sex trafficking—especially the debate about trafficked women as agents or victims—with the ways in which trafficking and its consequences are constructed in South Asia.

Sex Trafficking and Globalization

The U.S. Department of State has estimated that, globally, 70 percent of all trafficked females are trafficked for prostitution and other forms of sexual exploitation (U.S. Department of State, 2004). While some women, men and children are trafficked for organ harvesting, and others—primarily women and children—are trafficked to provide coerced domestic, agricultural, construction, industrial, militia labor, the vast majority end up as "resources" for a rapidly growing commercial sex industry. Commercial sexual exploitation includes prostitution, pornography, stripping, live sex shows, mail-order brides, military prostitution and sex tourism. Contemporary globalization has increased the scale of the trafficking industry which traverses multiple countries, and includes many layers of middle-persons between the consumers and providers of the service. In order to address the role of the varied people and organizations involved in trafficking, the UN's protocol on trafficking attempts to traverse both the process through which vulnerable people are moved as well as the profit making enterprise. The "Protocol to Prevent, Suppress and Punish Trafficking in Persons, Especially Women and Children, Supplementing the United Nations Convention Against Transnational Organized Crime" (in short, the Trafficking Protocol). Set in Article 3(a) of the Protocol, trafficking in persons is defined as:

> the recruitment, transportation, transfer, harboring, or receipt of persons, by means of threat or the use of force or other forms of coercion, of abduction, of fraud, of deception, of the abuse of power or of a position of vulnerability or of the giving or receiving of payments or benefits to achieve the consent of a person having control over another person, for the purpose of exploitation.

This definition of trafficking emphasizes the process through which vulnerable people are moved and received. Since there is some overlap with migration, especially illegal migration and smuggling,[3] there is a global movement by

---

3   The United Nations Convention against Transnational Organized Crime and its two distinct Protocols on "Trafficking" and on the "Smuggling of Migrants by Land, Sea and Air" (Protocol on Smuggling hereafter) seeks to resolve the conceptual ambiguity that arises from overlapping the two concepts. The Protocol on Smuggling defined smuggling as "the procurement, in order to obtain, directly or indirectly, a financial or other material

groups such as the Coalition Against Sex Trafficking to stop such trafficking by developing new laws, especially migration laws to address trafficking in the receiving countries.

Just as the earlier phase of globalization—via colonization of large parts of the world by European powers and the rapid growth of military and police cantonments surrounded by "comfort women" districts—led to an upsurge of sex trafficking, the contemporary phase has contributed both to an upsurge[4] in sex trafficking as well as the recognition of trafficking as a problem. Among the contributory factors that, directly or indirectly affect sex trafficking are the impoverishment of groups especially through Structural Adjustment Programs (SAPs),[5] the rapid growth of feminized jobs, and the lure of these "well paid" jobs for women in impoverished areas, easier access to long distance travel, the circulating global imageries via global media of life in other places that attract women who want to move to these

---

benefit, of the illegal entry of a person into a State Party of which the person is not a national or a permanent resident." Typically, smuggling involves a contractual relationship between those seeking to leave a country and those acting as agents to assist their client with entry to another country. Usually, the relationship ends once the migrants have arrived at their destination and have paid their legal fees. Illegal entry means "crossing borders without complying with the necessary requirements for legal entry into the receiving State" (UNODC; 2004). Illegal immigrants may or may not have been smuggled. What sets trafficking apart from smuggling and illegal immigration is notion of consent. While smuggling and illegal immigration involve the consent of those smuggled or illegally migrating, trafficked victims are recruited and transported by means of coercion, deception or some other form of illicit influence. The United Nations Office on Drugs and Crime (UNODC) explicitly states that, "the smuggling of migrants, while often undertaken in dangerous and degrading, involves migrants who have consented to the smuggling. Trafficking victims, on the other hand, have either never consented or, if initially consented, that consent has been rendered meaningless by the coercive, deceptive or abusive actions of the traffickers." The document furthermore states that children below the age of 18 years cannot give *valid consent* (UNODC 2004).

4   Data on sex trafficking are notoriously difficult to obtain or validate. So there may be room for debate about the potential "upsurge" in trafficking. All the data in this chapter is based on estimates or are projections based on very small-scale surveys.

5   There is a significant feminist literature on SAPs and their effects. Our assumption of SAPs follows Shah et al.'s (1999) discussion of Structural Adjustment Programs that lead to devaluation of currency, encourage exports (consequently affecting the balance of food grown for consumption and subsistence), lobby for government incentives for the private sector (shrinking public sector "welfare" programs and other programs that addressed people's social human rights), privatization of government-owned units, de-licensing, deregulation and disciplining labor (and labor rights/economic human rights demands) to create conditions that are supposed to demonstrate how the "magic of markets" positively affects all. In reality numerous studies have shown that while some sectors benefit, others suffer (e.g. Sen 1992; 1997). Sections that are impoverished are affected both in terms of dwindling incomes and their ability to subsist through agriculture, but also in terms of life chances as government resources are diverted to the rights of the wealthier sections of society and the world (Sen 2002).

"familiar places" in order to create better lives for themselves, disruptions and social disorder introduced by war and prolonged violent conflict, and the racial commoditization and marketing of women's bodies. All of these factors affect South Asia.

The overwhelming number of women and girls who are trafficked in South Asia are poor. Their vulnerability to sex trafficking has been enhanced through the effects of SAPs as well as the lure of new feminized jobs. All four countries have been subject to economic corporate globalization, which has enriched sections of the middle class, but has further impoverished the urban and rural poor, significantly diminishing their social and economic human rights to food, shelter, education, health etc. (Shiva 2005). At a global level continuing protection of domestic agricultural markets in the West have made it difficult for largely agricultural economies, like Bangladesh, to improve living conditions for the vast majority of its rural inhabitants. At the same time, the adoption of neo-liberal policies that that led to significant privatization of public resources, such as water, leading to severe drought, destruction of agricultural land, increased rural indebtedness and famine or near-famine conditions (e.g. Shiva 2005; Sainath 1997). Among the four countries in South Asia, India shows the greatest contrasts. Since the 1980s, it has developed both a very large increasingly affluent middle class (larger in size than the entire population of the U.S.), as well as growing numbers of desperately poor people who are witnessing the erosion of the meager government safeguards— through subsidized education, health-care, food, agricultural support—that they hoped to access before. Pakistan, Bangladesh and Nepal have been subject to SAPs for longer period of time with similar results for the poor but, unlike India, without the growth of a large middle class.[6] And, as Sassen (1999) and others have pointed out, the 1980s and 1990s have also been a period of massive expansion of feminized labor opportunities—ill paid, marginal jobs that are targeted to women—that appeared to provide opportunities to women with little education and few "formal" skills. The rapid growth of garment factories in Bangladesh (Kabeer 2002), or carpet industries in Nepal (Gurung 2003a) are indicators of this trend in South Asia.

The loss of livelihood through SAPs, the reality of poverty and destitution, combined with new gendered labor opportunities in the region, together, create an environment where more and more women were willing to look to more distant areas for jobs and parents were willing to send their children off with "labor" recruiters. For instance, as Shobha Gurung (2003a; 2003b), Hennink and Simkhada (2004) points out, from the 1980s, the implementation of structural adjustment programs

---

6   It is important to note that India has always been a multiparty democracy, Nepal, a monarchy till very recently, Bangladesh has been both democratic and subject to military rule in phases, while Pakistan has mostly been subject to military rule. These political conditions intersect with economic trends, so the effects of economic changes are not an outcome of economic forces alone. However that larger discussion is beyond the scope of this chapter.

in Nepal led to a huge cut in government spending on social welfare and massive layoffs of people employed by the government. In many rural areas, men went to cities in search of jobs paying family-wages (which they rarely found), and soon women were looking for jobs as well. Many Nepali women were lured into the sex industry by people who either promised them jobs weaving carpets in factories (for which their young nimble fingers were supposed to be specifically suitable), or by men who pretended to fall in love with young women who were employed in factories, convinced them to move to another place where they would "get married," and thus easily sold the women to the buyers who shop for trafficked women. Many of these women were then trafficked to India. While the hegemonies with South Asia are discussed later, the substantive point is the role of globalization in promoting poverty *and* holding out the promise of new work opportunities for women contribute to the context in which trafficking is facilitated.

While war and conflict are less recognized in the main literature relating globalization and sex trafficking, the enormous growth in the number of conflicts (Gledditsch et al. 2002) in the 20th century points to the massive dislocations to established ways of life because of wars and ethno-conflicts. The massive sale of arms by the G-8 countries to the rest of the world, including South Asia, a characteristic of contemporary globalization, then, also contributes to conditions that promote sex trafficking. As women's groups have pointed out at various international platforms, women are often raped, enslaved as "symbols of their communities," and simply kidnapped for sale during times of social disorder. The ongoing conflicts among South Asian neighbors, such as the India-Pakistan or the Pakistan-Bangladesh war/s, the internal conflicts such as the Maoist uprising in rural Nepal, periodic ethnic cleansing in the state of Gujarat in India, growing armed movements among religio-political factions in parts of Pakistan or Bangladesh, secessionist movements in India, all contribute to social dislocation and increased vulnerability of women and girls to sexual exploitation and, subsequently, for trafficking.

Much of contemporary globalization is about profit making and sex trafficking is an extremely lucrative source of income, not only for organized crime, but also for the people in the sex tourism industry. Increasingly specialized segmented markets—much like marketing of brand name products—link consumers with specific kinds of women who are expected to provide varied sexual gratification. As the spread of neo-liberalism enriches groups of people in different parts of the world, relatively wealthy men are able to travel to different countries, or to places within their own countries, in search of sex. A rapidly growing industry caters to the varied demands for sex (from sexually provocative dancers to prostitutes and sex slaves) for this group. Asian women in general—long considered pliable, willing, and able to go to any lengths to please a man, according to racist stereotypes (Espiritu 1997)—are a prized commodity in this market.[7] While the global level focus is still on "oriental" women (i.e. women from South East and East Asia), South Asian women satisfy the desires of men who are looking for the other type of Asian women. Such global trends intersect with locally constructed beliefs and practices. In fact, a series of local cultural myths based on religion, nationality, and age of the female—for instance, having sex with a virgin Nepali Hindu girl cures STDs—have been constructed to promote the marketing of specific kinds of women into specific niches of the industry.[8] Who ends up in brothels and who is directed to pornographic rings, is a function of the demand for women of particular race, age, religion, ethnic characteristic among the consumers.

The rapid and effective circulation of images of commoditized women's bodies supports trafficking. Globalization contributes centrally to the racialized/gendered imageries that are sold through the rapidly emerging pornographic websites. For instance, a simple Internet search on "Bengali women" (a term describing women from Bangladesh and from the neighboring state in India, West Bengal who speak the Bengali language) will yield a number of pornographic sites. Since the hierarchy of sites is dependent on the number of "visits," the virtual marketing of commoditized sex contributes, along with other efficient media forms, to the publicization of raced/gendered bodies for consumption. Thus globalized means of communication such as the World Wide Web have proved an indispensable ally and marketing tool for traffickers. Pornographers use sex trafficking victims in their films, websites, and so forth, while at the same time those productions promote the "sale" of women that help build the demand for sex trafficking victims (Guinn 2006). Different levels of involvement are offered to the buyers of sex in the virtual world. They can choose to watch what has been uploaded online, or they can choose to engage in web cam chats with models catering to all their whims and fancies in the virtual space. Options for sex tourism too are routinely advertised. According to the U.S Department of State (2004), child sex tourism (CST) is a dark side of globalization, with some two million children exploited in the global commercial sex trade. Buyers sitting in one country can choose or bid for their "models" in another as women and children procured in one part of the world are being "bought and sold" in another.

In sum, sex trafficking is not a "new" phenomenon, but globalization has significantly increased the reach of this trade (Richter and Richter 2004). While the women and girls have been trafficked on the Indian subcontinent for centuries, contemporary globalization—the burgeoning mediascapes, ethnoscapes, technoscapes, finanscapes, as Appadurai (1996) has described them—has increasingly transcended its local bases and become transnational in its organization and market. The routes however are always from lesser developed to

---

7   A certain proportion of men and boys are also exploited for sex but, given constraints of space and available information, we confine our attention mostly to women.

8   See for instance, Ruchira Gupta's documentary film, *The Selling of Innocents*, about Nepali girls who are sold to brothel owners in Mumbai, India.

more developed regions of the world. As Denier (2003) argues, poor, uneducated, young females from the global south involuntarily servicing older, rich, educated and privileged males from the industrialized global north. This same relationship holds within South Asia, where women from poorer regions continue to serve wealthier men in other parts of the country or in other countries.

South Asia as a Context of Sex Trafficking

A key factor that shapes sex trafficking in South Asia is that the four countries form a contiguous landmass with international borders that are relatively porous. Due to their ongoing political conflicts, the border between Pakistan and India are under surveillance but the borders between the other countries are more porous. For instance, the lack of overt political conflict between India and Nepal, as well as the mountainous character of much of the border area, make the borders between India and Nepal most porous. While technically, the Bangladeshi border is under greater surveillance, Sleightholme and Sinha (1996) report their first hand experiences of the porosity of the Bangladeshi border where border security guards profit from sex trafficking.

The significant cultural similarities between each of the four countries also facilitate the task of traffickers. It is harder to distinguish exactly who is being trafficked between the four countries on the basis of measures used in the West. In contrast to the mostly mono-lingual U.S., where a sense of "white, English-speaking person, as native" persists as a yardstick for identifying who the foreigners are, and who might, potentially, be victims of international trafficking (Landsman 2004), in the multiracial, multi ethnic, multi linguistic South Asian countries, which share much of the cultural pluralism, it is harder to identify "trafficking victims" based on any notion of foreignness. Perceived cultural similarities also make it easier to convince women that they are likely to find jobs in another country, the lure of feminized jobs that we discussed earlier. At the same time, the cultural similarities can facilitate the "assimilation" of trafficked women into niches of a multi-lingual, multi-religious, multicultural sex industry. The U.S Department of State (2001) report notes that children from Bangladesh and Nepal are routinely trafficked into India where they are forced into prostitution.

In his seminal work—*Modernity at Large*—Appadurai (1996) argued that globalization does not necessarily dissolve local hegemonies; instead local and regional hegemonies are likely to be enhanced depending on which places or groups are able to most benefit from globalization. India is the most populous, democratic, economic powerhouse in this region. It continues to act as a beacon for marginalized people, especially in Nepal and Bangladesh, who hope to find "well paid" jobs. It has become the source, transit region, and destination for sex trafficking in South Asia (Huda 2006, USAID 2001). India's large and rapidly growing tourist industry—driven by images of historical landscapes, beaches, multi-level tourist facilities, religious pluralism, and relative peace—provides the space for the more upscale sex tourism. Sex tourism attracts relatively wealthy consumers from within the country and from nearby destinations such as the Middle East as well as far off destinations such as Europe, North America and Australia. Similarly, India's technology revolution facilitates web-based dissemination of information and virtual links to the sex industry. At the same time lower costs brothels survive and grow fuelled by clients among migrant male laborers in urban areas, truckers who routinely carry products across the country, or any urban male in search of cheap sex. Mumbai, Kolkata and Delhi brothels are major destination for trafficked women and children from all four countries.

According to The Protection Project, "Of the 74 million South Asian women reported as missing, 20 million are said to be working in Indian brothels. An estimated 25 percent of women trafficked to India are under 18 years of age" (Mattar 2003). Bangladeshi and Nepali women are most likely to be trafficked into India, Bangladeshi women are additionally transferred to the Middle East. Like India, Pakistan is also a source and transit country, especially for commercial sex exploitation of women and girls. However, the scale is supposed to be smaller compared to India. Protection Project estimates that in the past ten years, 200,000 women ages 12 to 30 have been trafficked for purposes of sexual exploitation from Bangladesh to Pakistan.

Most evidence suggests that women from poverty stricken areas, in all four countries, are lured by traffickers with promises of a better job or better life (Sleightholme and Sinha 1996). Traffickers can be local recruiters, relatives, neighbors or even the immediate family. Of seven trafficking Nepalese victims interviewed by Human Rights Watch/Asia in March 1994, six were trafficked to India with the help of close family friends or relatives. In each case, the victim complained of deception. Women are sold for amounts as small as $4.00 to brokers who deliver them to brothel owners in India for anywhere from $500-$1,333 (Guthrie 1995). Debt bondage and forced labor characterize the sex trafficking nexus in South Asia. Debt bondage, prohibited under "The Supplementary Convention on the Abolition of Slavery, the Slave Trade and Institutions and Practices Similar to Slavery," is defined as "a situation in which debtors pledge their personal services against a debt they owe, but the person to whom they owe it fails to deduct the value of their services from the debt, or the length and nature of those services are not respectively limited and defined" (<http://www.hrw.org/reports/1995/India.htm - P400_94079>). However, in this scenario the trafficked victim is not a voluntary debtor but is instead forced to work in order to pay off the price that has been paid to "buy" them from their trafficker. Forced labor, is defined by the ILO as, "All work or service which is exacted from any person under the menace of any penalty and for which the said person has not offered himself/herself voluntarily" (Guthrie et al. 1995; Plant 2006).

Once sold into prostitution, women and children typically end up working to pay off the "debt" that they have been "deceived" into accruing. The brothel owners force them to work in abysmal conditions to "buy" their way to freedom.

A villager interviewed by Human Rights Watch reported that a typical "pillow house"[9] charged $1.66 for fifteen minutes, and that a woman earned between $50-83 a day which she turned over to the owner. In a day she might have more than twenty-five "clients" and she could earn small tips five to fifteen cents from clients. A bungalow-style brothel charged about Rs.100 [$3.33] for an hour and the girls kept the tips (Guthrie et al. 1995).

In all four countries, women and children most likely to be trafficked belong to minority and economically vulnerable groups (USAID 2001). In Nepal, seventy percent of women and girls trafficked are thought to belong to ethnic minority groups such as the Tamang, Gurung, Magar, and Sherpa; women and girls from Nepal's Hindu majority communities comprise about ten to fifteen percent (Guthrie et al. 1995.) Internally displaced persons are also under heightened risk of being trafficked. As recently as 20 December 2007, the disappearance of about 100 children from camps for displaced Reang tribes people in India's northeastern state of Tripura was reported. The poor illiterate parents were told that their children were being taken away to be groomed in better schools in the cities and were conned into signing a document saying that the child was an orphan and that they were only his relatives taking care of him (Bhaumik 2007).

Cross-border tension often exacerbates trafficking in these regions rendering women and children in refugee camps most vulnerable. For example, reportedly the events of 9/11 have further exacerbated the problem of trafficking as the boundaries between Afghanistan and Pakistan became fluid. UNHCR Ruud Lubbers said, "Afghans are the largest group of asylum seekers in the world, and many are falling into the hands of traffickers" (Protection Project). Bhutanese refugees in Nepal face a similar situation (HRW 2003).

Trafficking syndicates in these countries have a wide international network. For example, other than Bangladesh, Pakistan also serves as a destination for women and children trafficked by Russian organized crime groups, from Tajikistan and central Asian states such as Burma, Nepal, Thailand, and the Philippines. (The Protection Project 2000). Women and children from India, Bangladesh, Nepal, and Pakistan are also trafficked to other parts of the world especially the Middle East and Kuwait (The Protection Project 2000). U.S Department of State (2001) reported that Nepalese citizens are also trafficked to Hong Kong and Thailand.

Responses to Trafficking in South Asia

The problem of sex trafficking has been identified—through the efforts of governments, NGOs and other activist organizations—and defined by United

---

9   According to Human Rights Watch, the brothels have different types upon the price charged and services provided. A pillow house are the cheapest brothels where a room consists of several beds separated only by curtains. The "bungalow house" serves more elite clientele who are allocated personal rooms (Guthrie et al. 1995).

Nations protocols. At the same time local understandings and activism in South Asia continue to shape responses to trafficking. In her book Human Rights and Gender Violence, Sally Engle Merry has argued that throughout the world, international protocols are often interpreted and reworked in local contexts in ways that might be at odds with the legalistic framework of many "universal" protocols. The state and civil society responses together show how responses to trafficking reflect both the directions of universal protocols and some specifically local responses to the problem.

State Responses

In 2001, the United States Department of State developed a three-tier system to evaluate progress made by countries to combat trafficking. While countries ranked in tier 1 showed most progress in criminalizing trafficking, punishing traffickers, and providing rehabilitation to victims, those in tier 3 showed the least commitment and progress. According to the report, India, Nepal and Bangladesh are tier 2 countries while Pakistan is tier 3 country (U.S. Department of State 2001).

All four countries have signed or ratified important international covenants that criminalize trafficking. These countries have also adopted several domestic legislations to combat trafficking. For example, in India, the "Immoral Traffic (Prevention) Act" prohibits trafficking in human beings (including children), encompasses sexual exploitation for commercial purposes of members of both sexes, and provides enhanced penalties for offences involving minors. In Bangladesh, the "Suppression of Violence against Women and Children Act of 2000" punishes the crime of trafficking in children and women by capital punishment or by imprisonment for life and a fine. In Nepal, the "Human Trafficking Control Act of 1986" prohibits selling of persons in Nepal or abroad and provides for penalties of up to 20 years' imprisonment for traffickers. The Federal Cabinet of Pakistan in August 2002 also passed the Prevention and Control of Human Trafficking Ordinance in all countries except Nepal, prostitution is illegal.

The countries have extensively collaborated among themselves to increase border surveillance. The governments of Nepal and India announced in late December 2003 that their human rights commissions would sign an agreement to control cross-border trafficking. Pakistani and Iranian officials also held talks in Islamabad in May 2003 on tightening their common border. In January 2002, the governments of all seven South Asian countries signed the "SAARC[10] Convention on Prevention and Combating Trafficking in Women and Children for Prostitution". They collectively declared that, "the evil of trafficking in women and children for the purpose of prostitution is incompatible with the dignity and honour of human beings and is a violation of basic human rights" (SAARC 2002).

---

10   The South Asian Association for Regional Cooperation (SAARC) forum, founded in 1985, aims at promoting cultural ties and economic and social development among member states (Bangladesh, Bhutan, India, Maldives, Nepal, Pakistan, and Sri Lanka).

However, the gains made in terms of passing Acts and signing treaties has not been sufficiently translated into active enforcement or tangible relief for victims of trafficking. Lack of political will, poor implementation of programs, pervasive corruption, paucity of adequate information/data, patriarchal state policies, and the shortage of resources have often been cited as the main obstacles to effectively combat trafficking, prosecute traffickers and assist victims.

In India, for instance, police and local officials patronize brothels and protect brothel owners and traffickers. Brothel owners pay protection money and bribes to the police to prevent raids and to bail out under-age girls who are arrested. Girls and women who complain to the police about rape or abduction, or those who are arrested in raids or for vagrancy, are often held in "protective custody" where corrupt authorities have been known to allow brothel owners to buy back the detainees. Custodial rapes in "protective custody" are not unheard of either (Guthrie et al. 1995). Along the border, the border patrol personnel work with the traffickers to provide facilitative conditions for trafficking (Guthrie et al. 1995, Sleightholme and Sinha 1996). Even when apprehended, traffickers in South Asia enjoy high acquittal rates thereby contributing further perpetration of crime rather than its arrest (Huntington 2002).

In addition to laxity in abetting in the crime, the police and the legal system can further victimize trafficked women by treating them as criminals. In Pakistan, when caught, the women are booked under Pakistan's controversial Hudood Ordinance of 1979, which criminalizes Zina, defined by law as extra-marital sex. Sex outside marriage is deemed to be a crime against the state and women forced into prostitution are compelled to marry relatives of brothel owners to escape prosecution under Islamic Hudood laws that legalize polygamy (Mattar 2003).

Other domestic policies, which are paternalistic in character, restrict women's right to migrate voluntarily in the name of protection against trafficking. The Foreign Employment Act in Nepal (1985) prevents women from being employed across the national borders. Advising girls to stay home and "not be modern, work hard, be patient" is often a doomed strategy since it runs contrary to the needs and aspiration of the girls. For example, the survey conducted in Nepali villages by the Asia Foundation and in the NGO Horizons, shows that 40 percent of the girls interviewed sought to migrate and 85 percent wanted to move to urban areas. Often strict border controls have been instituted to curb the problem but paradoxically this only exposes women more to traffickers who lure them away with promises of better lives and livelihoods. In 1998, in an effort to combat trafficking, the Bangladeshi Government placed restrictions on Bangladeshi women traveling abroad to work as domestic servants—often a ruse to induct women into the sex trade—for non-Bangladeshi employers (The Asia Foundation 2001).

Thus, the strategies employed by South Asian countries have had more repressive than emancipatory repercussions. Brown (2002) states that even though states show apparent sympathy for trafficking victims, they are quick to distinguish between so-called "innocent" victims of trafficking and victims who the states can effectively blame and punish. A state's quest for finding an "innocent" victim, in an attempt to distinguish between candidates "deserving" and "undeserving" of support and services, often leaves out trafficked women who have become recruiters per force in order to "buy" their way out.

State agencies also tend to blur the status of trafficked women and immigration laws. Destination states can claim that trafficked women are undeserving of rights and respect just by virtue of not owning legal immigration papers and often being forced into trade that is regarded as illegitimate by the state. In such situations summary deportations, imprisonment and detention further victimize the victims (Brown 2002). For instance, approximately 2,500 Bangladeshi women have been detained in Pakistan on charges of illegal entry and of illegitimate sexual activities (Mattar 2003).

Overall, the construction of trafficking as a criminal justice issue has led to the gendered construction of women as innocent victims (otherwise undeserving of state protection) and traffickers as criminals. Little attention has been paid to male consumers whose desires and buying power fuel this industry. A policy suggestion in India, proposed by the Minister for Women and Children, Renuka Ray, in 2007, to criminalize, prosecute and assign jail sentences to men who frequent brothels, has generated sufficient controversy within her party that the measure, at present, seems unlikely to pass (Kasturi 2008).

Non-governmental Responses to Trafficking

Compared to the governments' responses, the non-governmental organizations in South Asia has been more active and effective in addressing the problem of sex trafficking. The framing of sex trafficking as a human right violation and not merely one of organized crime or illegal migration has provided the facilitative context for much of the anti-trafficking activism (Mattar 2003).

Many NGOs have adopted the declaration of the Beijing Platform that violence against women, and hence trafficking, is violation of human rights. It declared that,

> The effective suppression of trafficking in women and girls for sex trade is a matter of pressing international concern...The use of women in international prostitution and trafficking networks has become a major focus on international organized crime...Women and girls who are victims of this international trade are at an increased risk of further violence, as well as unwanted pregnancy and sexually transmitted infection, including infection with HIV/AIDS. Beijing Platform for Action, chap. I, resolution 1, annex II, para 122)

From a strategic perspective, viewing trafficking as a violation of human rights rather than simply a problem of organized crime has discernible advantages. Viewing trafficking as a problem of organized crime focuses on individual victims and perpetrators thereby shifting the focus away from structural causes. Additionally, criminal proceedings often victimize the victim by exposing them and their families to later vengeance by the perpetrators and their organizations. The victim is merely reduced to becoming the "witness and evidence." The narrow approach often obscures the trafficked persons' rights and provides little in terms of state protection, justice, rehabilitation and repatriation (Wijers et al. 1997, Wijers and Lin 1998). Viewing trafficking as only a problem of illegal migration has similar limitations as it upholds the sanctity of state borders and sovereignty over and above the fate of the trafficked individual. This approach conceptually merges smuggling of persons with trafficking and thereby criminalizing the trafficked victim as well. Strategically the state responds by stepping up repressive measures and more stringent border controls to prevent migration (Wijers et al. 1997). Compared to these approaches, focusing on trafficking as a problem of human rights violations offers a way around several limitations. Conceiving it as human rights violations brings the focus back upon underlying structural causes of poverty and gender discrimination that spurs trafficking. It is more sensitive to the agency and personhood of the trafficked individual who is viewed more as "human" rather than "criminal" violating state boundaries. It allows for more comprehensive understanding of trafficking as a social, economic and political issue.

At the grass roots level, the nexus of local NGOs and INGOs have been extremely beneficial in organizing against trafficking. These civil society actors have typically adopted a three pronged strategy for combating trafficking— lobbying the domestic governments to enforce anti-trafficking regulations more effectively; working with activists across border to bring international pressure to bear upon lax governments as well securing better sources of funding, and, finally, the NGOs and movements on ground have sought to rescue and rehabilitate victims of trafficking. In some cases, NGO activism has directly prevented the state from "criminalizing" the victim. For example, the UNIFEM lobbies the South Asian governments to take a stronger stance against traffickers and be more sympathetic towards victims.

Coalescing with NGOs across the border has proved effective in raising awareness across borders as well as transferring funds and resources from the North to the South. In 2000, USAID funded a large regional anti-trafficking effort for South Asia. Managed by the United Nations Development Fund for Women (UNIFEM), it focused on prevention and education in Bangladesh, India, Nepal, Pakistan and Sri Lanka. USAID-UNIFEM's funding for prevention strategy includes support for networking and alliance-building among NGOs, community leaders, and the law enforcement community in an effort to generate political and community support for anti-trafficking initiatives (USAID 2001). For example, USAID/Bangladesh provides support and funding to the Action Against Trafficking and Sexual Exploitation of Children (ATSEC), a regional anti-trafficking network of NGOs. It also supports the Bangladesh National Women Lawyers' Association (BNWLA) in its efforts to combat trafficking. BNWLA focuses on the protection of trafficking victims and the prosecution of trafficking perpetrators. The BNWLA provides legal aid, rehabilitation, and repatriation support services to trafficking survivors, and manages *Proshanti*, a shelter home for trafficking victims and abused women and children. BNWLA has provided shelter and services to nearly 1,000 women and children over several years. It also works in co-operation with the Government of Bangladesh to promote the prosecution of traffickers. USAID/ Nepal's anti-trafficking activities address the need for prevention and protection, focusing primarily on raising awareness, gathering information, promoting advocacy, and providing assistance to victims.

In addition to the NGOs that are allied to INGOs, a number of other local organizations exist in each of the four countries. Most of these focus on social and economic opportunities for trafficked women; others look to health care issues. In Nepal an NGO, ABC, emphasizes the creation of educational opportunities for women and girls across 32 districts to reduce their vulnerability to trafficking. Educational awareness is coupled with an economic empowerment program that promotes savings and provides credit and start-up funds to women. Another NGO, Maiti-Nepal, focuses on education, promotes community-based surveillance, and rescues and rehabilitates trafficked girls. Shakti Samuha, started in 1996 in Nepal, is the first NGO in the world formed by trafficking survivors. It conducts various activities to facilitate awareness among the targeted population groups (Shakti Samuha 2007).

Along with the organizations *for* trafficked women, South Asia, especially India, has been the site of organizing *by* trafficked women. Trafficked women have mostly focused on economic and social human rights issues. In Kolkata, India, the Sonagachi movements started by sex workers initially to demand safer conditions of work and safe sex practices has successfully intervened in stopping child trafficking in West Bengal (Nath 2000). The trafficked women have also organized themselves as sex workers[11] so they could demand certain rights to ameliorate their conditions. Using the political opportunity in West Bengal, India, where a Communist government, whose public rhetoric is about labor rights, has won elections for over twenty years, the "sex workers" have begun to frame their demands within workers' rights issues. Sleightholme and Sinha's unique study documents how the original movement among "sex workers" in Kolkata/Calcutta reflected the visions of middle class members of NGOs or quasi government agencies (1996). These middle class activist driven solutions focused on "small" income generation schemes to "rehabilitate prostitutes." Yet such rehabilitation

---

11   There is debate in use of the term "sex workers" in the literature as well as among movements of women. Anne E. Lacsamana (2004) gives an excellent critical and analytical discussion of this debate in "Sex Workers or Prostituted Women: An Examination of Sex Work Debates in Western Feminist Theory." She argues that those who are in the "pro-sex worker" camp tend to accommodate to the existing order rather than bring about a new social order. She gives voice to GABRIELLA a woman's movement organization in the Philippines whose stance on combating sex trafficking is to change the system that produces it. Naming prostitution as "sex work" does not change the exploitative and dehumanizing nature of it for women.

schemes were ineffective because the gendered perspectives on income generation did not recognize these women as the main breadwinners (rather than partial and supplementary income contributors) for their families. Apart from income generation, other NGO efforts focused on health issues. Rising from the concerns about the spread of AIDS, somewhat reminiscent of the British concern over the spread of venereal diseases, some NGOs tried to distribute condoms to red-light areas. Initially these types of initiatives did not take into account the power imbalances that leave the trafficked women vulnerable to the men who have paid to consume their bodies. Over time, initiatives by "sex worker" groups, supported by doctors such as Samarjit Jana, created the climate for condom use throughout the Sonagachi area and actually arrested the rates of spread of AIDs and other diseases (Basu et al. 2004). Building off these successes, Sanlaap and other NGOs in Kolkata have spearheaded the demands of sex workers for labor rights; their demands have been framed in terms of better work conditions, provision of child-care facilities, creation of shelters and homes, broadening the scope of health related projects and access to health care, promoting savings and credit schemes, addressing gendered labor conditions in the job market, creating more female police officers and training police officers on issues affecting sex work, creating a lobby for sex worker demands, better enforcement of anti-trafficking laws, and creating lobbies against media portrayals of women as sex objects (Sleightholme and Sinha 1996). While sex worker movements of this type are still unique in South Asia, the demands of these Kolkata-based groups point to some reforms initiated by the women that addressed the immediate conditions of trafficked women. On the other hand, however, such reforms raise the question of how to bring about broader radical change that will address the structural roots of sex trafficking in the context of globalization in order to ultimately end sexual exploitation and commodification of women. As well, it raises the critical question: how can human agency ultimately change the system that profits from the sexual trafficking of women and turn them into commodities for sale? How do responses to sex trafficking lead to radical transformation of the complex structures which in the first place creates the conditions trafficked women cope with or even escape from?

In sum, the responses to sex trafficking by the government and NGOs overlap only to limited degrees. While the government, lobbied by NGOs, focus on control of trafficking and rehabilitation of the trafficked women, other NGOs, including the sex worker NGOs, focus on a variety of human rights issues. This points to the complexity of combating sex trafficking.

Conceptualizing Trafficking and Policy

While there is a growing literature focusing on trafficking and globalization, much of the literature remains mired in the conceptual controversies over trafficked women as victims or as agents (Miriam 2005). Use of the imagery of women as victims has provided a strategic frame for successfully gathering support of people who wish to help victims on humanitarian grounds (McDonald 2004). On the other hand, constructing women as victims alone also deprives them of their ability to define their situation and the solutions they require (Kelly 2004). Even this brief overview of sex trafficking in South Asia and its links to globalization shows that this "victim-vs.-agents" dichotomy is not always helpful for highlighting the causes and consequences of sex trafficking. While victims, trafficked women can also be agents of change, although such arguments cannot be romanticized given the constraints trafficked women face.

This review of sex trafficking in South Asia also highlights the need to raise consciousness about men's roles in fuelling the supply and demand in sex trafficking. While the focus remains on women and victims, the relatively wealthy consumers of sex, those whose desires and buying power, fuel this industry, remain formally invisible in most policies and NGO efforts internationally and locally. The consumers are not studied, their race, class, cultural backgrounds are not monitored. Very few countries systematically punish these consumers. Policies, such as the one currently being debated in India about punishing male consumers, rarely garner support through widespread publicity. While some regions, like the European Union, have taken measures to combat sex trafficking (see for instance Zierer 2006), there is no cooperative effort—along the lines of the co-operation to identify, arrest and render across political boundaries, those suspected or accused of terrorism—internationally to punish consumers (or even purveyors) of the sex trafficking industry. While the efforts to help women and address the process of trafficking needs to be improved significantly, the lack of systematic attention on male consumers, suggests that most solutions are likely to be partial, at best.

There have been relatively little attention to sex trafficking as a economic and social human rights issue, as these are defined by sex workers. While a few studies have begun to feature "voices of victime" (e.g. Coonan 2004: Zavartnick 2005), few academics have produced extended ethnographies like Sleightholme and Sinha (1996). If there are initiatives like the sex worker initiatives at Sonagachi in Kolkata, in other parts of South Asia or in other parts of the world, there are little systematic "deep ethnographies" on these efforts. Thus the construction by sexually trafficked women of their situation as human rights violations—a claim borne out of globalization as well—are mostly missing from academic conceptualization of sex trafficking. Therefore, our informed understanding of sex trafficking in South Asia and elsewhere continues to be incomplete.

Addressing sex trafficking requires addressing the nature of corporate globalization—its relentless attempts to privatize resources and to dismantle governmental safeguards so that all resources, services and welfare supports become commodities for sale and profit—and how this plays out in the lives of the poor and marginalized. It also requires significant focus on the links between conflict (and the factors that promote conflict including the growing trade in arms) and women's vulnerability to trafficking. The solution to sex trafficking that most governments have espoused—i.e., treating it mainly as a criminal justice issue—is unlikely to significantly alter the push and pull factors that make women vulnerable to trafficking, although it may offer a legal basis for state action against it. The larger economic and social structural issues that shape women's vulnerability to sex trafficking, exacerbated under globalization, must be radically transformed.

References

Appadurai, A. (1996), *Modernity at Large: Cultural Dimensions of Globalization* (Minneapolis: University of Minnesota Press).

Asia Foundation and Horizons, Trafficking and Human Rights in Nepal: Community Perceptions and Policy and Program Responses, Research Summary, August 2001 <http://www.popcouncil.org/pdfs/horizons/traffickingsum1.pdf>, accessed December 20 2007.

Asian Development Bank (2003), *Combating Trafficking of Women and Children in South Asia*, Regional Synthesis Paper for Bangladesh, India, and Nepal. April 2003. <http://www.adb.org/Documents/Books/Combating_Trafficking/ Regional_Synthesis_Paper.pdf>, accessed December 20 2007.

Basu, I. et al. (2004), "HIV Prevention Among Sex Workers in India," *Epidemiology and Social Science* 36: 845-852.

Banerjee U. (2003), "Globalization, Crisis in Livelihoods, Migration and Trafficking of Women and Girls: The Crisis in India, Nepal and Bangladesh," <http://www.qweb.kvinnoforum.se/../misc/trafupala.rtf>, accessed December 22, 2007.

Bhaumik S. (2007), "Fears For Children Missing in India," *BBC News*, December 20, <http://news.bbc.co.uk/2/hi/south_asia/7145071.stm>, accessed December 22, 2007.

Blackwill R. (2003), "Dealing with Trafficking in Persons: Another Dimension of U.S-India Transformation," Transcript of Speech in Mumbai, India, February 18, 2003 <http://www.state.gov/p/sa/rls/rm/17900.htm>, accessed December 22, 2007.

Brown, W. (2002), "A Human Rights Approach to the Rehabilitation and Reintegration into Society of Trafficked Victims, Human Rights Watch," <http://www.hrw.org/backgrounder/wrd/trafficked-victims.htm>, accessed December 22, 2007.

Chuang J. (1998), "Redirecting the Debate over Trafficking in Women: Definitions, Paradigms, and Contexts," *Harvard Human Rights Journal* 11: 65-107.

Coonan, T. (2004), 'Human Trafficking: Victims' Voices in Florida,' *Journal of Social Work Research and Evaluation* 5: 207-216.

Demir J. (2003), "Trafficking of Women for sexual exploitation: A Gender-Based Well-Founded Fear?" <http://www.jha.ac/articles/a115.pdf>, accessed November 20, 2007.

Department of Women and Child Development (1998), "Plan of Action to Combat Trafficking and Commercial Exploitation of Women and Children, Government of India," <http://www.acim.es/ecpat/documentation/planes-nacionales/India. pdf>, accessed November 20, 2007.

Espiritu, Y. (1997), *Asian American Women: Love, Labor, Laws* (Thousand Oaks: Sage).

Gledditsch, N.,Wallerstein, P., Erikkson, M., Sollenberg, M. and Strand, H. (2002). 'Armed Conflict, 1946-2001: A New Dataset.' *Journal of Peace Research* 39: 615-637.

Government of Nepal, (1985), *Foreign Employment Act, 2042*, <http://www. nepalqatar.com/downloads/neplaboract.pdf>, accessed November 20, 2007.

Guinn, D. (2006), "Pornography, Prostitution and International Sex Trafficking: Mapping the Terrain," <http://ssrn.com/abstract=885389>, accessed November 20, 2007.

Gupta R. (2002), *The Selling of Innocents*, A Documentary. <www.apneaap.org/ about.html>, accessed February 2, 2007.

Gurung, S. (2003a), "Women in Factory-Based and Home-Based Carpet Production in Nepal: Beyond the Formal and Informal Economy," unpublished dissertation, Northeastern University.

—— (2003b), "Women Weavers in Nepal," in B. Purkayastha and M. Subramaniam (eds) *The Power of Women's Informal Networks: Lessons in Social Change from South Asia and West Africa* (Lanham, MD: Lexington Books).

Guthrie J., Jones, S., and Laber, J. (1995), "Rape for Profit: Trafficking of Nepali Girls and Women to India's Brothels," Human Rights Watch. <http://www. hrw.org/reports/1995/India.htm>, accessed November 20, 2007.

Hennink, M. and Simkhada, P. (2004), "Sex Trafficking in Nepal: Context and Process," *Asian and Pacific Migration Journal* 13: 305-338.

Huda, S. (2006), "Sex Trafficking in South Asia," *International Journal of Gyneacology and Obstetrics* 94: 374-381.

Huntington, D. (2002), *Anti-Trafficking Programs in South Asia: Appropriate Activities, Indicators and Evaluation Methodologies*, Summary Report of a Technical Consultative Meeting (New Delhi: Population Council).

Human Rights Watch (HRW) September 2003, *Trapped by Inequality, Bhutanese Refugee Women in Nepal*, <http://www.hrw.org/reports/2003/nepal0903/ nepal0903full.pdf>, accessed November 20, 2007.

Kabeer, N. (2002), *The Power to Choose: Bangladeshi Women and Labor Market Decisions in London and Dhaka* (London: Verso).

Kasturi, C. (2008), "Cracks in Government over Brothel Visitor Cuffs," *The Telegraph*, January 14, Section: *The Nation*: p.4.

Kelly, L. (2004), "The Perils of Inclusion and Exclusion: International Debates on the Status of Trafficked Women as Victims," *International Review of Victimology* 11: 33-47.

Kumar, R. (1990), *The History of Doing: An Illustrated Account of Movements for Women's Rights and Feminism in India, 1800-1990* (London:Verso).

Lacsamana, A. (2004), "Sex Worker or Prostituted Woman?: An Examination of the Sex Work Debates in Western Feminist Theory," in D. Aguilar and A.

Lacsamana, (eds) *Women and Globalization* (Amherst, New York: Humanity Books).

Landesman, P. (2004), "The Girls Next Door," *The New York Times* 25 Jan 2004, pp. 1-11.

McDonald, W. (2004), "Traffic Counts, Symbols and Agendas: A Critique of the Campaign against Trafficking of Human Beings," *International Review of Victimology* 11: 143-176.

Mattar, M. (2003), "The Role of the Government in Combating Trafficking in Persons—A Global Human Rights Approach" <http://www.protectionproject. org/commentary/ctp.htm>, accessed December 20, 2007.

Merry, S. (2006), *Human Rights and Gender Violence: Translating International Law into Local Justice* (Chicago: University of Chicago Press).

Miriam, K. (2005), "Stopping the Traffic in Women: Power, Agency and Abolition in Feminist Debates over Sex-Trafficking," *Journal of Social Philosophy* 36: 1-17.

Munir S. (2003), "Trafficking, South Asia and Pakistan," *Himal South Asian Mag* <http://www.himalmag.com/2003/september/report_2.htm>, accessed December 20, 2007.

Nath M. (2000), "Women's Health and HIV: Experience from a Sex Worker's Project in Calcutta," in C. Sweetman, (ed.) *Gender in the 21st Century* (Oxford: Oxfam Publishing).

Richter, W. and Richter, L. (2004), "Human Trafficking Globalization and Ethics," <http://www.aspaonline.org/ethicscommunity/documents/Human%20Traffick ing,%20Globalization%20and%20Ethics.pdf>

Plant, R. (2006), "Combating Human Trafficking: A Global Picture," < http://www. ilo.org/dyn/declaris/DECLARATIONWEB.DOWNLOAD_BLOB?Var_ DocumentID=6582 ->, accessed December 20, 2007.

SAARC (2002), "SAARC Convention on Preventing and Combating: Trafficking in Women and Children for Prostitution," <http://www.saarc-sec.org/old/ freepubs/conv-traffiking.pdf>, accessed November 20, 2007.

Sainath, P. (1997), *Everybody Loves a Good Drought* (New Delhi: Penguin Books).

Sassen, S. (1999), *Globalization and Its Discontents* (New York: New Press).

Sen, A. (2002), *Development As Freedom* (New York: Knopf).

Sen, A. (1997), *Poverty and Famines: An Essay on Entitlement and Deprivation* (Oxford: Clarendon Press).

Sen, A. (1992), *Inequality Reexamined* (New York: Russell Sage Foundation).

Shah, N., Gothoskar, S., Gandhi, N. and Chhachhi, A. (1999), "Structural Adjustment, Feminization of Labor Force and Organizational Strategies," in Nivedita Menon (ed.) *Gender and Politics in India* (New Delhi: Oxford University Press).

Shakti Samuha (2007), <www.giftasia.in/nepal/shakti_samuha.php>, accessed November 20 2007.

Shiva, V. (2005), *India Divided: Diversity and Democracy Under Attack* (New York: Seven Stories Press).

Sleightholme, C., Sinha, I. (1996), *Guilty without Trial: Women in the Sex Trade in Calcutta* (Kolkata: Stree Publications and New Brunswick: Rutgers University Press).

The Protection Project (2000), "The Three P's Approach to Combating Commercial Sexual Exploitation," School of Advanced International Studies, Johns Hopkins University <http://209.190.246.239/pdfmaps/g31.pdf> accessed November 20 2007.

USAID, Office of Women in Development, (2001), "Trafficking in Persons: USAID's Response," <http://www.usaid.gov/our_work/cross-cutting_programs/wid/pubs/Trafficking2001.pdf>, accessed December 20 2008.

United States Department of State, (2001), Country Reports on Human Rights Practices.

—— (2002), Trafficking in Persons Report.

—— (2004), Trafficking in Persons Report Released by the Office to Monitor and Combat Trafficking in Persons June 14, 2004.

Wijers M. et al. (1997), "Only Rights Can Stop Wrongs: A Critical Assessment of Anti-trafficking Strategies," <http://www.nswp.org/pdf/WIJERS-ONLYRIGHTS.PDF >, accessed November 20, 2007.

Wijers, M. and Lin, L. (1998), "Trafficking in Women, Forced Labor and Slavery like Practices in Domestic Labor, Marriage and Prostitution," STV/GAATW, Utrecht, April 1998/1999, <http://www.nswp.org/pdf/WIJERS-ONLYRIGHTS.PDF>, accessed November 20, 2007.

Zavratnik, S. and Pajnik, T. (2005),"Trafficking in Women: A Victim's Perspective," in *Praksa* 42: 113-135.

Zierer, B. (2006) (ed.), *Social Work and Trafficking in Women* (Vienna: University of Applied Sciences, Department of Social Work).

Index